Manufacturing Matters

Research for this book was supported by grants from Carnegie Corporation of New York and Carnegie Forum on Education and the Economy, Washington, D.C.

Manufacturing

Matters *The Myth of the Post-Industrial Economy*

STEPHEN S. COHEN

JOHN ZYSMAN

A COUNCIL ON FOREIGN RELATIONS BOOK

Basic Books, Inc., Publishers New York

Library of Congress Cataloging-in-Publication Data

Cohen, Stephen S.
  Manufacturing matters.

  "A Council on Foreign Relations Book."
  Includes index.
  1. United States—Manufactures.   I. Zysman, John.
II. Title.
HD9725.C58   1987   338.4'767'0973   86-47737
ISBN   0–465–04384–4   (cloth)
ISBN   0–465–04385–2   (paper)

For Julia

For Victoria

CONTENTS

PART III

Creating Advantage

ACKNOWLEDGMENTS

This book, more than many, has grown out of the efforts of others. Our colleagues at BRIE (The Berkeley Roundtable on the International Economy) have created an environment of remarkable intellectual excitement, creativity and energy. This book is one of many presentations of BRIE research and thought; it takes its substance and impetus from that common endeavor. The work of Michael Borrus, BRIE's deputy director, on international competition in high technology and telecommunications is integral to the second part of the book. Our colleagues at the University of California, Berkeley, Professors Manuel Castells, Chalmers Johnson, Alberto Sangiovanni-Vincentelli and Laura D'Andrea Tyson, mainstays of BRIE, are sources of some of the major ideas in this book and also helped to discipline the way those ideas took form.

In a way, the book is an effort to answer a question posed to us by Robert Heilbroner in a discussion about trade—why, he asked us, does manufacturing matter?

Ann Mine and Jay Tharp at BRIE produced the text and edited it for typos, inelegancies, and stray foolishnesses.

The research and analysis on which this book is based was funded in part by a grant from Carnegie Corporation of New York. The views expressed, however, do not necessarily reflect those of Carnegie Corporation, its staff, or trustees.

Carnegie Forum on Education and the Economy financed early stages of the work. Marc Tucker and David Mandel, of the Forum, have been more than project funders. They have worked with us as analysts, commentators, even as fastidious editors and, in the process, have reshaped our thinking about the role of education in the economy. They also helped assemble a distinguished and hard working group to critique our work.

The Council on Foreign Relations has likewise helped organize evaluation and advice at a vital step in our writing. In particular, Michael Aho, David Kellogg, and Paul Kreisberg have been of real help, substantive as well as moral.

Others who contributed as participants in the review sessions organized by the Forum and the Council include: Charles S. Benson, Jane Biba, Harvey Brooks, Philip Caldwell, Peter Cowhey, William Diebold, E. Alden Dunham, Joshua Gotbaum, Burton Klein, Ray Marshall, Murray Smith, P. Michael Timpane, Robert Valkenier, Ray Vernon, Robert M. White, and Lewis Young.

The Office of Technology Assessment (OTA) of the Congress of the United States supported earlier work that led to this book. In particular, Henry Kelly of OTA converted a relationship that began as one of institutional support to one of exciting intellectual effort.

In addition, we would like to acknowledge the colleagues and friends who offered ideas, comments, information and advice. They include Barbara Baran, Peter Jones, James Millstein, T. J. Pempel, Peter J. Siris, David Teece, and Kozo Yamamura.

INTRODUCTION

The newspapers remind us daily that basic changes are afoot in the world economy and that the United States is neither shaping them nor responding to them very well. There are stories of restrictions on the import of automobiles, accompanied by pieces about how the Japanese produce cars much less expensively than American firms, and seemingly to higher quality standards. At first those stories focused on wages: ours high, theirs low. But now, as the wage gap disappears, the stories report that the Japanese advantage lies in the organization of production and the effective use of automation, not in low wages. There are stories—confusing, disparate pieces—about General Motors's response to the Japanese pressure: some are about GM arranging to source in Korea; others report on joint production in California with Toyota; and still others tell about a strategy for factory automation in which robots and computer vision systems are to be linked through telecommunications nets that tie design to production and the point of sale to the shop floor. Does the new automation mean more jobs? Fewer jobs? More than what? Fewer than what? Does knowing something about GM, even a most confusing something, really tell us anything about the rest of American industry? GM—and IBM and AT&T —can try all strategies at once, or at least experiment with a few. Smaller companies have to pick one, and pick it soon. What will they decide to do? What will determine their choices? What do those choices mean for the rest of us? All these stories have migrated from the business page to the front page, and they will not quietly drift back.

There are other stories. American companies find themselves trading for Polish ham and Malaysian wicker, discovering that in the twentieth century the premarket game of barter is back. Entrepreneurial semiconductor firms, a symbol of venture capitalism, find themselves suddenly fighting for survival with giant integrated Japanese corporations. Collective research and development projects in Japan are forcing cooperative efforts at R&D and new production technologies among independent Silicon Valley firms whose executive offices are hung with brash slogans of gunslinging individualism. Under the pressure of Japanese competition, ever-plastic California culture is adjusting. We are eating sashimi despite our keen concerns about water pollution, and we are re-creating the ad-hoc cooperation that was the real hallmark of the Far West while reluctantly abandoning some of the lone-rider individualism of a cultural style that took the Western, not the West, as its historic past.

It is easy to see that dramatic changes are taking place in world markets: in who is competing with whom, in what determines competitive success, in who is winning and losing, in the technologies of product and production, and in the very rules of international competition. It is much harder to make sense of those changes and of their meaning for the United States. There is no shortage of interpretive pieces to complement the news stories —that's part of the problem. There are interpretations to satisfy just about every opinion, every interest, and every mood, to reinforce calm in the complacent and panic in the paranoic. The confusion is real. The stakes are also real, and very high. If a crisis can be defined as an important situation where informed opinion, the best opinion, is utterly confused, then we are in one now.

The difficulty—and the reason for this book—is that the interpretive lenses through which the American policy debate views these events distort American perceptions of what is happening and prevent us from seeing what our choices are and what our priorities must be. For example, as imports pour in and some U.S. production moves offshore while other factories close, an odd debate goes on. Some believe we must protect our economic base by building barricades around the blue-collar production jobs and plants of the past. But will protected American industries undertake the massive investments, changes, and innovations needed to keep us at the leading edge in technology, incomes, and power? And what will American protectionism do to world prosperity and, more important, world order? Many, probably the majority, counsel calm and faith. They explain patiently that the problem is primarily one of an overvalued dollar —even though the dollar has been pushed down enormously this past year and the trade deficit has continued to widen. Still, they insist, faith, patience, and some good old-fashioned deficit reductions will ultimately prevail.

Sometimes wages take the spotlight. We have to bring ours down to competitive levels. The party is over. But are they serious about Korean and Taiwanese wage levels for American workers and managers? What about our entire history as a high-wage economy and about our most powerful and successful competitors, Japan and Germany, who have wage levels quite comparable to ours? Finally, there are those who view these changes as signs of progress, a shift out of our industrial past and up forward, toward a post-industrial service economy. But just what is a post-industrial economy? Who has one? Las Vegas? Manhattan? The Bronx? England? Will American companies really dominate international trade in communications if they are not leaders in computers, semiconductors, telephone switching equipment, launchers, satellites, and fiber optics? Will American engineering firms be able to sell turnkey plant designs to foreign steel makers who themselves build state-of-the-art steelworks while obsolete American steel mills shut down? Will Japan or France or Brazil really let our banks control their economies, and will American banks, with their uniquely weak balance sheets and eroding positions even in the U.S. market, be better able to compete with the Japanese and Germans than American manufacturers? Of course services matter; they dominate the employment statistics. Of course the character of work is changing. But the notion of a post-industrial economy, supported precariously by a peculiar substitution of statistical categories of job classifications for analysis and thought, is grossly misleading. It blinds America to the reality of the profound changes in the economy, the new international division of labor, and the new technical division of labor that has extended the production processes outside the confines of the traditional manufacturing firm. We are experiencing a transition not from an industrial economy to a service economy, but from one kind of industrial economy to another.

This book is an effort to offer a different set of lenses to explain and understand those changes and the enormous significance they have for the wealth and power of this nation. It attempts to provide an alternative account of where we are, where we are going, and what we can do about it. The argument of this book is simple. It reduces to five slightly overstuffed propositions. (1) Manufacturing matters. Manufacturing is critical to the health of the economy; lose manufacturing and you will lose—not develop—high-wage service jobs. The wealth and power of the United States economy would decline drastically if major segments of manufacturing were to shut down or to move offshore. (2) Changes in the extent and practices of international competition, coupled with the application on a mass scale of new microelectronics-based technologies (digital telecommunications, robotics, flexible computer controls) are revolutionizing production; together they are creating a fundamental economic transition that puts the position of every nation in the international hierarchy of wealth and power, including the United States, up for grabs. (3) America is not adjusting well to the changes in the world economy. Evidence from a variety of indicators and perspectives suggests serious competitiveness problems. (4) Weaknesses in production are eroding our competitive position, and this is critical. Manufacturing capabilities are decisive to the competitiveness of industrial firms; over time, you can't control what you can't produce. American firms will have to give priority to redeveloping their production skills. (5) Policy sets the terms of the new competition and the context in which the new technology will evolve. It can help to upgrade a nation's competitive position in substantial and enduring ways or it can handicap national producers and accelerate a downward spiral of weakening production capability, slow and timid introductions of new production technologies, offshoring, and a flight into pure distribution and defense contracting. If we are going to be able to choose our own future and not just submit to it, the focus of American policy-making attention will have to change: competitiveness will have to become a primary concern.

No one element, no single policy or reform can, by itself, restore our competitiveness; trade policy, investment policy, macro policy, management practices, labor relations, and technological diffusion all play key roles. But decisive in the mix of policies and reforms that will decide our future are those that will create our future skill base. Technology is not an external force that drives our society, autonomously shaping our future and ourselves. The evolution of technology does not unilaterally determine the mix of skills a nation requires; rather, to an important extent, during the key formative phases of a technology's evolution, the mix of available skills shapes the evolution of the technology. If America wants the technologies to support a high-wage, high-value-added economy, it will have to ensure the education and skills to make that possible. It isn't doing so at present.

The dominant, traditional approaches of American economics to the dynamics of economic development and trade have obscured the nature of the problem and the choices we confront. In particular, they have clouded the critical role of manufacturing in the economy and in competitiveness. We must move beyond an economics based on comparative statics and the misleading myth of a post-industrial economy.

The organization of this book is simple. In Part I we show why manufacturing matters and examine America's eroding competitiveness. In Part II we contend that America confronts a fundamental economic transition driven by abrupt shifts in markets and technology. In Part III we insist that our priority must be to create advantage in world markets by recognizing, in policy, the central importance of manufacturing and, in corporate strategy, the decisive significance of production skills.

PART I

Manufacturing

Matters

1

Why Manufacturing Matters

MANUFACTURING MATTERS mightily to the wealth and power of the United States and to our ability to sustain the kind of open society we have come to take for granted. If we want to stay on top—or even high up—we can't just shift out of manufacturing and up into services, as some would have it. Nor can we establish a long-term preserve around traditional blue-collar jobs and outmoded plants: American competitiveness in the international economy is critical to long-term domestic prosperity, social justice, international leadership, and world order. We must reorganize production, not abandon it. In a catch phrase, if the United States is to remain a wealthy and powerful economy, American manufacturing must automate, not emigrate. The difference is decisive. There is absolutely no way we can lose control and mastery of manufacturing and expect to hold onto the high-wage service jobs that we are constantly told will replace manufacturing. At the heart of our argument is a notion we call "direct linkage": a substantial core of service employment is tightly tied to manufacturing. It is a complement and not, as the dominant view would have it, a substitute or successor for manufacturing. Lose manufacturing and you will lose—not develop—those high-wage services.

Despite all the upbeat talk to the contrary, the United States cannot hope to let manufacturing go and reconstruct a strong international trade position in services. Exports of services are simply too small to offset the staggering deficits we are running in industrial goods. They will remain so over the foreseeable future. Furthermore, a decisive band of high-wage service exports are linked to mastery and control of manufacturing. Services are complements—not substitutes or successors—to manufacturing.

These contentions should be obvious, and are taken as solid premises in policy debates abroad. In such countries as Japan, France, Sweden, West Germany, Korea and Brazil, they are—for better or worse—the views that guide policy. But in American policy and academic debates they constitute a distinctly minority—and often suspect—view. In part this is due to the intellectual, political, and ideological power of a central tenet of American economic thought: the composition of national product should be a matter of indifference to policy. (Defense is exempted on noneconomic grounds.) This conventional view is supported in books, in the journals, the op-ed pages and in expert testimony by easily marshaled data. The data show a relentless decline in manufacturing employment, from about 50 percent of all jobs in 1950 down to about 20 percent now, and an irresistible increase in service jobs, up to about 70 percent of all jobs.[1] The data underwrite the basic view that economic development is an ongoing and never-ending process of shifting out of activities of the past and up into the newer, higher-value-added activities of the future. We shifted out of farming and into industry, although the country rocked to the bad economics of "Burn our farms, and grass will grow in the streets of our cities." Now that we are shifting out of industry and up into services and high tech, similar cries are being heard; they have similar validity and should be ignored. The policy point is clear: keep hands off. Things are going as they should. Life, especially economic life, does not stand still. A substantial capacity in steel or in semiconductors is no more an economic necessity than one in buggy whips or oats. If the interventionist temptation proves irresistible, concentrate on smoothing and softening the "adjustment process": retraining and relocation programs.

The strength of this dominant view—that the American economic future is assured by a smooth shift into services—is based on data that although overwhelming in their seeming consistency and scope to a large extent reflect a statistical muddle. That muddle derives from the particular ways in which economic data are organized; it is not without consequence. For example, in the data that economists and policy makers use to shape theories and guide policy, tight linkages of the sort that inextricably tie the crop duster (a service firm) to the farm (agriculture) are indistinguishable from the linkages which loosely and indifferently tie an advertising firm to GM (domestic production) or to Toyota (imports). This leads to policy based on a notion of industrial succession—up out of one sector and into another.

For example, in a recent report to Congress on trade agreements, the president of the United States sets out the following framework for understanding what many take to be a troubling trade situation. "The move from an industrial society toward a 'postindustrial' service economy has been one of the greatest changes to affect the developed world since the Industrial Revolution. The progression of an economy such as America's from agriculture to manufacturing to services is a natural change."[2]

The New York Stock Exchange, in a recent report on trade, industrial change, and jobs, put it more pointedly: "a strong manufacturing sector is not a requisite for a prosperous economy."[3]

Or, in the words of *Forbes*, "Instead of ringing in the decline of our economic power, a service-driven economy signals the most advanced stage of economic development. . . . Instead of following the Pied Piper of 'reindustrialization,' the U.S. should be concentrating its efforts on strengthening its services."[4]

Compared to the argument of this book, these views are more soothing in their message, calmer in tone, more confident in style, and more readily buttressed by applications of traditional economic data and methodologies. They are also quite possibly wrong in their analysis. And because they encourage and justify policies that create risks of colossal scale—the wealth and power of the United States being the stakes—they are, for all their conventionality, terribly radical as guides and rationalizers for policy.

By contrast, our message is disturbing. Our tone is one of urgency, and our approach, precisely because it differs from conventional economic analysis, appears to be handcrafted and radical. No attempt has been made to disguise these appearances. As a guide to policy, however, it is quite conservative. It argues against taking major and potentially irreversible risks on a basis of uncertain knowledge consisting of inadequately examined and unexplained economic data (mostly about employment in jobs labeled "services") and unproven and untried, albeit dominant, economic theory.

Our argument takes issue—fundamentally—with the widely articulated view that sees a service-based, "post-industrial" economy as the natural successor to an industry-based economy, as the next step up a short but steep staircase consisting of "stages of development." In this view agriculture is the first stage, industry is the second, and services—especially knowledge-based services—is the third, and for the moment the ultimate stage.[5] From this view comes a comforting interpretation (which dominates policy debate) of America's present economic difficulties. Aside from difficulties caused by exchange rate and interest rate differentials which are due to incorrect macroeconomic policies (inherently a bothersome, but temporary, problem amenable to tough, but conventional, treatment), the loss of market share and employment in such industries as textiles, steel, apparel, autos, consumer electronics, machine tools, random-access memories, computer peripherals, and circuit boards, to name but a few, is neither a surprise nor a "bad thing." We should take no special measures to halt or reverse it. It is not a sign of failure but a part of the price of success. America should be shedding the sunset industries of the past, and they should be taken over by countries that trail us while America moves on to services and high tech, the sunrise sectors of the future. It is part of an ever-evolving and ever-developing international division of labor from which we all benefit.

Linkage, Not Succession

The ideas and the basic vision behind the dominant policy positions are not new, nor were they when Daniel Bell popularized them more than ten years ago.[6] Since then their diffusion has been extensive. They have found their way into central positions in economics and literature, in sociology (popular and recondite), into such official policy documents as the *Report of the President on the Trade Agreements Program* and the report of the Council of Economic Advisors and, of course, they constitute a mainstay of economic journalism.[7] But since they first gained currency, a lot of evidence has accumulated that clouds the picture and complicates the core notion of development through industrial succession.

For example, agriculture has by no means become an activity of the past, something easily and perhaps advantageously sloughed off. To the embarrassment of those who view the persistent cultivation of large quantities of soy beans, tomatoes, or corn to be incompatible with the proper image of a high-tech future, agriculture has sustained, over the long term, the highest rate of productivity increase of any sector.[8] Total output has increased steadily, and the sector has been a vital generator of broadly diffused wealth and technical innovation. New technologies, based on microelectronics and microbiology, promise to accelerate innovation and increase productivity in that oldest piece of the simple and misleading sectoral slice that underlies (and undermines) this rudimentary stages-of-development position. Hands-on technical mastery and direct control of a substantial and internationally competitive production capacity in agriculture is the source of a substantial quantity of high-end—and also low-end—industrial and service employment. Were that production to have moved elsewhere, sooner or later, those tightly linked industrial and service jobs would have followed.

At the heart of our argument is a contention that similar tight linkages tie a broad core of service jobs to manufacturing—but on a much larger scale. Shift out of manufacturing and it is more likely that you will find that you have shifted *out of* such services as product and process engineering, than *into* those services. This is true of a large number of high-level service activities, the very services that are supposed to drive the argument for development by sectoral succession—out of industry and up into services. These services are complements to manufacturing, not potential substitutes or successors. The wages generated in services that are tightly linked to manufacturing exert an enormous effect on wage levels in services quite independent of manufacturing, activities as distant as teaching, government work, hairdressing, and banking. Were America to lose mastery and control of manufacturing, vast numbers of services jobs would be relocated after a few short rounds of product and process innovation, largely to destinations outside the United States, and real wages in all service activities would fall, impoverishing the nation.

High Tech

Along with services, high tech is held out as the successor to manufacturing. It is not always clear what people mean when they say "high tech." For most, it is a list of processes and products that they find particularly exotic or complicated and new—microelectronics, biotechnologies, new materials—and their applications—robotics, computers, lasers, magnetic imaging. For our official statistics it is a list of industries with a high proportion of R&D expenditures or a high proportion of employees with advanced or scientific degrees. Though a bit more sophisticated than a simple listing of the new but arcane, it, like the manufacturing/services classification scheme, creates more problems and blind spots than it helps to solve. Many industries—including such big ones as farming, textiles, and insurance—do not perform their own R&D. But they are the users of R&D performed in supplying industries and at specialized nonindustry

research centers. It is the historical development of the industry, its relations with its suppliers, and its competitive and institutional structures, not
necessarily the nature of the product, that determines whether or where
R&D will be performed. No one farmer, we learn in elementary economics
texts, has the means or even the incentives to do R&D. But if all the farms
in Nebraska were owned by a single firm, it could find itself doing much
of the R&D now performed in the chemicals, electronics, and machinery
industries as well as in the Department of Agriculture and the universities.
Would we then count farming as high tech?

High tech is not defined only by the nature of the product; a better
definition would include the way the product is produced. Within a relatively short time, the U.S. economy will have only high-tech industry—
whether it be producing computers, trousers, or tennis balls. The others
will have long gone offshore.

But the relationship between high tech and manufacturing, like that
between services and manufacturing, is not a simple case of evolutionary
succession. High tech, however defined, must be understood as intimately
tied to manufacturing, and not as a free-floating laboratory activity. It is
tied to manufacturing in two distinct and important ways. First, despite the
popularity of home computers and burglar alarms, most high-tech products are producer goods, not consumer goods. They are bought to be used
either in the products of other industries (like microprocessors in autos) or
in the production process (like robots, computers, and lasers across the
range of manufacturing and services) or both. If not American producers
of autos, machine tools, telephones and trousers, who is going to buy a bag
of American silicon chips? The answers, like the interdependencies of
real-world production processes, are, as we shall see, anything but simple.

The second tie to manufacturing is even tighter. If high tech is to
sustain a scale of activity sufficient to matter to the prosperity of our
economy and not shrink down to a marginal research activity, America
must control the production of those high-tech products it invents and
designs—and it must do so in a direct and hands-on way. There are several
reasons for this. First, as we shall see, production is where the lion's share
of the value added is realized. It is where the "rent on innovation" is
captured. And given the dependence of American high-tech firms on a
private capital market, this is where the returns needed to finance the next
round of research and development are generated. Second, and most important in the overwhelming majority of cases, unless R&D is tightly tied
to the manufacturing of the product—and to the permanent process of
innovation in production now required for competitiveness in manufacturing—R&D will fall behind the cutting edge of incremental innovation.

For example, by abandoning the production of televisions, the U.S. electronics industry quickly lost the know-how to design, develop, refine, and competitively produce the next generation of that product, the VCR. As a result, we make no VCRs in this country, and we are likely to lose whatever positions we still maintain in research and development of products that derive from mastery of that product and production technology. High tech gravitates toward the state-of-the-art producers.

Statistical Categories and Economic Realities

The conventional analytic categories that provide the basis for an image of economic development, distinguishing a movement up a succession of industries defined by the nature of their final product, do not work. Those categories—agriculture, manufacturing, services, high tech—organize employment, output, and profit data in ways that are easy to collect and count. They satisfy a popular understanding of how an economy works and ought to work: it is simply clear as a bell that a country that does brain surgery and computer programming is, in a fundamental way, ahead of a country that doesn't and can't. But it is a slippery path from that hard truth to a model of development—and worse, a policy for development—based on those categories which now become analytic categories though they embody no real theory, though they do not square with the realities of economic organization and linkages, and which, like the Brand X candies in the M&M's ads, melt in your hand when you try to use them.

The demarcations between *services* that find their finality in the production of a product (such as product design, process engineering, and the repair of automated equipment, as well as accounting, dispatching, and billing) and *production* tasks (such as the monitoring of automated equipment, the regulation of an on-time inventory system, testing, quality control, and systems integration) are generally the results of statistical categories and institutional arrangements external to the logics and realities of actual economic activity. These statistical categories tend to become analytic categories. This is especially true when both the evidence and the very vocabulary of analysis must be drawn from those same statistics.

Even when these initial doubts about the viability of the categories are pushed aside and the employment data are studied closely within their own framework, the statistics reveal what is, at best, a mixed message about whether a shift toward service jobs is an indicator of economic development. Though many of the figures, such as increases in programmers, systems integrators, designers, and bioengineers, are positive signs of development, the overwhelming preponderance of service jobs created in the past fifteen, ten, or even five years are not futuristic in any recognizable sense of that old-fashioned image. They are not especially knowledge-based, "advanced," high-paid or difficult to emulate abroad or to import. Instead, in every way except the best ways, they are very traditional: wholesale and retail sales, routine office work, restaurant work, hospital work, welfare work, janitorial work, security, and so on. Overwhelmingly, they are simple, low-skill, hands-on, part-time, low-wage, dead-end jobs.

But a simple dismissal of this sectoral-succession view would be wrong, or at least premature, whether based on the obvious inadequacies of its division of the economy by final product or on the ambiguous statistical relationship of increased service employment to any notion of progressive development, or both. It would give short shrift to both the impressive array of people who articulate variants of that view and to the equally impressive body of information they have marshaled to support that view. It would also flaunt common sense and casual observation: we are, after all, overwhelmingly a service economy. And so are the French, the Dutch, the Swiss, and the Germans. We are quite prosperous and consider ourselves to be as "advanced" as anyone. And we know that just digging harder or hauling more coal is really not the important source of our present prosperity and certainly will not be the source of our future development. It is a big and rich argument, and it calls for a big and rich discussion, rooted in a sympathetic understanding. A swift, preemptory rejection, based on the obvious difficulties of the approach, not only risks sweeping away the elements of truth we sense to reside at the base of that easily, perhaps too easily, punctured argument; it also risks blocking our own understanding of how and why manufacturing matters mightily for the wealth and power of a modern economy.

The argument of this part, "Manufacturing Matters," is developed in the next three chapters. Chapter 2, "Linkages, Wealth, and Power," addresses the question, What would happen to the wealth and power of the United States if we shed more and more manufacturing and actually became a service economy? Its central contention is that direct linkages exist between manufacturing and a substantial core of service activities. Our conventional statistical and analytic categories are blind to these linkages, and so are theory and policy that derive from these categories and conceive of development in terms of sectoral succession—out of manufacturing and up into services. Strong manufacturing capabilities and high-wage service activities are complements rather than, as generally presented, substitute or successor activities; lose control and mastery of manufacturing and you will lose—not make room for—the high-value-added services on which America's future must be based.

Chapter 3, "Services and the American Trade Balance," addresses the question, As our merchandise account accumulates staggering deficits, can the United States move on to reestablish a strong international trade position as an exporter of services? It demonstrates that at the present time, and for the foreseeable future, services cannot replace manufactured goods as the principal sources of high-value-added exports needed to sustain a strong American position in international trade.

Chapter 4, "Services and Development," asks, What is a service? and reviews the rubbery answers commonly available. It then examines the growth of service employment, to see what, if any, relation those changes in employment bear to economic development (or decline). Having defined and tabulated it, the chapter proceeds to deconstruct its subject—the use of services as an analytical category in development theory.

The fifth and final chapter, "The Eroding Competitiveness of American Industry," surveys the competitiveness of the American economy. Competitiveness is not defined by a nugatory identity: the ability to balance imports with exports. At some exchange rate, say one dollar equals fifty yen, balance can always be achieved. Even the poorest nations balance their accounts. The important meaning of competitiveness is the ability to compete in an open world economy with high and rising American wages. The primary cause of our deteriorating competitive position is, we suspect, to be found in production; we are being beaten on the shop floor.

2

Linkages, Wealth, and Power

WHAT WILL HAPPEN to the wealth and power of the United States if we really do shift out of manufacturing and actually become a service economy? Will we be impoverished? Enriched? Remain the same? More specifically, what will happen to employment in services if major chunks of manufacturing close down or move offshore? Will the jobs remain? At high wages? Does the *way* we shed manufacturing employment —automating or offshoring—matter very much? If so, in what ways and to whom?

Most celebrations of the developmental shift out of industry and into services begin by constructing a parallel to the shift out of agriculture and into industry. Daniel Bell, to take the best known for example, begins his argument by noting that while agriculture employed over 20 percent of the U.S. work force in 1929, it now employs about 3 percent.[1] We shed all those jobs and are better off for it. That classic shift—from low productivity, low-paid labor on the farm to higher productivity, hence higher-paid employment in industry—is precisely what economic development is all about. The same developmental movement, the same "creative destruction," is now being repeated in the shift of resources out of industry and into services and high tech.[2]

This conventional view of economic history as a long process of shifting from sector to sector in order to shift to higher and higher levels of productivity is familiar and reassuring. But it is also misleading. It leads us to confuse two separate transitions: a shift out of agricultural production (something parallel to the curtailing or offshoring of U.S. manufacturing production); and a shift of labor out of agricultural production (something exactly like increasing labor productivity by adding other resources, whether land, capital, or technology). Only the first shift never occurred. The United States did not shift out of agriculture, as we are now often advised to shift out of manufacturing. American agricultural production did not go offshore or shrivel up. Instead, it increased by colossal amounts, whether measured in tons or dollars or whatever. Agricultural output rose, but farm labor inputs decreased; they were replaced by capital, education, and new technologies.[3] To extend an analogy, we automated agriculture; we did not offshore it or shift out.

The difference between the two approaches—keeping production by automating versus shifting out—makes all the difference in the world to the wealth of nations and to the composition of employment. The most important difference, as we shall see, is not in blue-collar employment in manufacturing—though that is not at all trivial—but in service employment itself, high-paying mostly white-collar service employment.

Linkages and Development

Even the employment shift out of agriculture—the most important and best documented demographic/economic shift ever in every country in the world—is complicated enough to merit a second look. The generally accepted ballpark figure for agricultural employment in the United States is now about 3 million, or about 3 percent of the work force.[4] But this takes us back to the problems of categories used to classify employment. Those categories derive, not from the reality of production, but from institutional arrangements. Looking at agricultural employment that way (using a figure like "3 million") is a bit like looking at industrial employment and counting only people on the production lines. Are crop-duster pilots or large-animal veterinarians employed in agriculture? The 3-million figure is blind to important economic realities, and it blindsides policy makers. To take an important example, it does not give an appreciation of what would have happened were we to have offshored, or simply abandoned, agricultural production rather than automated it. It is therefore the worst possible basis for an analogy designed to provide a comforting interpretation of a massive offshoring of industry.

If we pose the question this way: What would have happened to employment (or wealth) if we had shifted out of agriculture instead of just moving labor off the farm?, we quickly encounter the notion of linkage: the relationship of agricultural production to employment in tractor repairing, veterinary medicine, ketchup making and grape crushing.

In general, productivity increases usually imply an ever greater indirectness in the production process and an ever greater specialization of inputs (including labor). The more advanced or modern the production process, the longer and more complicated the chains of linkages. A primitive farmer has his wife scratch the ground with a stick. He needs no outside stick repair-person and very little else from outside. He also has a very low productivity. A modern American farmer is really the point man in a long, elaborate chain of specialists—most of whom don't often set foot on the farm—all of whom are vital to its successful operation and directly depend on it.

Linkage is not a new notion to economists. Development theorists talk about forward and backward linkages. Input/output analysis is a device to highlight intersectoral linkages. But conventional economics does not like the notion of linkages to be used as evidence of some special economic importance for a particular sector or set of sectors. Linkage has no place in a discussion of a subject such as why manufacturing matters. The objection is not that linkages are dubious or rare, or impossible to demonstrate. Rather it is that they are robust and ubiquitous. In economics, everything is linked to everything else, in a way that is similar to—but surely very different from—the Hare Krishna view that everything is one. Robert Z. Lawrence of the Brookings Institution puts the conventional position clearly and in the context of our debate: What is the nature of linkages among industries? Should those linkages matter to policy?

> Some . . . proponents of selective industrial policies for the United States . . . point to "forward linkages" from key inputs such as steel, textiles, semiconductors, and machine tools and suggest that domestic production of these products is essential for industries such as automobiles, apparel and machinery. Others point to "backward linkages" from complex products such as automobiles and aircraft and suggest that domestic production of these final goods is essential for the suppliers of component materials.
>
> But the economy is an interdependent system of industries. Almost all industries are interconnected; therefore this criterion does little to narrow the selection process. It is widely acknowledged that private markets may fail

when there are spillovers (or externalities), such as pollution, which are not accounted for in private incentives. Simply because one sector supplies input to another, however, does not imply the presence of such spillovers. Since a supply in industry can capture in its profits the benefits of such production, there is no reason to expect underinvestment in a sector that produces inputs.

He goes on to administer the coup de grace to protectionists, industrial policy types, and such misguided foreign institutions and bad economists as Japan's MITI (Ministry of International Trade and Industry):

Protecting input industries may, in fact, be particularly costly. If protection raises input costs, it will exert pervasive damage on the international competitiveness of finished products. For example, high prices for steel and machine tools will hurt numerous industries such as metal products, machinery, aircraft, shipbuilding and automobiles. To survive in global competition, it is crucial that makers of complex products obtain their inputs from the cheapest sources. On the other hand, protecting finished products will not prevent producers from using offshore sources. Indeed, recognition of this fact lies behind proposals for domestic content legislation.[5]

In brief, efforts to privilege any sector on the basis of its linkages to the rest of the economy will only raise costs to consumers and contribute to a loss of the economy's overall efficiency and international competitiveness. This refutation is quite total, and it is rehearsed in a manner so routine as to seem obvious and unquestionable. Still, it might just be wrong. For starters, it has two fundamental problems. The first concerns concreteness: it is misplaced (as in the formal fallacy) and therefore it misleads. The second has to do with the categories of linkage. They may well be conventional, but they are not exhaustive, or even particularly apposite. There are characteristics other than direction (forward, backward) to define and categorize linkages in the economy, and they may be much more relevant to the question.

Despite its illustrations of concrete linkages from across a convincingly broad range of activities—forward from steel and semiconductors, backward from autos and aircraft—Lawrence's refutation of the linkage argument contains no real concreteness. It is the industries that are specified concretely—not the linkages. All the linkages he enumerates, whether they go forward or backward, are of the same special kind. They are loose couplings, loose linkages. Each is a simple market relationship of buyer and seller with no other interdependence. And each involves a good, a traded good. None involves a service. If you excise, or offshore, one industry from a loosely linked pair, in principal you should not affect the other. You can make cars or textiles with imported machines. In the United States we do it every day, though at a steadily shrinking volume. Offshore the machine makers and you do not necessarily disturb the auto makers. And you can, in principle at least, make semiconductors in the United States and sell them anywhere in the world, even if all American semiconductor users, such as auto makers or computer makers, have vanished. Polish golf carts, Japanese lawn mowers, and Korean CB radios are examples of products produced exclusively for export markets. There is some basis—in theory, if not in experience—for imagining a world in which Japanese televisions or computers are made with U.S. semiconductors and Korean shirts with U.S. textiles. All are traded goods, and in principle, though less often in reality, they are unbounded spatially: the purchaser-supplier relationship is not necessarily confined to one place or to one nation. These are the loosest linkages imaginable. Nothing is attached. No one activity is bound to another. The interface is strictly unidimensional: a buyer-seller relationship via competitive markets. It is the only kind of linkage that the basic analytic method underneath Lawrence's work can address, and therefore the only kind of linkage it permits into the discussion.

There are, however, other kinds of linkages in the economy, such as those which tie the crop duster to the cotton fields, the ketchup maker to the tomato patch, the wine press to the vineyards (to return to our focus on agriculture). Here the linkages are tight and quite concrete. True, they are market relations, and all the laws of substitution and competition prevail, but only within a bounded submarket. Beyond the limit of possible recombinations provided by that bounded space, the linkage is a bind, not a junction or substitution point. Offshore the tomato farm and you close or offshore the ketchup plant. No two ways about it. There is a spatial bind that provides a concreteness all its own. It is a real concreteness that differentiates one linkage from another. It also blunts the abstract, surgical niceties of Lawrence's industrial excisions and insertions by substituting a real economic tissue for a set of economist's logo logs.

It is quite possible that an economy like ours is characterized by an enormous number of such tight bonds and is not simply a system of slide-in-slide-out linkages like those that exclusively dominate the models from which conventional economics produces its conventional prescriptions. Certainly the possibility ought to be explored before routine, and therefore horribly glib, refutations and prescriptions are allowed to affect policy.

Tight Linkages

The massive importance of tight linkage, or binding, is clearly visible in agriculture, once we ask our question, What would have happened had we offshored agricultural production instead of automating it? Even at first glance, it is easy to spot a tight bind between agricultural production and the food-processing industry. Food processing [SIC 2011–99] employs about 1.7 million Americans; much—though surely not all—of it would have gone away along with farm production.[6] The linkage is quite different in kind, and in consequence, from that used to make policy pronouncements in Lawrence's work. No American farming, not much American food processing. The linkage is real and direct. It is physical—a bind, not a junction. Food processing must generally be performed in physical propinquity to farm production. It is technically possible, but economically improbable to mill sugar cane in a country far from the sugar fields, or to process tomatoes far from the tomato patch, or to dry grapes into raisins or crush them for wine far from the vineyard. It is a forward linkage starting with farming; food processing is downstream in the production chain, like cars and machine tools in Lawrence's example, but the similarities in the linkages end there. In agriculture, both in theory and in what is too often dismissed as mere real-world examples, tight linkages bind in both directions. There are many activities tightly bound to farming that are backward linkages: crop dusters, animal vets, harvesters, tractor repairers, mortgage appraisers, fertilizer salesmen, blight insurers, agronomists, chemists, truckers, shuckers.

There are other U.S. industries—such as finance, insurance, and the manufacturing of agricultural machinery and agricultural chemicals—that are less tightly linked to agricultural production. Admittedly, it is theoretically possible that they could survive equally well onshore whether agriculture is automated or offshored. Such a premise is, after all, at the heart of conventional economics. It is possible, but it is also a poor guide to an operational understanding of how the economy works. It is extremely implausible that the United States would have a major industry in agricultural chemicals absent the world's largest and most advanced market for those products. It is also theoretically possible that we would have developed the world's largest agricultural machinery industry in the absence of the world's largest agricultural sector, but it is most unlikely. And in today's world of extremely imperfect international competition, were the wheat fields to vanish from the United States, the machinery makers would shrink (or offshore) and so would their suppliers of parts, trucking, and janitorial services.

Though such linkages are of vital importance to the strength of our economy and the character of our communities, they extend beyond the very restricted category "tight linkages" that we have been using in this argument. They are, if you will, substantial additions to the effects on which we have been concentrating. They could be called "medium linkages," and, as in the preceding example, they can be caused by market forces or social or community structures as well as by the technical factors we have used to define clear and simple cases of tight linkage. The medium linkages can only be understood and appreciated in a dynamic, or developmental sense (and we will return to them, from just such a perspective, in part II where we discuss the dynamics of industrial development and decline). A static analysis of their presence simply misses their role in development and decline. Finally there are weak linkages where excision has minimal or no consequences. These, as in the above example, are the kinds that hold center stage in conventional economics.

The obvious need is for a solid empirical analysis of linkage. For starters, an analysis of employment (or value added, or both) directly tied to agriculture would be extremely interesting. We tried to locate a study of employment that directly depended upon agricultural production, and not some multiplier analysis of a hypothetical marginal dollar spent on farm output that would count pizza parlor personnel in Nebraska or cotton millers in Carolina. We were unable to locate any serious numbers. The Farm Bureau uses a 7:1 income and employment multiplier to tell the nation how important farming is to our economy.[7] The United States Department of Agriculture provides estimates of agriculture-dependent employment, but they outrageously overstate their own case by tracing the food and fiber chains up through textile mills and food stores to arrive at numbers such as 28.4 million for U.S. 1982 agricultural employment.[8] Based on rather conservative assumptions and procedures—such as trucking jobs only to the first distribution center, no employment effects at all in farm machinery or agricultural chemicals on the ridiculously conservative assumption that the United States could remain the world's biggest producer of tractors absent a domestic market, and of course, no second-round multiplier effects whatever—we made a quick estimate of our own. We found that 3 to 6 million jobs are tightly linked to farm production, which itself directly employs 3 million. Rather than the 3 million jobs commonly assigned to agricultural production, a total of between 6 and 8 million jobs should be considered part of direct farm production in any discussion of offshoring that activity, or in any contemplation of the awesome productivity of American farming that enables a mere 3 percent of the work force to produce the food for all of us and for a considerable amount of the rest of the world. The economic reality is closer to 6 percent or even 8 percent rather than 3 percent.[9]

Tight Linkages Between Services and Manufacturing

If we turn from agriculture to industry—where the conventional base of direct employment is not 3 million but 21 million jobs—even a remotely similar "direct linkage rate" would radically change the meaning of most interpretations of the place of manufacturing in our economy. And it would radically change the drift of policy suggestions about encouraging, or at least not worrying about, the shift out of manufacturing. Manufacturing employment would not be discussed, as it now is in conventional economic presentations, as something that was about one-third of all jobs in 1953 and is now down to one-fifth and doomed to continue down that trend line.[10] Instead, we would have to say that the particular organizational structure of manufacturing production in the United States (and probably in most other highly advanced economies) makes the employment of perhaps 40 or 50 or even 60 million Americans, half or two-thirds or even three-quarters of whom are conventionally counted as service workers, depend directly upon manufacturing production. "Depend" is used to mean that if manufacturing goes, those service jobs go with it. Value added probably follows in rough proportion.

If this tight-linkage argument has anything at all going for it, we must recast our national discussion of the place of manufacturing in the economy. We must start with a new vocabulary and a new perspective. The proportion of jobs in the economy classified as manufacturing or services must be dropped as a defining and operational concept. In its place we must substitute: (1) an analysis of the ways economic activities are linked to one another, something completely absent from the current stock of ideas from which conventional economics draws to set the terms for policy making, and (2) an analysis of how a declining proportion of manufacturing jobs brought about by the loss or offshoring of the production process would compare, in its overall impacts, with a declining proportion brought about by maintaining production while substituting capital, technology, and indirect labor for direct labor. It is our strong suspicion that in the aggregate, onshore development extends the chains of linkages that are the generators of development; offshoring weakens and ultimately unlinks the hauberk; it generates decline.

We do not claim that direct linkages on the order of 1:3 or 1:2 (or even 1:1 or 1:.5) exist between manufacturing and service jobs, and that, therefore, the dominant economic approaches informing policy are all wet in an intellectually fundamental and socially disastrous way. But we do argue that such linkages are real, despite their absence from the vocabulary of conventional economics and that they may be of such scale as to necessitate revision of accepted economic theory and recision of accepted policy. At a minimum, this possibility certainly ought to be examined before policy and attitudes continue along their current path.

Clearly, what is needed is a major reworking (or rather development) of the notion of linkages from the perspective of economic development and decline. Analytically, linkages must be categorized by the degree of dependence—tight, medium, weak—and by the direction of dependence. These must be crossed against the causes and principles of linkage. In the simple and clear illustrations used in this text, the tight linkages are determined by technology; their principle is physical propinquity. There are also other causes of tight and medium linkages and other principles affecting their operation, including market forces, social and communal structures and mores, cultural concerns, and political rules and uncertainties. Finally, quantitative work must be undertaken to gauge their importance, so that we have a body of theory and information that can inform policy. This is no small task.

Without a body of substantial, empirical studies of the concrete nature of economic linkages—and not just empty input-output notions of linkage—and given the prodigious consequences if substantial employment and value added in services are indeed tightly—or even pretty tightly —linked to manufacturing, we will have to argue for the possibility of such a situation by demonstrating its logic and at least its surface plausibility. After all, this takes us right to the heart of the matter.

If the United States loses control and mastery of manufacturing production, it is not simply that we will not be able to replace the jobs lost in industry (narrowly defined) by service jobs; nor simply that those service jobs will pay less; nor that the scale and speed of adjustment will shock the society—and the polity—in potentially dangerous ways. (Many of these terrible problems would also present themselves—though in substantially less severe forms—if we were to automate instead of shifting out of manufacturing.) It is that if we lose mastery and control of manufacturing, the high-paying service jobs that are directly linked to manufacturing will, in a few short rounds of product and process innovation, seem to wither away (only to sprout up offshore, where the manufacturing went). In the final analysis this is the core of the manufacturing matters argument, the proverbial bottom line. It is the high-value-added service roles tied directly to manufacturing (whether they are located in service or manufacturing categories) that we must hold and develop if we are to remain a powerful economy. It is not manufacturing jobs per se. In brief, in order for the shift of employment to services to be developmental and not become a shift to poverty, we must maintain mastery and control of manufacturing production.

Linkages and Wealth

Most, though certainly not all of the service jobs that are likely to be tightly linked to manufacturing are upstream (backward linkages). The great battalions of service jobs downstream from manufacturing, such as wholesaling and retailing, would not be directly affected if manufacturing were ceded to offshore producers; the same sales effort is involved in selling a Toyota as in selling a Buick. Nor would there be any *direct* negative impact on services such as health or education, or fire insurance or sanitation, or hairdressing or dry cleaning. These constitute the great bulk of service employment, and they have no direct linkages to manufacturing, tight or loose. They are related to manufacturing in only two ways, both indirect but both important: (1) through multiplier effects on the demand side: large manufacturing incomes create demands for pizza; shrinking manufacturing incomes reduce the size of the pie; and (2) through wage-setting forces behind the supply side in the labor market for services: eliminate manufacturing jobs in a major way, plus those service jobs directly tied to manufacturing, and the level of wages in the rest of the service sector will drop precipitously as demand for them shrinks and supply mushrooms, in a vortex of impoverishment. This is not a trivial relationship.

To sum up, it is not across the broad expanse of service employments that the critical, or motoring linkages to manufacturing are to be found. Rather, direct linkage is concentrated in the relatively narrow band of services to manufacturing businesses and (awkward though it sounds) in services to services to manufacturers.

Examples of such closely linked activities include design and engineering services for product and process; payroll, inventory, and accounting services; financing and insuring; repair and maintenance of plant and machinery; training and recruiting; testing services and labs; industrial waste disposal; and the accountants, publicists, designers, payroll, transportation, and communication firms who work for the engineering firms that design and service production equipment; or the trucking firms that move the semifinished goods from plant to plant, up the links of the manufacturing chain.

Two questions pose themselves immediately; many more follow. The first involves scale: How important are these upstream services to manufacturing? Do they constitute a scale of employment and value added sufficient to justify a new set of concerns, a rethinking of theory or a recasting of policy? Or do we simply need to add a few more jobs to manufacturing employment as conventionally defined? The second concerns the nature of the linkages between these upstream services and manufacturing: What are their concrete relationships to manufacturing? How can we go about determining how many of those jobs would vanish from the U.S. economy if U.S. producers lost control and mastery of manufacturing and U.S. markets were sourced from offshore? How can we make a new understanding of linkages operational?

The *Report of the President on the Trade Agreements Program* provides an approximate answer for the first question. It is staggeringly large: "25% of U.S. GNP originates in services used as inputs by goods-producing industries—more than the value added to GNP by the manufacturing sector."[11]

The magnitude of this estimation of the importance to the economy of upstream suppliers of services to manufacturers is so colossal that if it is even close to accurate it compels us to stop and immediately reconsider the treatment of manufacturing by conventional economics categories. After all, manufacturing plus services sold to manufacturing firms equals half the economy. Talk of shifting out of it is not something that should be complacently contemplated. Categories of thought that lead to such conclusions should, at a minimum, be subject to quality control and reality checks.

Given the enormity of the magnitudes involved, the first task is to check the president's estimates (derived by an input-output methodology) against an estimate derived differently. Two other readily available numbers can help us check the president's estimate to see if it squares.

First, if we analyze the economy by *value added,* manufacturing represents about 24 percent of GNP.[12] When you count the value added by a firm to GNP you do not count the goods and services that firm buys from other firms. You count just the value of what it does to those inputs (receipts minus purchases). That value added comes out of the firm in the form of the wages, rents, profits, and so on, that it pays. The value produced by service firms that sell their services to manufacturing concerns, and have the value of their services embodied in the manufactured goods, would not be counted in the value added by manufacturing. But it would be included in the price of the manufactured good and in the proportion of GNP by final demand represented by goods. So, if we take the 24 percent of value added that is created by manufacturing firms and add to that the president's estimate of 25 percent of GNP by value created by service-producing firms and used as inputs by goods-producing industries, we get about one-half of GNP embodied in manufactured goods. Second, if we analyze the economy *by final demand* (omitting agriculture and con-struction), we find that goods represent about 47 percent of GNP, services about 53 percent.[13] As rough approximations the numbers square.

These numbers are a rough estimate of an upper limit of upstream service employment. They are not at all an estimate of tightly linked jobs. Many of these upstream services, such as advertising (150,000 jobs), would do quite as well with foreign or offshore manufacturers. All upstream service jobs and value added that are tightly linked to manufacturing will be in this category (upstream sales of services to manufacturers), but not all jobs in this category—maybe only a small percentage—will be indispu-tably tightly linked to manufacturing.

Charting just how the different pieces of that upstream service em-ployment are linked to manufacturing is the difficult problem. It should be right at the top of the economics research agenda, so that it can get to the top of the policy debate. For, unless it can be shown that the overwhelming bulk of those services are very weakly linked to manufacturing (so weakly linked as to be indifferent to whether manufacturing stays or moves off-shore), we must quickly reformulate the terms of that policy debate. It does not take much research to see that some of those upstream services are clearly not indifferent to offshoring manufacturing.

Some upstream service jobs are so tightly linked into manufacturing that they are best understood as direct extensions of that employment base. These would include, for example, truckers (and those who service them) who specialize in interplant shipments of raw materials, compo-nents, and semifinished goods. The U.S. textile industry, for example, because of its enormous size and the geographical spread of specialized plants, is a major employer of trucking services. There are some 15,000 to 20,000 trucking jobs, specialized in moving and warehousing, chemicals, raw materials, yarn, cloths, pieces of garments, and even packaging, right up to, but not including, the completed garment (at which point imports would have the same employment effect).[14] Few of these roles would exist without an onshore textile/apparel industry. The same is obviously true for those who repair and service the machinery used in manufacturing: in almost all cases, they have to be located close to the machines that will need servicing. The same conditions apply to the numerous security guards, janitors, bookkeepers, and data processors hired, not directly by the manufacturing firms, but through specialized janitorial, security, or general service firms (who often are able to pay lower wages than the unionized manufacturers). Printers; industrial waste disposal specialists; environmental health, safety, and pollution specialists; hydrologists; and payroll, paying, and receiving services are also directly linked to the manufacturing process. So are specialized financial services, factors, insurance adjusters and raters—right on up to the top of the financial line, venture capitalists. Whatever the scale and location of those who collect the funds for venture investments, those who place those funds, and hand hold and monitor the ventures, and decide whether to go further to second-round financing or just write off the grubstake must operate in tight propinquity with the start-up companies. If "the action" in high-tech start-ups moves from the United States to Korea or Spain or Japan—regardless of whether the pension funds that collect the venture cash remain in New York, Paris, and Zurich—the venture industry will find itself slouching toward Seoul or Madrid or Tokyo. All the services we have mentioned, and many more, simply must be performed in close propinquity to the manufacturers. If manufacturing goes, they disappear—or, more exactly, those same service roles get filled by new people at the new offshore locations next to the manufacturers.

The category of services tightly linked to manufacturing is real, and it is peopled. But we do not know how big it is. Given the reality of these tight linkages—the complementarity rather than the substitutability of service jobs and manufacturing jobs—the critical questions emerge: How big are they? How many jobs are involved? How much income? Those questions can be answered only after careful empirical study. But asking them, and getting the questions to be taken seriously, may define a good first step.

Power and Wealth

This chapter has argued that manufacturing is critical to the wealth and power of the United States; lose manufacturing and you will lose—not develop—high-wage service jobs. The argument focused on economics, on the process of generating wealth. Throughout, power has been viewed as an aspect of wealth, as having the resources to create the kind of society we want. Its military manifestation is not a central concern of this book. Military needs have been treated in parenthesis, as they are treated in conventional economics. The parentheses suspend not just the rhythms of the text, but the laws of efficiency and the rules of resource allocation. Like so many of the conventions of economics, this way of signaling exceptions misleads as much as it informs. It is not easy to make exceptions for something as big as the U.S. military effort. Exceptions on that scale are never without consequences for the rest of the system.

However costly it may appear, the costs of our defense effort are radically reduced by the existence of a strong domestic manufacturing capability. Strong, diverse, and leading-edge producers of such technologies as semiconductors, computers, and telecommunications, and of the advanced equipment needed to design and produce, swiftly and without defects, generation after brief generation of these products makes the costs of the advanced weaponry and information systems that constitute the basis of our national security much less than they would be if we had to create such an industrial structure—extending all the way back to training in materials, computer, and electronic sciences—exclusively for military use.

If American commercial producers in, say, semiconductors fell behind foreign competitors, it might not just be extremely costly for the military to maintain, for its own use, a permanently superior technical and production capacity; it might not be possible. Domestic capability in critical links of the production chain, as, again in semiconductors, mask making, clean room and production equipment, and design tools, could quickly disappear as foreign producers win the competitive contest. There are indications of new concerns at the Pentagon for precisely such circumstances. Such an erosion of our competitive position in a critical set of industrial chains would constitute a massive reduction of our strategic independence and diplomatic options. Loss of leading-edge capacity in chip making quickly translates into a loss of diplomatic and strategic bargaining chips. At the very best, in some cases, it would merely increase massively the real costs of defense. And it would do so in a way that will create a necessity for ever more massive cost increases at every level of technological development and commercial erosion.

It should be recognized that this line of argument suggests that commercial development can often drive military capability. It is the reverse of the generally received scenario where military needs drive commercial development. In some areas, military investment can still drive commercial competitive development, particularly where it can finance generic R&D

and then serve as a launch market for new product areas. Space technology is a conspicuous current example; aircraft bodies and engines and, in the very early days of the technology, semiconductors are earlier instances of military requirements successfully driving and launching new areas of commercial advantage. However, there are now a great many important cases—semiconductors, computers, machine tools, and robotics, to name but a few—where commercial markets are mature and commercial requirements are large in scale, competitive in price and application and as sophisticated as, though different in form from, military requirements. In these not uncommon circumstances, military investment in research and procurement can neither drive nor decide the lines of technological development nor leverage competitive advantage.[15]

Diverse, robust, and leading-edge U.S. producers in these and other industrial chains are more critical to U.S. national security at the current time than to most other nations or to ourselves at earlier periods in our history. For, in a fundamental sense, whatever the ups and downs of military spending and the changes in defense strategies, our basic security posture is built on the assumption that America will maintain, round after hurried round, a permanent lead in a rather broad range of advanced industrial technologies.

If America were to lose the scale and the leading-edge quality of its productive base in semiconductors, computers, telecommunications, robotics, and machine tools, to name but a few key sectors, we would end up having to support the full weight of an arsenal economy that is not only vast but also premised on the difficult necessity of permanant technological superiority. Our economy would become vis-à-vis Japan not so different from the arsenal Soviet economy vis-à-vis ours. This is another critical sense in which a strong and broad manufacturing sector matters mightily to the power and wealth of the United States.

Sometimes new notions capture our fancy, resonate to some element of our experience, and color the way we see the world. The concept of a post-industrial society is just such a notion. It gives voice to our experience of big changes, shapes our perceptions of their tone and texture, and organizes our understanding of their direction. But the notion obscures the precise location of those changes and their meanings.

Things, of course, have changed. Production work has changed. People go home cleaner; more and more of them leave offices rather than assembly lines. Service activities have proliferated. The sociology of work and the organization of society have changed along with the technologies of product and production.

But the relationship of those changes in technology and society to changes in the fundamentals of economics—the process of wealth creation —is less clear. There is not yet, nor is there likely to be in the near future, a "post-industrial economy." The division of labor has become infinitely more elaborate and the production process far more indirect, involving increasingly specialized inputs of services as well as goods and materials located organizationally (and physically) far from the traditional scene of production, the proverbial shop floor. But the key generator of wealth for this vastly expanded and differentiated division of labor remains mastery and control of production. We are shifting not out of industry into services, but from one kind of industrial economy to another.

3

Services and the American Trade Balance

C AN the United States run a surplus on trade in services with the rest of the world, of a scale to offset significantly our merchandise deficit? As this is not a whodunit mystery novel, there is little suspense to be lost, and perhaps some clarity to be gained, by revealing the answer up front: no. Whatever claims may be made by politicians, economists, or leaders of some of our more successful service industries, service exports at present do not and, for the foreseeable future, will not be able to offset massive American deficits on merchandise.* Behind that answer lie four funda-mental arguments that we will explore in this chapter:

*Financial identities are conventionally used to structure discussions of the current account balance. The balance of trade in goods and services must, by identity, equal invest-ment flows and equal the domestic balance of savings and investment (private and govern-ment), so that,

$$X+T = NFI = S-GD-I$$

where X= Balance on trade in goods
  T= Balance in services, interest, and transfers
  NFI= Net foreign investment
  GD= Government deficit (net gov. borrowing)
  I= Investment

This accounting identity can be read either way: causality is reversible. It can, and frequently is, used to show that as long as our savings are insufficient to cover investment plus government deficits the United States must import capital and, therefore, must show a trade deficit. It can equally well be read in the opposite direction: trade deficits necessitate capital imports.

Our concern in this chapter is not with the static macro accounting of the U.S. current

1. The scale of trade in services is simply too small to offset difficulties in our merchandise accounts.

2. There is no reason whatever for assuming—or perhaps "wishing" is a better word—that the United States is better at exporting services than it is at exporting manufactured goods or that our comparative advantage and our competitive advantage are in services, not manufactured goods. Recent data provide no basis for such satisfaction, and current trends could be interpreted as pointing toward serious difficulties on the services front.

3. Large segments of trade in services are directly tied to the existence of a strong and technologically advanced manufacturing sector. There is as much reason for seeing service exports as a complement to manufacturing as for seeing them as a substitute or successor.

4. The international environment for trade in services is even less liberal than that for trade in goods. Despite U.S. cries for international liberalization, there is every reason to believe that liberalization will be slow in coming, limited in scope, and unliberal in form.

Trade in Services

The weight of services in international trade bears no proportion to its place in the composition of GNP. Services constitute a very small proportion of our international trade, and despite recurrent predictions to the contrary and policies predicated on them, there is no indication that the situation will soon change in ways that matter quantitatively.

The difficulty in arguing this simple position, a position that can easily be supported by statistical evidence of impeccable banality, is that the discussion of the contributions of services to our trade balance is confused by the data at two separate levels. First, it is confused by some simple but

---

account. Nor is it with the complex and perverse effects on exchange rates and interest rates of offsetting massive trade deficits with financial flows (and vice versa). Nor is it with the unique role of the dollar in international finance that permits "permanant" massive trade deficits and thereby changes the operational meaning of the static accounts approach as well as raising questions about the congruence of the political and economic boundaries to which the accounting should be applied.

Instead our concern is with the dynamics of U.S. international competitiveness, on our ability to sustain high-value-added exports and increase domestic productivity. It is with the composition of our trade account.

very misleading classifications in the trade accounts. That confusion then becomes a convenient support for official and unofficial positions that minimize—where they don't fully discount—the difficulties, both short- and long-term, to the U.S. economy created by the disastrous trade balance in the merchandise account. We can quickly and easily clear away that confusion and also the arguments based on it. But second, beyond that simple confusion lies a deeper murkiness in the data. There is a feeling that the data simply do not provide a complete picture of what is going on. They invite, therefore, all sorts of hypotheses, estimations, and projections.

The Council of Economic Advisers exemplifies simple confusion from on high. It explains in reassuring terms what many feel to be, at the very least, a disturbing trade deficit:

> Although the 1983 and likely 1984 trade deficits are without precedent, they are not difficult to explain. To begin with the United States has a normal or "structural" deficit in merchandise trade that is offset by a surplus in exports of services and therefore need not be a cause of special concern.[1]

That our manufacturing trade balance continues to decline is, there- fore, no cause for alarm. It is to be expected (except for excesses due to the short-term aberration of an overvalued dollar). It is compensated by a surplus in exports of services. The 1981 trade balance, as the Council reads it, shows a $28 billion deficit in merchandise and a $39 billion surplus in services. In 1982 the merchandise deficit was up to $36 billion, but it was largely offset by another $33 billion surplus in services.[2] (The 1984 and 1985 numbers are simply too ugly to consider in this context of calm, reassured discussion.) The evolution of our foreign trade mirrors the evo- lution of our domestic economy: a decline in manufacturing and a shift to services. Of course the official view recognizes problems, such as obstacles to the exports of services erected by foreign governments, but they can be dealt with. Indeed, they should be the focus of our negotiations. It is in trade in services that our future lies. If trade-offs have to be made, and indeed they will, we should not lose sight of our long-term interest, which is the export of services, not routine manufacturing.[3]

The problem with this reassuring and widely received argument is that it does not hold up to careful analysis. It squares with the desire to find that things are going fine and that the invisible hand has put us, once again, in the lead position on the winning path. But it does not quite square with the facts. The 1982 current account (which compared with 1983 was a "good" year, and a wonderful year if compared with 1984 or 1985) lists a "balance of goods and services" of minus $3 billion. The key to this acceptable performance was a $33 billion surplus in services which largely offset the $36 billion deficit in merchandise. But $25.5 billion of that $33 billion surplus was investment income—interest—from U.S. investments abroad. The overwhelming mass of what the Council of Economic Advisers calls the service surplus[4] is not service exports at all, but returns on old investments, more precisely U.S. loans to foreign borrowers. These should not be confused with the export performance of an economy. Most of these "earnings" represent interest payments on Third World loans, which, though not yet technically in default, are rather close to de facto default. (Doubtful Third World debt owed to U.S. banks can be conservatively estimated at $300 billion. At 10 percent per year, there goes the "service surplus.") Furthermore, the United States is now a net debtor— rather than a creditor nation—so that the balance is now reversed, and we will pay out more interest than we take in. In the words of the president's latest *Report on the Trade Agreements Program,* "The United States has borrowed so much money from overseas to finance its deficits and domestic investment that it has become a net debtor to the world for the first time in 70 years. In fact, America has gone from being the world's largest creditor to its largest debtor in less than three years."[5]

Thus, almost all of the services surplus—which is supposed to offset our "natural" merchandise deficit—is, first, not services but rather interest on foreign loans and investments; second, not very bankable; and third, already gone, as our obligations to foreigners now exceed theirs to us. It is certainly nothing on which to base an argument that there is no reason for concern about our balance of trade. The part that is *potentially* services is quite small. At the most only $7.5 billion could be real, net service earnings (and we will return to that later in this chapter, because a lot of that is not really services either). In no way can we count on it to offset a $36 billion deficit in merchandise—and remember, that was the last reasonably good year. For 1984 the deficit on merchandise was $123 billion, and for 1985, about $150 billion, and 1986 should be even worse.[6] The scale of trade in services is simply too small to offset the deficit in our merchandise account.

Comparative Advantage in Services?

The relatively small volume of trade in services is not necessarily the beginning of something big. International trade in services is not growing any faster than trade in goods. According to the Department of Commerce, service exports were about one-fifth the size of world merchandise exports in 1983, about the same relative size as in 1973.[7] So there is nothing in our statistics of the recent past that should lead us to expect services to suddenly grow to offset our merchandise deficit. More important there is nothing in those same trade statistics to encourage the belief—let alone the making of policy based on the belief—that the United States has either a particular competitive advantage (we are flat out better than the others) or even its comparative advantage (our least inefficient exportable) in services.

Let us look more closely at the concrete composition of our trade in services. If we begin by excluding the items we identified as not being services—interest and investment income and profit repatriation (by now a giant deficit anyway)—we find that the United States does indeed run a net surplus on real services. But it is a very small surplus realized on a relatively small volume of trade. In 1984 the surplus amounted to $2 billion (against a merchandise deficit of over $120 billion). The volume of trade in services (exports plus imports) was only $85 billion in contrast to about $560 billion in merchandise trade.[8]

In table 3.1 the first three categories of services—Travel, Passenger Fares, and Transportation—are quite straightforward. The travel account represents money spent by tourists and business travelers. When U.S. citizens spend dollars abroad, that counts in balance of payments terms as a U.S. import; when foreigners spend money in the United States, we export the service. Almost one-half of our travel account is with Canada and Mexico, the other half is overseas travel. Over the past three years, the relentless rise of the dollar has held this item in deficit; we ought to note, however, that it has rarely been a surplus item. The recent surplus years, about two in all, followed the low point on the trade-weighted dollar, around 1980.

Passenger fares represent payments to international carriers, mostly

TABLE 3.1

U.S. Trade in Services for 1984

	Export	Import	Balance	Total Trade (exports + imports)
Travel	11.4	15.8	−4.4	27.2
Passenger Fares	3.1	6.6	−3.5	9.7
Transportation (goods)	13.7	14.7	−1	28.4
Proprietary Rights	8	.5	7.6	8.5
Other Business Services	7.2	3.9	3.2	11.1

SOURCE: Department of Commerce, *United States Trade: Performance and Outlook,* June 1985, p. 140.

airlines. When Americans fly on foreign flag carriers, those payments are counted as a service import. For the United States this is traditionally a deficit item, reflecting in part the greater tendency of U.S. nationals to travel overseas compared with overseas visitors who choose to visit the United States. The high dollar has pushed this item into serious size deficit for 1984.

Transportation is a category that covers the movement of goods, not people. It is a composite of different services, including, principally, freight handling and shipping, and port services. On the movement of freight we ran a major deficit last year. But we managed to narrow the overall categorical deficit by being a major exporter of port services: fees paid by foreign shippers to our ports for docking and unloading imports of manufactured goods into the United States amounted to $9 billion, while U.S. shippers paid only about $5 billion to unload a smaller volume of goods into foreign ports.

The most interesting categories, and the ones most central to our argument, are the next two: Proprietary Rights (licensing of know-how and technology), and Other Business Services—which includes all the services that proponents of "Services as Our Future" argue will take the burden of our international trade position: engineering, banking, brokerage, construction, advertising, accounting, legal, medical, management consulting, financial, and data processing and design services, plus all other private business services (except for those we have already discussed: investment income, travel, passenger fares, transportation, and proprietary rights).

At first glance the Other Business Services category looks like a Western river: it's a mile wide and an inch deep, and it doesn't move much water. It is by far the broadest of all the trade categories: it would take the better part of a page just to list its components. But the dollar amounts are quite small. Certainly they are too small to support the burden of the argument placed on it, to say nothing of the burden of the merchandise deficit. In 1984 total exports plus imports of Other Business Services equaled only $11 billion (with a $3.2 billion surplus of exports over imports). But it is on this bundle of services that the entire services position hangs: no one is seriously arguing that the United States will become a major tourist center—in that sense we are closer to Japan or Germany than Italy or England. There is little reason to think that we will become a major provider of shipping to the world; and of course those port receipts, though growing at an impressive rate, are a kind of ironic service export to project upward.

Our analysis of international trade in services has been based on official U.S. government statistics on service exports and imports. Those statistics reflect all the fundamental failings of the statistical categories and data on the role of services in the domestic economy that underlie the argument that America's economic future is to be found in the developmental succession of services for manufacturing. Their fundamental inadequacies, and the consequent confusion they create for both analysis and policy making, are the major theme of chapter 4.

As both a cause and an effect of the movement to place the opening of foreign markets to American service providers—especially financial and telecommunication services—at the very top of the U.S. trade negotiating agenda, a small group of analysts are arguing that the United States is a much bigger and better service exporter than the data indicate. The data, they argue, simply miss huge volumes of U.S. service exports.*

Let us, for the moment, simply take as given that the statistics on

---

*Perhaps the most intelligent as well as the sanest treatment of the role and potential for exports of business services can be found in the collaborative work of Jonathan Aronson and Peter Cowhey.[9] The most influential of these studies was prepared by a small consulting firm for the U.S. Department of Commerce.[10]

The Department of Commerce study argues that conventional statistical reporting systematically and massively undercounts the volume of trade in services, and that much of what is really service trade gets reported as investment. To provide what they consider to be a more accurate estimate of American service exports, they count one-half of U.S. investment receipts as service exports.

Methodologically, this strikes us as somewhat extreme, though not lacking a certain ruthless panache. Taking one-half of investment receipts and calling it service exports is just a bit too heroic. Of course, data on service exports and imports are not very good. It is also quite likely that the investment category is stuffed with transactions that are not properly investments but that have no clear and convenient place in the statistical accounts. Fees and commissions earned by Wall Street firms on services to foreign investors might often be so misclassified. But there is also likely to be a set of fees and commissions that go the other way—that go, in whole or in part, to Zurich or London or Tokyo—given (as argued in the following pages) the colossal role of foreign financial institutions in the U.S. market. And there are also likely to be parallel misclassifications for such items as certain headquarter activities in U.S. manufacturing companies that are really part of export sales. But such items are not the only large-scale transactions that often elude correct classification and are therefore dumped into the investment category or simply counted as domestic activities. Illegal transactions, especially those related to the drug trade, might occupy a place of prominence in any revised accounting.

We could easily marshal evidence for this hypothesis of equal plausibility (and, therefore, dubiousness) as that used to support "taking half of investment receipts and calling it service exports." For example, the volume of phone calls is often used as a proxy for the volume of transactions between two market centers. Colombia ranks strikingly high on the list of telephone destinations from Manhattan (not Queens, where there is an immigrant population).[11]

Now that the flow or net investment income has reversed and receipts are outbound, not inbound, are we to assume that the colossal sums (one-half of receipts) attributed to service exports will be attributed to service imports?

There is every reason to distrust the official statistics on service exports. There is no reason, however, to make a leap into self-confirming "evidence" as does the Department of Commerce report and those who carry its "findings" into argument. All omitted or undercounted service transactions do not go one way: some, perhaps very many, are imports. Also, the undercounting may have been consistent over time. As trade in services has not grown international trade in services are not very good, and assume that exports (and perhaps imports) of business services may be greater than we think.

If we increase exports of business services (while holding imports constant) by ten percent, or even 50 percent, nothing changes in our argument. A recent study by the Congressional Office of Technology Assessment (OTA) increases exports by 50 to 100 percent and imports by up to two-thirds.*

Even if we double or triple the volume of exports (and, most peculiarly, not touch imports), we would still not substantially affect the thrust of our argument.

Initial perusal of the data on exports of services to business raises a simple quantitative response: at present, and for the foreseeable future, volumes in this crucial category are just far too small to offset international trade losses in value-added and high-wage employment in the manufacturing sector.

A second examination of that data generates deeper and perhaps more important questions, not just about the quantities traded, but about the plausibility of assuming a developmental sectoral succession in exports from manufacturing (where American advantage is apparently eroding) to services to business (where it is supposedly solid). There is little in U.S. performance in these service activities to indicate any special U.S. advantage. And there are as many and as solid reasons for thinking that the United States might be relatively weaker in this category in the near future than it was in the near past. Most prominent among those reasons is that,

---

over the past ten years any faster than official tabulations of trade in merchandise, revising our data to include the undercount might not, in the end, affect the problem: What does the change in today's international trade position from that of several years ago mean for the wealth and power of the nation?

No one distrusts more than we the usefulness of economic data categorized by economic sector. A major purpose of this work is to show why such a categorization should be mistrusted and to demonstrate that a fundamental rethinking of the analytic categories under which statistical data are collected—and used—is necessary. Such a redoing of our statistics would be, to say the least, a substantial and complex undertaking. Quick and very, very dirty dumpings of disingenuously rough estimates of the margin of ambiguity into categories that suit the analyst's purposes is not the way to do it.

*As this book goes to press, the OTA has published a set of estimates of exports and imports for twenty-two major service industries. (The major omission is banking and finance.) As part of the effort for the Uruguay Round of GATT (General Agreement on Tariffs and Trade) talks, other such studies are likely to follow. The OTA study concludes that the official U.S. data on trade in services are woefully inadequate. Its estimates of service exports for 1984 increase the official figures by somewhere between $25 billion and $47 billion (in other words, as much as 100 percent) and increase imports by from $16 billion to $33 billion (as much as two-thirds).

Taking OTA's midrange estimate the U.S. surplus for 1983 would increase from the official $6.4 billion to about $17 billion. This is a substantial increase, but, as indicated, even a $10 billion increase doesn't affect the thrust of this chapter's argument.[12]

as we shall see, many of these services are quite closely linked to the technological level and competitive performance of U.S. manufacturing.

This is clearly seen if we look at the Proprietary Rights category in table 3.1. In 1984, the United States exported $8 billion in proprietary rights and imported only $0.5 billion. Here is a comparative advantage that produced a competitive advantage with a ratio approaching (but not quite reaching) those for Japan in autos or consumer electronics. And it is in exactly the right place: exports of knowledge in immaterial form, the quintessential post-industrial activity. This category mainly counts payments—fees and royalties—for the use or sale of intellectual property: copyrights, patents, processes, technology. It reflects, as the Department of Commerce puts it, "U.S. dominance in the development and sale of technology."[13]

Some 80 percent of all our exports of proprietary rights are contained within U.S. multinationals:[14] they are paid by the foreign branches and directly controlled affiliates back to headquarters. In addition to licensing fees for technology, the Proprietary Rights Category includes payments from the affiliate to headquarters for management, professional, and technical services, payments for allotted shares of research and development costs, and payments for assigned shares of other major expenses, such as overhead. These payments do not include returns on investments such as interest and dividends. The fact that payments from affiliates to headquarters within U.S.-owned multinationals constitute 80 percent of this category blurs the sharply etched image of developmental movements up from production to the provision of intangible, high-valued information. For example, it would be relatively easy for headquarters to manipulate payments from affiliates for such difficult-to-monitor transactions as management services, technology, and shares of overhead. Special considerations —such as different national tax practices, or claims on profits by labor in different countries—might lead a multinational firm to adjust, where possible, payments from its affiliates to square less with compensating the services they are paid for, and more with strategic notions about where and in what form it wanted its income (and expenditures) to come out. It is conceivable that some companies might assess the affiliates more for services from headquarters to establish lower profit rates in certain high-tax countries and bring those gains out as profits in low-tax countries.

Whatever the intricacies of intracorporate international accounting (and they are many and wondrous), and however their strengths might weaken the basis for using the Proprietary Rights category to support the argument that the U.S. economy can build up its service exports to offset substantial declines in its merchandise accounts, we feel, nonetheless, that it is not unreasonable to conclude with the judgment of the Department of Commerce that U.S. strength in this critical service category "reflects the historical U.S. dominance in the development and sale of technology . . . and is a reflection of the prevalence and advanced technology used by foreign affiliates of U.S. companies."[15] After all, that supports our central argument: exports in these critical service areas are not substitutes for manufacturing strength; they are complements. They depend on the technological and competitive strength of U.S. industry, and of course contribute to maintaining that strength and to holding onto the value added it generates. Complementarity or interdependence is a more accurate description of the relationship than substitution or succession.

Trade in Services and Competitiveness in Production

This is equally the case in the broader Other Business Services category, which, if we may repeat, includes *all* the services that are supposed to carry the burden of the U.S. balance of payments. In some cases the dependence of service exports on manufacturing capability is absolutely clear. We export satellite launching and satellite broadcast services because we produce communication satellites and launching systems. We invented this technology and had the world market to ourselves until very recently. Now there is competition in launchers and in satellites from Europe, and soon there will be competition in satellites from Japan despite the noncompetitive cost of Japanese satellites. (We have already lost the lead in receiving stations to the Japanese.) American advantage in services delivered in the high heavens (satellite launching, broadcasting, mapping and meteorology) and under the deep seas (exploration and foraging services) depends upon our being the producer of the most advanced and competitive equipment.

Few examples of anything are so dramatic as the dependence of satellite launching services on advantage in equipment production, but many other services evidence a substantial dependence on state-of-the-art production capability. This is certainly the case if one adopts a long-term, dynamic perspective, and not just a short-term, static notion of advantage. The appropriateness of such a perspective is also evident: it is the only one that counts when the subject is development and decline. Consider American exports of engineering services. These are top-of-the-line service exports. They are knowledge-intensive and employ a high percentage of highly paid professionals who in turn purchase significant amounts of other services, including enhanced telecommunications, data processing, computer programming, transportation, accounting, and law.

Product and process engineering is a major service export. It is often suggested that the United States should shift up and out of selling steel, and petrochemicals, and other routine manufactured goods to the world— or even to ourselves—and concentrate instead on selling the know-how, the high-end services that go into those products: engineering services for the design, construction, and operation of steel mills and petrochemical plants. Indeed, the argument goes, it is not in competition with lower-wage nations in the direct production of goods but precisely in this high-value-added niche that a high-wage America will find its comparative advantage. But the ability to stay competitive in the sale of such services depends on U.S. producers of steel or petrochemicals, or automobile engines or disc drives, maintaining highly competitive, state-of-the-art production facilities. Competitive advantage in engineering services depends upon mastery and control of the latest production technology by U.S. producers.

When leadership in production changes hands, it is soon followed by a switch in the direction of service flow. Not very long ago the United States exported high-end services in the steel industry. Then U.S. steel producers fell behind in technology, in the organization of production, and in the design and operation of the production technologies and facilities. Now we import those same services from our former customers in Europe and Japan, and before long, we will probably import them from Korea and Brazil. Services to the steel industry is not an isolated case of producer services.[16] We used to export automobile engineering services. Now we are importing those services, as the GM-Toyota and Chrysler-Mitsubishi joint ventures conspicuously testify. Petrochemical engineering is another major area of high-level service exports where a reversal of flow is quite probable over a reasonably short time. And so is the production of computer peripherals and components—if there are any American producers left to buy those services and if we force the Japanese to sell to United States manufacturers the know-how as service instead of product. Fermentation technology—at the heart of the industrialization of biotech—is another possible market, but one as likely to become an import market for foreign engineering services as a market for U.S. engineering exports. In the design and construction of nuclear energy plants, American engineering firms such as Bechtel, in conjunction with American producers of nuclear-energy-generating equipment such as Westinghouse, were major, perhaps dominant, suppliers of engineering services to countries around the globe who were building light-water reactors. Then, new construction of such plants in the United States dried up. Critics began to find fault with the engineering work and to turn elsewhere. Companies based in other countries, such as France, Japan, and Germany, were building new plant at a faster rate than in the United States. They were learning as they went along. France graduated from its licensee obligations to Westinghouse, and the French firm Framatom quickly became a major competitor to the U.S. service exporters.

Competitiveness in these high-end services is directly related to hands-on experience in state-of-the-art production. When that position in production is lost, so, over time, is the competitive advantage in the service. When American manufacturers fall behind competitively, and market share and profit margins erode, they cease adding new plants. Those competitors who add new plants eventually master the technologies and the know-how, apply it themselves, and begin to upgrade it little by little through experience and through the opportunities for process and product innovation afforded by adding new plants. Then they export it—first the product, and then, if forced, the know-how. The export of production technologies cannot, over time or at any significant scale, substitute for sustained mastery of production. They are complementary, not alternative, activities. There is interdependence in time as well as in function; under most circumstances, the succession from selling product to selling services that embody the know-how that goes into that product is only a brief stretch-out of returns on old investment and old know-how.

The process of succession—not the succession of services replacing production, but the succession of new producers in different nations replacing old production leaders in the provision of services as well as goods —is just as clear in another major service export area: construction engineering.

In recent years construction engineering accounted for about 10 percent of all U.S. service exports.[17] Especially in big job projects, giant and highly sophisticated U.S. construction engineering firms like Bechtel had a commanding presence in international markets. Now they are watching the rapid erosion of their markets in the face of a complex set of negative factors: first, an overall shrinkage of big international construction jobs; second, a comparable erosion of big job construction projects in the United States; and third, and most important to our purposes, the rise of new foreign-based competitors. Korean firms are the most discussed, but not the only new (and surprisingly strong) foreign competitors; there are also such newly venerable players as France's Bouyges and Japan's Chiyoda. International construction firms such as Korea's Lucky and Hyundai were originally (and until just yesterday) mere providers of unskilled construction gangs. Then they began to upgrade, increasing the scope of their services to include higher and higher value-added elements. They were, after all, now part and parcel of an industrial structure that was the low-cost producer of structural steel. The materials for a big construction job are vastly more costly than the engineering services. This gave them a potential advantage in pricing: the engineering services could be bundled up in the costs of the materials. They could be pushed at low cost, at no cost as a loss-leader, or simply as part of the sales costs for materials. In some markets, like the Persian Gulf, they could supply the whole package: engineering, materials, and labor, and then take payment in countertrade. Accumulating experience in their home markets and in international markets, and aided by a national development strategy of upgrading skills (such as Korea's policy of producing engineers), they were able to learn to do the project design, programming, and organization that give the big engineering firms their competitive advantage. Now they have become lead engineers on big international jobs, winning contract after contract. The U.S. engineering firms find themselves being pushed out of vital export markets, and substantial penetration of the U.S. market by foreign construction engineers is now a distinct possibility.

Many American engineering groups, whether independent firms like Bechtel or integrated outfits like Westinghouse, are among the best in the world in their specialties. But they are no longer the only sophisticated operations in the business. Unless American industry adds new and state-of-the-art plants and equipment, American engineering groups, especially the big, integrated firms, will fall behind their foreign competitors who continue to upgrade their hands-on expertise, and the U.S. competitive position in that big segment of service exports will erode. The Americans have few special advantages that cannot be countered. Many of their foreign competitors, as we have noted, are owned by the firms that produce the materials—aluminum, steel, cement, or equipment—or the final product—steel, autos, or petrochemicals. Some, for example France's Technip,[18] that do big projects such as petrochemical plants, are owned by consortia of all of them. Since design and engineering, like architecture, is always a small percentage of any major project, these "integrated" service producers may be able to build a competitive advantage over U.S. firms which may have to price their engineering services at full cost plus mark-up because they may no longer be closely tied to competitive materials or equipment producers, or state-of-the-art final-product companies, or may simply be independent.

It is not only engineering services that go through this development cycle offshore. A whole range of services will grow at the locations where industrial production is growing and becoming more complex and sophisticated. What services grow, at what rate, to what extent will depend upon a complex set of interactive factors among which will figure prominently: the organizational form of offshore production (multinationals, contractors, single plant, lots of plants, and so on); the skills and infrastructure available in the host country; the local "climate" for spin-offs; and, of course, the role of government policy in the host country in pushing the offshoring companies to source more and more value-added locally. Many countries, such as Taiwan and Korea, have put together impressive packages of these diverse elements—skills, infrastructure, policies, institutions—and are in fact developing substantial on-site capacity in many services that until recently had to be imported along with the manufacturing plant and the capital.[19] Some of these services will soon be exported, along with indigenous manufacturing plant, technology, and capital.

Financial Services

Banking—and, more generally, "financial services"—is the most often cited example of a service whose export earnings could offset deficits in the merchandise account in a very big way. It is a sector in which the United States is said to have a strong competitive advantage. It is high in knowledge, high in technology, and is supposed to take its developmental cues from the patterns of the most advanced economy: ours. Optimistic forecasts of U.S. advantage in financial services are a commonplace of trade policy discussion.

But the situation in banking services may be less clear and less rosy than we like to think. At first blush at least, there is no compelling reason to assume a special advantage for U.S. banks compared with their competitors in Japan and Western Europe.

First, foreign banks are bigger, and they are growing bigger faster than the U.S. banks. A recent listing of the world's one hundred biggest banks counted twenty-three Japanese banks but only eighteen American banks: it also included forty-four European banks.[20] Size may or may not mean much in banking, although outside of highly specialized niches, a fairly huge minimum size is needed to provide worldwide service and to support investment in the new technologies of worldwide banking. Second, there is every reason to expect U.S. banks to increase in size dramatically over the next years. The unique American phenomenon of an enormous number of small independent banks is determined not by "economic forces" but by regulation forbidding interstate banking and the mixing of various kinds of investment banking with commercial banking. Those regulations are currently being dismantled, and it is likely that over the next few years the big money-center banks will take over the smaller banks and set themselves up as a big four, a seven sisters, a pac ten, a tremendous twenty, or something. And then we too will have giant banks. Some of the biggest U.S. banks have already invested in the technology to support such an operation.

U.S. banks are not only failing to dominate the world market in banking services, they are not particularly succeeding in holding onto their home market. For example, in California, the harbinger market, foreign banks are doing quite as well as foreign auto producers. Six of the ten largest banks in California are now foreign owned (up from two out of ten just five years ago).[21] As for money-center activity, the high end of the business, foreign banks now account for about 40 percent of big commercial loans in New York and San Francisco.[22]

A major cause of this relatively poor competitive showing is the fact that the U.S. market is really wide open to foreign banks, while most of the major foreign markets are not open to outsiders. The press and even our government, not to mention the banking industry, is keenly aware of this market asymmetry, far more so than in other sectors where similar arrangements prevail. The conclusion has become that if we could remove those barriers, financial services would be a major, and probably the major, U.S. export service. Their elimination is a top objective of U.S. trade negotiations; it may even be *the* top priority, but it is very hard to judge our government's trade negotiation priorities. Opening foreign markets in a serious way to U.S. financial service firms would, of course, greatly improve the competitive position of the American banks—or at least the biggest ones. But it will not be easy to negotiate. As we shall see, many of those barriers go down deep, right into the way a foreign economy is organized. And the competitive capabilities of the U.S. banks are not necessarily superior to those of the Europeans or the Japanese, at least not by such a wide margin as to make the outcome of "fair" competition a foregone conclusion.

At the moment, foreign banks are not only bigger than American banks and successfully competing with them in the foreigner's home markets, in the United States, and in third markets, but in many ways they are stronger. U.S. banks are currently suffering from severely impaired balance sheets. This not only makes them less "strong" in that traditional financial sense of the word. It also deprives them of the capital and confidence needed for international expansion and the development of new services so as to better compete with their foreign rivals when competition requires deep pockets and financial staying power.

For example, one of the biggest growth areas in international financial services is the complex business of barter, countertrade, buybacks, and offsets. Barter, countertrade, buybacks, and offsets are not new. Indeed, money was invented, quite some time ago, to alleviate many of the more obvious inconveniences of those venerable forms of trade. For the longest time, they have been treated as marginal phenomena in a dominant and expanding system of monetized international trade. The enduring persistence of barter has always been acknowledged, but it was usually located in situations of greater interest to anthropologists than economists. It was assumed to grow up quickly under conditions of disorder, but also presumed to disappear just as quickly once normalcy had been restored. Like so many other primitive and bureaucratic practices, barter was taken for granted as somehow incurably part and parcel of any deals with centrally planned economies. Like the suburban homeowners who get together and swap services to cut the taxman out of his take, international barter was seen as wrong and potentially upsetting to the system, but so marginal that it was no cause for concern as long as it was kept within bounds.

But barter and its more elaborate varieties (such as countertrade, buybacks, and offsets) have broken out of all imaginable bounds.[23] Like some disease-causing microbe once thought safely eradicated by modern science, they have made a startling comeback in the past few years, and they now pose a challenge to the rules, procedures, and structures of international trade. Estimates of the extent of these practices vary widely. The U.S. Department of Commerce estimates that between 20 percent and 30 percent of world trade is now subject to some form of counterpurchase, buyback, or offset and that the proportion could reach 50 percent in fifteen years.[24] In surveys by the National Foreign Trade Council Foundation, the number of reported transactions involving some form of barter has been increasing at rates of 50 percent, 64 percent, and 117 percent respectively in each of the past three years.[25] *Business Week* and the General Electric Trading Company each independently estimates the volume at 30 percent of world trade.[26] The General Agreement on Tarriffs and Trade (GATT), in a recent report, makes by far the lowest estimate: 8 percent of world trade.[27] Since the volume of world trade is about $2 trillion, any point on this intolerably broad range of estimates nevertheless constitutes a staggering sum—especially for such an obscure and ill-regarded "marginal phenomenon." When variance is in the hundreds of billions of dollars, we know two things: first, that something big is going on; and second, that we have no control over it.

Countertrade would not be a very substantial phenomenon if all international transactions were conducted company to company, without government playing a directive role. The swift acceleration to its present importance and its continuing rapid growth are indicators—even a measure—of the extent to which the nation-state now directs the terms of international sales and systematically sets policies and rules to influence the terms of supposedly private bargains. There simply would not be very much countertrade unless some nation-state (the buyer) dictates that access to its market can be gained only by sellers willing to take payment in countertrade or to provide offsets.

Countertrade deals are elaborate, inventive, and extremely diverse. Sometimes they are also embarrassing, as when McDonnell Douglas found itself with, among other countertraded items acquired in a partial payment for aircraft equipment it sold to Rumania, a rather stupendous supply of canned ham "which the firm's staff is expected to munch its way through at the company's canteen for years to come."[28] The Algerian wine that Caterpillar Tractor took on in countertrade, and found itself unable to sell, "was served in the company's cafeterias for many years."[29]

With their bank-based *Keiretsu* that include mammoth trading companies, the Japanese are perfectly organized and extremely successful at this game. The big trading companies, such as Mitsubishi, do billions in this high-profit, high-risk, high-skilled and high-value-added game. The Germans, based on a long experience of funny money trading with Eastern Europe, also have significant skills and know-how. Metellgesellschaft, for example, is an acknowledged world leader. Sears, now also a "financial services" company, tried its hand. It failed. But its effort provided what should be a textbook example of getting it all wrong from the outset. Among its other difficulties, such as very many and very expensive top personnel, Sears foundered on an inability and unwillingness to use its stupendous power as a purchaser to leverage its clients' sales. Otherwise, why Sears? Buying is the easy part. It wound down the business with a big loss and an embarrassment. Bank of America, the nation's second largest bank, also made a relatively disastrous foray into the trading company business with its B of A World Trade. Despite the power of its name, the depth of its domestic client base, and the range and sophistication of its worldwide network, it brought to its new business no consistent strategy and no special skills. To compound the matter, under the pressure of its embarrassingly eroding balance sheet, it proved to be risk-averse and capital-shy. It posed no challenge to the competition. Of the numerous entries by American financial service firms into complex trading, one of the most successful seems to be First Boston, perhaps in part because it formed a partnership with a foreign firm that knows the business: Germany's Metellgesellschaft.[30]

Beyond these important but temporary disadvantages of the American banks, there lie more fundamental and perhaps more intractable problems. The problem of foreign barriers in banking only hints at the profound difficulties involved in trade in many services. Foreign banks operate in this country quite as nationals, both in the eyes of the law and in the eyes of most of their clients. In the markets that matter—Japan and most of Western Europe—U.S. banks don't. They can't. It is, for example, difficult to imagine a way that Chase or Morgan or Bank of America could be the lead bank to Fujitsu, the way that Crocker (British) or BankCal (Japanese) or Hibernia (Hong Kong, despite the name), or Bank of the West (French) are lead banks for Silicon Valley firms, big real estate developers, and even utilities. Fujitsu is largely owned by the Fuji Bank, and it in turn is one of the principal owners of the Fuji Bank. Similar interlocking arrangements prevail in Germany, where the big banks, such as Commerzbank and Deutschesbank, control the stock of the major companies.[31] These obstacles to market penetration are more than superficial and are unlikely to be swept away in a round of talks. For the short run at least, banking is unlikely to provide the major offset to our hemorrhaging merchandise balance that the "service" argument so desperately seeks. And banking may not be the only major area of services where opening foreign markets could prove to be orders of magnitude more difficult than we now suppose.

Liberalizing Trade in Services

Nations erect barriers to trade in services with better conscience than to trade in goods—and with greater success. Actually, there is not much erecting going on, for the barriers are already in place. Most have always been there. Usually, maintenance is all that is needed. For example, commercial air transportation is a big service that could be opened to international competition with relatively little of the dislocation and complexity that would be needed to open up construction work, or value-added telecommunications services, or direct broadcast of advertisements and news. It raises few questions of preserving a national culture, a traditional political constituency, or a traditionally protected guild (for example, doctors). Most important of all, it does not threaten national sovereignty, however grandiosely interpreted, or national demographics, defined with even the finest paranoia. Yet air transportation remains organized by a series of crude bilateral negotiations of landing rights arranged to protect national flag carriers. Rarely, if ever, can a TWA flight, for example, load additional passengers in London, drop them in Paris, and then continue on to Rome with a new load of bodies the way ocean ships loaded, and still load, freight and passengers at each stop. Even in this most obviously internationalizable service (which is also the biggest one), liberalism remains a very distant point. Whatever the U.S. government may claim in its current effort to do something about our trade position by trying to open international trade in services, it will find that most nations—including the United States—do not want to liberalize trade in most services. Each nation has its particular list of services it does not want to open; each has its particular reasons. Some are simply classic cases of protected industries: many countries do not permit value-added telecommunications networks to carry data for processing offshore, where labor (or computer power) is better and cheaper.

But the reasons quickly get more complicated. American (or French) telecommunications companies are not allowed to offer a full range of telecommunications services to clients in most countries even though new technologies make such a business quite possible. National governmental policy comes in here, mightily and from several directions. For example, should the German Bundespost, the agency that controls telecommunications services, permit IBM or some new DATAZIP outfit to provide high-quality, very low-cost by-pass services (via microwave and satellite) to major German users such as the big banks and the big companies? It is a question the German government is currently wrestling with, and the outcome is far from clear. If such a service were to succeed, it would cut into the revenues of the Bundespost. Nobody likes competition, especially government agencies. More important, it would raise a political problem. The complex economics of telecom services have at least one simple aspect. In the United States, for example, 4 percent of the users generate 50 percent of the revenues.[32] The ratios are unlikely to be wildly different in Europe. In most countries the revenues from selling services to the big users, the giant organizations, are used to subsidize service to the smaller users, voting households. Does the Bundespost really want to open this can of worms? America recently did just that, and the political problem of who would pay the costs of the local loop has yet to be solved. Nasty as it is, that is the easy political problem.

Shouldn't a nation's telecommunications be under national control? What would happen if IBM indeed came to dominate telecommunications services in Germany and the German government found itself not liking IBM for some other reason (perhaps something having to do with differences among German, American, and IBM policy toward Eastern Europe)?

Would it be in a weakened bargaining position? Would it be compromised? Would it have ceded sovereignty? Does control of telecommunications services involve matters of sovereignty, political control, emergency, or military preparedness? There are no simple answers to these and countless other questions like the fate of Siemens's telecommunications equipment business, long a central concern and responsibility of the Bundespost.[33] There are also questions of privacy. And questions of long-term policy for telecommunications, seen more and more as the basic infrastructure of a nation's economy and the basic tissue of the society. Opening trade in telecom services raises many of these questions. It's as bad as agriculture, where open trade is a permanently open question. Perhaps it is worse. We have less experience in it. In any case, opening competition in telecommunications services will not be a short-term fix for the U.S. balance of payments. And international openings in value-added telecom services is one of the best bets for progress in liberalizing trade in services.[34]

The U.S. government thinks it very important to open trade in telecommunications services. In part, this is because it believes that we have highly competitive firms that could provide such services and it is just doing its duty by the American economy. In part, it is because it was only a few years ago that we thought of opening our own market to competition, and we are now, quite naturally, spreading our new-found faith. Ten, or even five years ago, the United States had a very different agenda on international trade in telecom—an empty agenda. In part, the vigor of our demands stems from embarrassment at our own stupidity. When we opened our telecom market to foreign equipment manufacturers, we never asked for any quid pro quo.[35] Now the imports are pouring in while the key foreign markets remain largely closed. We do, however, admit that the others neither made us open our market or even thought of asking us to do so. They just took advantage of an existing situation. We also have similar, and similarly new views in banking. As noted, many Americans think that trade in banking ought to be opened and that it is colossally unfair that our market is open while the others are not. Many American banks (or more accurately, a few very big banks) and our government believe this quite strongly.[36]

Trade in banking has its allure. It would, for example, be a relatively simple matter to convince the average Mexican, or Taiwanese, or Italian that his money would be safer in Citibank, or MorganBank, than in the local brand under the control of local businessmen and governments. But the Mexican, or Taiwanese governments may have very different views. Do they want to put control of their financial system in foreign hands, especially in the hands of giant foreign corporations? Banking is special; it controls a nation's money supply, it can shape the course of development, it can tumble governments quietly, insidiously. Also, other governments may have their own agendas for service exports, and they run smack into the "deep structure" of U.S. service protectionism.

Mexican truck drivers, for example, cannot deliver a load into El Paso, pick up a new load in Houston, deliver it to Oklahoma City, and change loads again and continue on to Kansas City. Is the United States ready to open in trucking? Will we permit construction brigades to fly in from Korea (or China), camp in the Sierras, and rebuild our railway tracks (which they built in the first place)? Will we let them, with their colossal comparative advantage in straight wage labor, build our water projects or skyscrapers and realize a huge savings for the "American consumer and taxpayer"? Of course, we maintain a miniversion of just that in agriculture with the braceros programs, but this is generally held out as some kind of an exception and not a prototype for trade in "services." The U.S. agenda for trade in services calls for activities that are low, or actually zero, in cross-border flows of large numbers of people; it prefers transborder data flows that are high in capital. Other countries have the opposite agenda. Negotiations will not be simple or swift.[37]

4

Services and Development

SHIFTING out of manufacturing would be a disaster for the wealth and power of the United States. We must automate production not cede or offshore it. In the past we did not shift out of agriculture: we automated. As a result we developed massive quantities of high-value-added, high-paid jobs that are tightly linked to agriculture and even more in industries and services such as agricultural machinery and chemicals that, though less tightly linked, owe their development, scale, and survival to a broad and strong American agricultural sector. The competitiveness of the American economy, which we define as the ability to maintain high and rising wages under conditions of openness to international competition, is not likely to be enhanced by abandoning production to others. As the previous chapters of this book have argued, manufacturing matters to our national economy. It matters to the firm too. As the second part of this book will argue, the firm will not, over time, be able to control what it cannot produce competitively. Instead of ceding production, we should be converting low-productivity, low-wage, low-skill production processes into high-technology, high-skill, high-wage activities—whether they are included in the manufacturing unit itself or counted largely as service firms. Services are not a substitute, or successor, for manufacturing; they are a complement. One needs the other. The process of development is not one of sectoral succession but instead it is one of increased sectoral interdependence driven by an ever more extended and complex division of labor. It is also quite clear that, for the present and for the immediate future, exports of services do not provide an offset to our staggering balance of payments deficit in manufacturing. In brief, we are not entering a post-industrial economy; we are shifting from one kind of industrial economy to another.

The most nagging problems in this line of reasoning are not about its correctness. Rather they concern how we got into an intellectual muddle about such fundamental trends in the economy. How does a line of argument in which most of the statements are unexceptionable, prudent, and fairly evident, and also underlie the economic policies of our most successful competitors, come to constitute a maverick view—one that is outside the mainstream of both professional economics and the dominant discourse of our policy debates?

Thus far the argument has been constructive in its expositional and methodological form. This chapter has the burden of "deconstructing" some widely used notions, particularly the classification "services" as an organizing principle for economic data and as a central category in the dominant development-through-succession theory. Because it defines, tabulates, and ultimately, dissolves its subject—the use of services as an analytic category in development theory—it is perhaps best, even at risk of a certain heavy-footedness, to alert the reader to what is coming and why.

The chapter begins with a brief examination of the notion of services. It asks, What is a service? and reviews the rubbery answers commonly available. Then it surveys the powerful growth of service employment. The two easiest and most popular interpretations of that growth—the one, that service growth represents post-industrial development, and the other, that service growth indicates stagnation—are rejected.[1] An empirical review of the growth of service employment opens to question the automatic and positive relationship between that growth and productivity, progress, or development, which is the heart of the most widely received view. A survey of similar trends in Europe and Japan forecloses the other easy solution: growth in service employment is simply a way to distribute economic stagnation, as argue those who contend that the post-industrialists are apologists, and that America is becoming a flabby economy of fast-food sellers.

The chapter then tries to see whether the category "services," a classification in our employment data, makes any sense in its most popular and important use, as an analytic category in the most widely received theories of economic development. It argues that it does not—that it does not help us to understand the process of development but instead acts to impede understanding. When put to work to analyze the dynamics of development, it dissolves, and so does the tidy and popular view of economic development as industrial succession—as in "up and out of agriculture to industry, then up to services and high tech."

Part of the answer lies in the way American economics tricked itself by commandeering statistical categories which administrators use to count things and employing them as analytic categories with which to organize its thinking. The effect was to obscure our understanding about the broad movements in our economy. The first and most important of these thought-obscuring categories is that of services.

What Is a Service?

What, precisely, is a "service"? Enumeration is simple, though exhausting: a shoe shine, a heart transplant, a wedding (or divorce), a computer program, a tax consultation (or audit), a legal proceeding, a math test, a bank withdrawal (or deposit), a speeding ticket, a memo to the files, a tennis lesson, a burial, a car wash, a crop dusting. But what, if anything, do these diverse activities have in common? In many ways they are more like Borges's Chinese categorization of the animal kingdom than a set of categories useful for analysis: "Animals are divided into: (a) belonging to the Emperor, (b) embalmed, (c) tame, (d) sucking pigs, (e) sirens, (f) fabulous, (g) stray dogs, (h) included in the present classification, (i) frenzied, (j) innumerable, (k) drawn with a very fine camelhair brush, (l) et cetera, (m) having just broken the water pitcher, (n) that from a long way off look like flies."[2] It is in abstracting from that heterogeneous list and comparing it to anything else that problems arise.

The category "services," if it is a category, exists in implicit distinction to the category "goods." The construction parallels such interdependent categorizations as supply/demand, debit/credit, import/export, and male/female. But under midnight oil at lightning glance it sometimes seems closer to dancer/dance. Services are said to share defining, abstract properties: nontangibility being the most important.[3] This separates them from goods, which are defined as having tangibility. But not all nontangibles in our economic accounts are "really" services: interest payments for instance. And some services, like architecture, product design, and shipping take their finality in goods; they are part of the production of tangible things. Nonstorageability is another attribute that is often used to define services, as in *Forbes*, "You produce and consume a service more or less instantly, so you can't build up inventories and live off them."[4] The SES-

AME report for the French government also uses nonstorageability as the defining characteristic of services.[5] But on-line data banks, an archetypical post-industrial service, do just that: they store intangible information; and so do the keepers of the "files" in bureaucracies, whether by computer or by hand.

Daniel Bell himself never provides a definition of services. He tries for an abstract definition based on a key characteristic: "A post-industrial society is based on services. Hence it is a game between persons. What counts is not raw muscle power, or energy, but information."[6] But Bell generally relies on a residual definition: services are what is left after you subtract jobs on farms and in factories. This is the same residual definition that Colin Clark used to launch the stages-of-development concept fifty years ago, the one that is still generally used, though sometimes reluctantly, by most writers on the subject.[7] Classification—even by final product—is tricky and rubbery. Software is a service; computer chips a good. But what about "firmware," a program on a chip? A movie broadcast on TV is a service; on cassette it is a good—that is, if it is purchased; rented, it is a service.

Ronald Shelp spends upward of 200 pages analyzing the role of services in international trade, but remarks early on, with admirable candor:

> I began this study with a fairly clear idea of the meaning of services. However, as often happens when one examines a subject in greater depth, the increased awareness of its complexity created confusion where before there seemed to be clarity. . . . I can offer no solid definition of services. . . . The most that can be said at the general level is that services encompasses an extremely heterogeneous group of economic activities often having little in common other than that their principal outputs are for the most part intangible products.[8]

Or as George Stigler concluded almost thirty years ago in his study entitled *Trends in Employment in the Service Industries,* "There exists no authoritative consensus on either the boundaries or the classification of service industries."[9]

Whether they try for an abstract definition based on something inherent about services or not, writers on the subject inevitably base their operational definition on classifications used in readily available government employment statistics. These are of two sorts. The first and most commonly used is based on the nature of final product. Here services are defined as a slice, more or less generous, more or less fastidious, of the Standard Industrial Classification Scheme. U.S. SIC codes 40 through 90 are the most common definition. The problems posed by such an approach are enormous. First, classification schemes differ from country to country. This is especially the case in services. The U.S. SIC code breaks down manufacturing into some 140 largely obsolete 3-digit categories, but services into only 66. But more important than their incomplete and obsolete disaggregation, they reflect institutional patterns that are created for many special, particular, and often temporary reasons. Thus, data on the German steel industry usually include engineering services that, because they are located in legally separate firms in France, are counted as Services. Proctor and Gamble had its own in-house TV production facilities, while Lever Brothers relied exclusively on outside agencies to make similar soap operas and commercials.

Focusing on institutional arrangements at the level of the firm or even the "establishment" blurs the functional economic reality. Classifications based on final product underrepresent the importance of service roles in our economy. In an extraordinarily complex division of labor, the margin for error, and for policy based on muddled or misleading information, is correspondingly high. Thus a typist in an insurance company is classified as producing services; a typist in a ball-bearing factory produces goods. Though detailed and precise, the data generated by this classification scheme are as useless to our purposes of understanding the complex work relationships in a modern economy as an analysis of Marilyn Monroe—or Lassie for the matter—that finds that a great film idol consists of two-thirds water and a few grams of iron, phosphorous, and calcium.

The second classification scheme is by type of job or role: service worker/production worker. Job classifications in such a scheme are independent of the nature of the final product the firm or the plant produces. For certain purposes they make sense. They tell us what people do. They make sense because in many hard-core manufacturing industries, such as chemicals, more than half the jobs are service roles—mostly white collar. Data organized according to this type of scheme are generally less readily available, comparable, or complete than SIC code data. While they give a more accurate picture (a kind of sociological snapshot) of the kind of work people do, they have their own disadvantages. The principal shortcoming is that they radically overrepresent service employment by reducing manufacturing employment to production-line tasks. The data serve to avoid understanding manufacturing as an activity in our economy that is linked in concrete ways to most other activities, and to reinforce an obsolete image that drives policy of manufacturing as dull, repetitive, assembly-line tasks.

Data classification schemes are designed to answer specific questions, but they are often used to answer different questions, sometimes with better success than others. Each of these two classification schemes answers a particular question. One scheme tells us what an enterprise produces as its principal product, the other about what people do all day. Neither tells us about what a service is, about the importance of services in a modern economy, about how they depend or are independent of manufacturing—the questions we must answer in formulating a national development strategy. The category "services," though bursting with busily employed occupants, is empty of meaning, but fraught with significance.

Employment Growth in Services

The service argument is rooted in employment statistics which evidence as deep, wide, and enduring a trend as one is ever likely to encounter in economics. In the United States the percentage of employment in services has increased steadily across the decades: 54 percent in 1950; 58 percent in 1960; 62 percent in 1970; 67 percent in 1980 and over 70 percent now.[10] The share of services in GNP by value added has increased roughly proportionally: it is now about 67 percent, while that of manufacturing has fallen to about 24 percent.[11] Over the past two decades, some 86 percent of job growth in the economy has occurred in the service-producing sector,[12] and the share of manufacturing in total employment has fallen to about 21 percent.[13]

The sheer mass and long-term consistency of these numbers make them impervious to quibbling. But they also invite interpretation. A finer mesh analysis broadens, rather than narrows, the range of possible interpretations. It opens to question the assumptions of productivity, progress, and development that form the basic burden of the services argument.

Between 1955 and 1980 the U.S. economy added some 40 million jobs, and only about one out of ten of those jobs was in manufacturing. By comparison, over the full twenty-five years, the health sector all by itself added as many jobs as all of manufacturing combined—ships and shoes and sealing wax and armaments, computers and toys. And education added more than health.[14] Since 1973 manufacturing has not added any jobs at all.[15] All jobs added between 1975 and 1980, some 12 million in all (less a generous 1 million for construction and mining), were in "services." Of these, the public sector made only a modest contribution, certainly compared with its performance between 1955 and 1975, when

total public employment rose by about 7.8 million jobs.[16] Despite carefully fostered impressions to the contrary, federal government employment did not change very much between 1975 and 1980 (up 100,000)
nor, for that matter, between 1968 and 1980. But state and local government added some million-and-a-half jobs (about half a million of them
in schools) between 1975 and 1980. This is a substantial amount, but
well off the 1955–75 pace when it added 7.2 million jobs.[17]

All the rest, about 10.5 million, were in private sector services. But of
these, almost half were in two very specific activities—retail trade and
health services—and one broader, vaguer, and more heterogeneous category—services to business. Retail trade was the most important, adding
2.35 million jobs between 1975 and 1980, of which about one-half (1.2
million jobs) were in "eating and drinking places."[18] This sector consists
of a disproportionate number of low-paid, part-time jobs held by minori-
ties and teenagers. In 1979 the average wage in eating and drinking places
for nonsupervisory personnel was $3.45 per hour, and the average work
week was only 26 hours. Average weekly earnings came to $91.00. (Earn-
ings estimates do not include tips; but for much of the growing portion of
eating and drinking places, especially "fast-food" places, there is little in
the way of tips.) The contrast with manufacturing as a whole is sharp:
$6.69 average per hour wage; 40.3 hours average week; $269 per week for
nonsupervisory personnel. Also, in eating and drinking places over 90
percent of employees are "nonsupervisory," whereas in manufacturing as
a whole it is 72 percent.[19] "Fringe benefits," such as health and life insurance and old age pensions, are much higher in full-time manufacturing
jobs; they are rarely available to the part-time workers in eating and
drinking places.

Health services was the second major generator of employment, adding some 1.2 million jobs between 1975 and 1980. Despite images of
fabulously remunerated doctors, employment in health has many parallels
with employment in eating and drinking places: about 90 percent of employees are nonsupervisory; in 1979 about 80 percent of employees were
women; and average weekly earnings for nonsupervisory employees came
to $171 in 1979, or $5.17 per hour, with an average work week of 33 hours.
In autos that same year, average hourly wages were $9 per hour, average
weekly pay $373, over 80 percent of the work force was male, and fringe
benefits were substantial.[20]

Services to business, an omnibus category, was the third major generator of employment and the principal focus of attention for post-industrial
theorists, including, as it does, think tanks, programmers, designers, and
venture capitalists. It added 900,000 jobs between 1975 and 1980. Of these,

some 110,000 were in "services to buildings" (mostly janitorial) and another 250,000 were at agencies supplying temporary employees to businesses. If one adds together retail trade services, health services, "services to buildings," and employees of temporary employment agencies, almost half the increase in private sector services employment is explained. Security guards—a zero net productivity item—should make up any remaining differences.[21]

Even this first glance at the detailed composition of service employment opens up serious questions about any automatic relationship between growth in service employment and productivity, development, and progress. Other hypotheses present themselves. Service growth is a way of utilizing, at low wages and in dead-end roles, an influx of women into the labor market. After all, these three sectors—retail trade, health services, and services to business—along with the fast growing FIRE group—finance, insurance, and real estate—are disproportionately high employers of low-wage female labor. Rather than an element and a sign of economic development, much of the growth of service employment may be a way of spreading around economic stagnation, as we all take in each other's linen for wash or, at least, each other's relatives for care. (On an average day in 1969, in California—the first, the best, the most advanced, and the most prosperous of the post-industrial economies—the clients of the state's institutions exceeded 7 million people, including 5 million in the schools.) On that same day, another 1 million people were employed as their caretakers. Together these groups represented 40 percent of the state's entire population. Others were treated to outdoor care: in 1975 one of every six children in the state was a recipient of Aid to Families with Dependent Children (more popularly known as the Welfare). Thousands were employed administering that system.[22]

One defense against this critique is to point to mushrooming employment in information-related services, the defining genie of post-industrialism. In the words of the president's *Report on Trade Agreements,* "Virtually all of the 20 highest-growth occupations . . . for the 1980s are involved with the handling of information. Computer programmers, analysts and operators are among the fast growing categories, as are operators and mechanics for data processing machines. Economists, travel agents, aero-astronautical engineers, psychiatric aides and paralegal personnel are some of the others."[23] (Shades of the Borges list cited earlier in this chapter!) Despite the projected rapid growth of this heterogeneous grouping, *together* they don't add up to the increase in fast-food workers.

Growth of Service Jobs in Foreign Economies

Though their magnitudes are measurable and of such scale as to indicate their great importance, the meaning of these trends remains far from clear. A glance abroad will help to eliminate, or at least clarify, one popular family of explanations: namely, that growth in service employment is due to some particularities of the U.S. system—political, demographic, or economic—or that it is related to a slow growth economy.

As Ronald Shelp, an enthusiastic advocate of the services view, remarks, "the United States is clearly the most advanced service economy."[24] But it certainly is not the only one. Most of the "advanced" economies have followed a similar evolution in the structures of employment and GNP, but at a less leisurely pace. They started later, but they have been catching up quickly. The 1950s data for France more resembles the 1920s than the 1950s data for the United States. In 1954, services represented 35 percent of French employment (a level reached by the United States in 1925, the same year that services in post-everything California had already passed 50 percent). By 1968 services in France had shot up to 45 percent, and by 1975 passed 50 percent, the definitional threshold of post-industrialism.[25]

The aggregate French data show that the trend is not confined to the United States and is therefore not explainable by any particularities of the American economy or society. Also during that period, the French economy grew far faster than the American. Between 1950 and 1960 French GNP grew at an average rate of almost 5 percent compared with 3.2 percent in the United States, and between 1960 and 1970 at 5.8%—well above the 4 percent rate. French growth has continued, although it slowed down in the long recession of the 1970s.[26] Most important, French growth was industry-led. Industrial production increased far faster than GNP, averaging roughly 6 percent during the 1950–70 period.[27] But despite that superior performance, which is unlikely to be repeated in the next few years, France did not add any industrial jobs. Unlike the United States, total employment in France grew only slightly during the 1960s and 1970s—and that only beginning about 1975. The reasons are largely demographic. French demographic curves, like its service employment curve, lagged behind that of the United States. But the very slight increase in industrial jobs accumulated during that period (a total of 7 percent over the thirteen years between 1962 and 1975) was lost after 1975, so that by 1980 industrial employment was back below the 1962 level. It is still headed downward. Even at its height, in 1975, industrial employment in France had added only 418,000 jobs since 1962—substantially fewer than education and less than half the number added by health![28] Even Japan, the industrial powerhouse, had about 56 percent of its GNP in services by 1978.[29]

The easy outs are closed. Growth of service employment is not simply a way to distribute stagnation. But neither is it an unambiguous indicator of development—of a shifting out of the low-productivity activities of a condemned past and a shifting into the high-skilled activities of a high-productivity, though increasingly dematerialized, future.

The employment data are rich in accuracy and detail, but poor as indicators of relative development or stagnation. What we need are data conceived, collected, and presented to show the concrete linkages and dependencies among the extraordinarily diverse and increasingly indirect activities of production.

5

The Eroding
Competitiveness of
American Industry

A STRONG manufacturing base is essential to national welfare and power, and American industrial competitiveness is eroding. We are not responding very well to the new challenges of international competition. The trade conflicts that have pushed their way from the business page onto the front page are not ordinary trade frictions about cars or blouses or semiconductors. They are not just about the profits or even the survival of particular firms. They involve serious, long-term conflicts about shifting national positions in the world economy. The wealth and power of nations are the stakes. Until recently, American firms dominated world markets; now they must adjust to them. Twenty-five years ago America produced about as many cars in a week as Japan did all year.[1] Europeans wrote books about the American Challenge and the Secrets of the Giant American Firms,[2] while they fretted about technology gaps and insurmountable American advantages in product, production process, marketing strategy, and management techniques.[3] Now the Japanese produce more cars per year than we do.[4] European GNP per capita has pretty much caught up with the United States.[5] Instead of foreigners studying the successful methods of American management, American managers and even politicians, to their great discomfort, are having to hear about the East Asian Edge and Japan as Number One, and even about flexible production in Italy. *Business Week* runs special features on the "Deindustrialization of America" and on the "Hollow Corporation: the Decline of Manufacturing Threatens the Entire U.S. Economy." And Akio Morita, the chairman of Sony, warns America: "Unless U.S. industry shores up its manufacturing base, it could lose everything. American companies have either shifted output to low-wage countries or come to buy parts and assembled products from countries like Japan that can make quality products at low prices. The result is a hollowing of American industry. The United States is abandoning its status as an industrial power."[6]

To argue, as we do in this chapter, that the competitive position of American industry is declining, is not to say that American industry is disappearing. Indeed, over the past fifteen years, manufacturing's share of GNP has remained roughly constant.[7] In that specific, restricted sense, we are not "deindustrializing." But to speak of deindustrialization is to pose the problem badly. To some, deindustrialization means a loss of industrial primacy, power, and incomes, while to others it means an absolute, or proportional, decrease in value added attributed by statistics to "manufacturing," usually with no differentiation being made between military and competitive markets. It is a framework in which it is difficult to reconcile the thrust of one set of statistics with another, the conclusion of one sophisticated study with that of another. Robert Lawrence of the Brookings Institution tells America that we are not deindustrializing: "This examination of the performance of U.S. manufacturing indicates that, contrary to recent fears, America is not deindustrializing."[8]

Using different data in different ways, and aware of the Lawrence findings, a sophisticated researcher like Professor Ray Marshall of the University of Texas and former U.S. secretary of labor concludes that "We will not be able to solve our economic problems until we come to grips with the realization that we are living through a period of rapid and serious *deindustrialization*—we are losing our manufacturing base."[9]

The notion of deindustrialization has been ensnarled in a confusing and sterile debate. It obscures crucial questions about our ability to sustain the incomes of our citizens and the wealth and power of the nation. We prefer to focus instead on the notion of American competitiveness, and to be very clear about what we mean. Competitiveness means the degree to which a nation can, under free and fair market conditions, produce goods and services that meet the test of international markets while simultaneously expanding the real incomes of its citizens. It is not defined by a nugatory identity: the ability to balance imports with exports. At some exchange rate, balance can always be achieved. Even the poorest nations balance their accounts. Competitiveness is associated with rising living standards, and an upgrading of employment. It is the nation's ability to stay ahead technologically and commercially in those goods and services likely to constitute a larger share of value added in the future. The operational meaning of competitiveness is the ability to compete in an open world economy with high and rising American wages.[10]

Unfortunately, the evidence is substantial that the competitiveness of the American economy is eroding, and manufacturing is taking the brunt of the downward shift.

Measures of U.S. Competitiveness

Measured in each of seven different ways—by unprecedented trade deficits in manufactured goods; by declining shares of world markets for exports; by lagging rates of productivity increases; by eroding profit margins; by declining real wages; by the increasing price elasticities of imports; and by an eroding position in world high-technology markets—American industry confronts a severe problem of competitiveness, which it has never known before. Each measure has its limitations and can, perhaps, be explained away, but taken together they defy easy dismissal and portray a serious long-term problem.

The first and most obvious indicator of trouble is the trade balance. The U.S. merchandise trade balance was positive from 1893 to 1970, turned negative in 1971, and except for 1973 and 1975, has stayed that way, growing worse and worse, until it reached the catastrophic levels of 1984, 1985, and 1986. (See tables 5.1 and 5.2.) The dramatic magnitude of the U.S. deficit in the early 1980s was unquestionably attached to the overvaluation of the dollar; it is, from one perspective, a counterpart of the flows of foreign funds into the United States to finance our government deficit. In classical trade theory there is no such thing as a sustained overvaluation of a floating currency. Trade deficits, as we are taught in class, have as a counterpart the piling up of the deficit country's currency abroad, which eventually lowers its value until trade flows come back into balance. In recent years, however, dollar exchange rates have reflected financial flows as much, if not more, than trade flows. Consequently the automatic adjustment mechanism no longer functions, or at least no longer functions promptly, efficiently, and constructively. The dollar stayed over-valued, and there was a hemorrhage of American industrial lifeblood. There are, therefore, substantial reasons for taking the trade balance—especially in the last two years—as an imperfect indicator of American industrial competitiveness.

Many who argue that the trade deficit, especially in the past three years, has been largely the result of an overvalued dollar believe that as the dollar's value declines, our troubles will pass. They contend that we do not have an underlying competitiveness problem; that we have a sur-face problem of macroeconomic policy: too low a rate of savings, and too high a rate of government spending means that we have to borrow money from abroad to finance our government deficit and the little investment that we do. That means our trade accounts must show a deficit. In our view, their diagnosis is too limited; and unfortunately there is substantial evi-dence of a fundamental, underlying competitiveness problem to support that view. As we complete this book in September 1986 the trade deficit continues to grow, although the dollar has been declining for more than a year. Perhaps it is still too soon to claim definitively that the falling dollar —down in value 30 to 40 percent from its highs—is not sufficient to reverse the problem. Nonetheless, our view is that the problems are deeper and disturbing.

TABLE 5.1

U.S. Merchandise Trade Balance (in billions of dollars)

Year	Trade Balance	Year	Trade Balance
1960	4.9	1973	0.9
1961	5.6	1974	−5.5
1962	4.5	1975	8.9
1963	5.2	1976	−9.5
1964	6.8	1977	−31.1
1965	5.0	1978	−34.0
1966	3.8	1979	−27.6
1967	3.8	1980	−25.5
1968	0.6	1981	−28.1
1969	0.6	1982	−36.4
1970	2.6	1983	−67.2
1971	−2.3	1984	−114.1
1972	−6.4	1985	−141.6

SOURCE: Council of Economic Advisers, *Economic Report of the Presi-dent*, 1986, p. 366. For 1985 (unrevised and annualized) from Office of the U.S. Trade Representative, *Annual Report of the President on the Trade Agreements Program*, 1984–85, p. 5.

To begin, there is the U.S. trade performance before the dollar's high. Table 5.1 shows that during the period 1972–1980, after the Nixon-Connally devaluation of the dollar—while the dollar was appreciably undervalued—the United States was still unable to sustain a positive merchandise trade balance. Unquestionably, dramatic increases in the price of imported oil was a major factor. But it was less so for the United States than for its principal competitors, Japan and West Germany, each of which depend on imported oil for a far greater share of its energy needs than the United States—the world's biggest oil producer.

The sharp and troubling contrast with West Germany and Japan (see table 5.2) was the United States's inability to offset its substantial and growing deficit in energy with substantial and growing surpluses in manufactured goods—despite a decline in the value of the dollar. The U.S. trade position in manufactured goods moved about erratically, the surpluses never grew beyond relatively small numbers, while the trade performances of West Germany and Japan in manufactured goods grew steadily more positive. Their surpluses in manufactured goods grew to big, important numbers; year after year each of those much smaller countries achieved a surplus a full order of magnitude greater than that of the United States.

A counterpart to the trade deficit is share of world exports. America's share has sharply and clearly dropped, falling in value terms from 26

TABLE 5.2

Trade Balance in Manufacturing (in billions of dollars)

	United States	Japan	West Germany
1970	3.4	12.5	13.3
1971	0.0	17.1	15.0
1972	−4.0	20.3	17.7
1973	−0.3	23.3	28.7
1974	8.3	38.0	42.4
1975	19.9	41.7	38.7
1976	12.5	51.2	42.1
1977	3.6	63.0	46.9
1978	−5.8	74.2	53.5
1979	4.5	72.0	59.2
1980	18.8	93.7	63.1
1981	11.8	115.6	61.7
1982	−4.3	104.0	67.5
1983	−31.0	110.3	58.7
1984	−78.4	93.9	43.0

SOURCE: U.S. Department of Commerce, International Trade Administration.

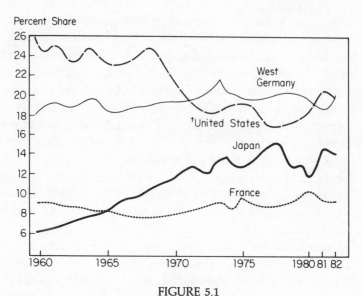

Percent Share

FIGURE 5.1

United States Share in World Trade in Manufactures: 1960–1980

Source: Bruce R. Scott, "National Strategies: Key to International Competition," in Bruce R. Scott and George C. Lodge, eds., *U.S. Competitiveness in the World Economy* (Boston: Harvard Business School Press, 1985), p. 27. The Scott table was computed from data supplied by the Federal Trade Commission. Data for 1980 to 1982 is taken from *OECD International Economic Indicators* (Paris: OECD, 1984), p. 34.

percent of world markets in 1960 to 18 percent in 1980—before the dollar aggravated matters. (See figure 5.1.) It would seem the United States is doing very badly, but does this measure really show we have a problem? As with any single measure of competitiveness, there are problems with this one. Setting aside the question of precisely how shares of world trade are calculated,[11] it can mean one of two things. If the total sum of trade in the world were constant, then a decline in share of exports would indicate a direct and absolute loss. It would be a zero-sum game in which a competitor's gain is the United States's direct and absolute loss. However, the total of world trade has been growing. Consequently, America's declining share of world exports means only that our exports are growing more slowly than world exports. Maybe a decade ago we could explain such data as a result of the rest of the world catching up to our standards of product and production and our levels of technology development and GNP. In the most advanced nations that is no longer the case. Japan has caught up and perhaps passed us in product quality and production technology; Germany's GNP per capita is now quite as high as ours.[12] They are pushing ahead, not just catching up with us. And West Germany as well as Japan is gaining market share even in a growing world economy, while the rest of the world is hurriedly catching up to their standards of production and

GNP. Figure 5.1, we should note, begins in 1960, when the postwar rebuilding was over. It reflects twenty-five years of a long-term shift in industrial position. It ends in 1980, before the dollar could be thought to have become a "special" negative factor and the problem had become a crisis.*

PRODUCTIVITY GROWTH

The third measure of declining U.S. competitiveness is that for several years now, productivity in manufacturing has been growing much more slowly in the United States than in its major competitor nations. Indeed, slow productivity growth relative to our major trade competitors is, in a general sense, the cause of our problems. Over time, only rising productivity can raise levels of income, and with productivity growing more slowly than our competitors', our incomes will have to grow more slowly than theirs or even decline in order to keep our goods competitive. Devaluing the dollar, steadily over time, to match the effects of the productivity differentials, is a device to solve (the trivial) trade problem by accepting a decline in competitiveness; it balances our accounts with the rest of the world by lowering our real incomes. A steady stream of devaluations to offset an ongoing productivity disadvantage is a steady reduction of American incomes and a reduction of our abilities to realize our national purposes and our power around the world.[13] We may debate the causes of our low rate of productivity growth, but the consequence is evident. Figure 5.2 underscores that our problem is not simply an unfavorable comparison with Japan but also with such solid European economies as West Germany. These differences in productivity trends accumulate to shift the national position. America's preeminent wealth and power is based on American productivity being higher than that elsewhere. As Figure 5.2 a–c shows, our unique productivity advantage has largely eroded. The United States is a great and wealthy nation, but its capacity to generate wealth and technological advance that can be converted into market position is no longer distinctive.

The next indicator should, therefore, be no surprise. Real weekly

*While the American share of world exports has declined, American multinationals—as a subset of American companies—have done much better in world markets. The most obvious conclusion is that the United States is an unattractive production location, but that the American multinationals retain a strong position in world competition based on management and technology. From a national viewpoint the decline of the United States as a production location is, of course, the entire question. National income, wealth, and power rest on producing competitively in the United States. Consequently, the evidence on multinationals does not challenge the argument developed in this book. However, the meaning of the data that argue that American MNCs, have remained strong is itself less than obvious to us. (See end notes.)[14]

Output Per Hour

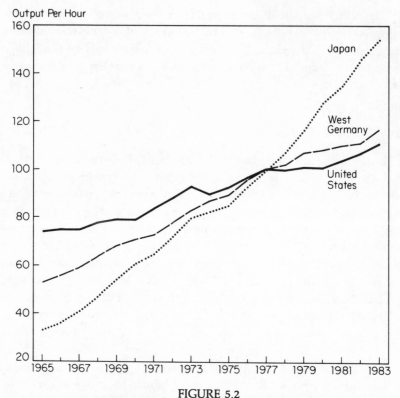

FIGURE 5.2

Manufacturing Productivity: Japan, West Germany, and the United States, 1965–1983
(index: 1977=100)

Source: U.S. Department of Labor, Bureau of Labor Statistics, "Manufacturing Productivity and Labor Costs in 1983 in Twelve Countries," 31 December 1984.

wages in the United States declined over the period 1973 to 1984 by about one-eighth. By 1984 they had fallen back to the levels of the early 1960s.[15] The contrast with the American past is stark: during the previous twenty years, 1953 to 1973, real average earnings rose steadily. (See figure 5.3.)

Of course, declining real wages might suggest nothing more complicated than a simple shift in income from wages to profits. But declining real wages have not permitted management to increase profits, and part of the loss in competitiveness has come out of profits: the pretax rate of return on assets in the manufacturing sector has declined steadily since 1978. (See figure 5.4.) Indeed, the decline in the return on manufacturing investment has made purely financial investments relatively more attractive. The concern with the flow of resources into purely financial instruments would seem to have a real cause. Paper capitalism may be as much the result as the cause of our difficulties.

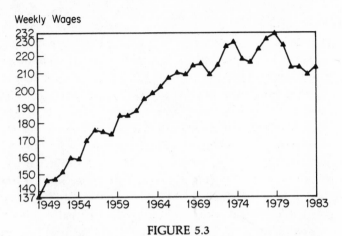

FIGURE 5.3

U.S. Real Wages, Manufacturing, 1949–1983 (in 1977 dollars)

Source: U.S. Department of Labor, Bureau of Labor Statistics.

Sixth, and more technically, the price elasticity of imports has increased—that is, a given price advantage for imports, whether created by exchange rate movements or differential rates of productivity growth, translates into larger sales volume for foreign firms in the United States.[16]

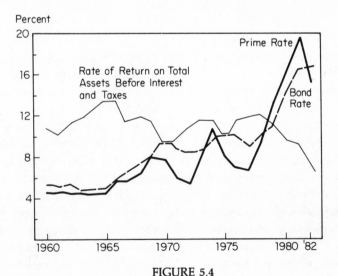

FIGURE 5.4

Rate of Return on Total Assets in Manufacturing Corporate Bond Rate and Prime Rate, 1960–1982

Source: Bruce R. Scott, "National Strategies: Key to International Competition," in Scott and Lodge, eds., *U.S. Competitiveness in the World Economy* (Boston: Harvard Business School Press, 1985), p. 31. The profitability data is from Federal Trade Commission, *Quarterly Financial Report for Manufacturing Corporations,* various issues; the bond and prime rate data is from Council of Economic Advisors, *Economic Report to the President,* February 1983.

For instance, a drop in the price of Japanese widgets (to talk some economics here) of, say, 5 percent would produce an increase in sales of 6 percent. As elasticities increase, that same 5 percent price drop would yield a 7 percent or 8 percent or 9 percent increase of sales. What this means is that foreign products are more and more like U.S. products. Ours are no longer so different and superior as to be insensitive to price competition. They command, therefore, less of the premium necessary to pay high wages to labor, high taxes to government, and high profits to finance new investments and pay to rentiers. As the dollar has risen we have therefore drawn in a greater flow of imports for each unit shift in relative price than we would have done before. This shift in price elasticity helps account for the failure of the dropping dollar to bring American trade back toward balance.[17]

The problem of price elasticity points to another problem, that of reversibility. There is little doubt that the flow of funds into the United States to finance the government deficit drove the dollar up, and that the rise of the dollar was a major source of the recent explosion of our trade deficits. We would feel comfortable attributing as much as half of the colossal increases in our trade deficits recorded in 1984 and 1985 over the previous years to the effects of the dollar's overvaluation.[18] The problem is that, however much the rise in the dollar contributed to the loss of position in international markets, an equal decline of the dollar will not leave the national economy where it was before the rise began.

Though symmetry is the organizing principle of economic theory, as many students learned while practicing origami in Economics 101, it is not the organizing principle of international competition. Temporary disequilibria, brought about by superficial causes—as the overvaluation of the dollar is generally treated—can have profound and enduring consequences. Foreign companies that establish sales, distribution networks, and even brand recognition in the U.S. market will tend to retain them as the dollar declines. Similarly, U.S. corporations that moved production to offshore factories during a period of a high dollar will not necessarily move their facilities home when the dollar falls. Indeed, as we argue in the next chapter, the move abroad to find cheap labor may end up representing more than just a sunk investment of cash, know-how, and political obligation. It may preclude a strategy of sustained production innovation at home. The super-profits garnered by foreign industries as a result of the dollar's high have, in many cases, been used for reinvestment in more efficient production that will generate a competitive edge in the years to come. It is perhaps worth noting that when the dollar rose by almost 50 percent between 1980 and 1984, the prices of imported goods declined by only 2 percent.[19] That means—despite what we are regularly told—it was not so much the U.S. consumer who benefited from the high dollar as foreign producers, middle men, and retailers.[20]

Such traditional notions as symmetrical effects and rubber-band responses where the system snaps back to the predisturbance equilibrium are inappropriate principles to organize our understanding of the dynamics of world markets. Strategic choices made in response to one set of factors—often relatively small factors—can have consequences that are not likely to be reversible and be far greater in scale than what caused them.

Seventh, our supposed comparative advantage in high-technology goods, which has been taken as a sign of successful and proper adjustment, is, we believe, deeply misleading. It suggests less a distinctive international advantage in high technology than a deep incapacity to compete even with our industrial partners in more traditional sectors. Moreover, our position in high-technology trade is quite narrow and consequently fragile. Some analysts, such as Robert Lawrence of Brookings, take comfort that high-technology exports have grown in importance for the United States. They see that as a sign of a healthy, normal development process in which American producers cede the lower-value-added and less technology-based sectors and position themselves in the sectors of tomorrow.[21]

Where Lawrence finds comfort in the expansion of the high-tech categories, others find a more somber picture: as Bruce Scott and George Lodge argue, the data "do not show a broad based pattern of adjusting exports toward high technology areas."[22]

We find a troubling, if not openly disturbing, picture. Let us look more closely at figure 5.5. The range of high-technology sectors from which a surplus is generated is quite narrow. The data show that the expansion of exports in high technology is concentrated in a limited number of sectors —aircraft, computers, and agricultural chemicals. What is not shown is that by 1984 the surplus was gone, and in 1984 and 1985 this category too ran growing deficits.[23]

Moreover, a substantial portion of high-technology exports in the sectors indicated in figure 5.5 are military goods, which indicates the character of America's strategic ties more than its industrial competitiveness. At a minimum, the price of such goods for export often comes as part of a strategic package in which the decision to buy reflects everything but simple commercial calculus.[24] If we adopt a slightly broader definition of high technology that includes a broader range of goods, we find an even more disturbing picture: the pre-1983 surplus narrows; the post-1983 deficit expands.

But the high-tech trade problem grows more serious as we proceed. Analysis by the French Center for International Economic Forecasting

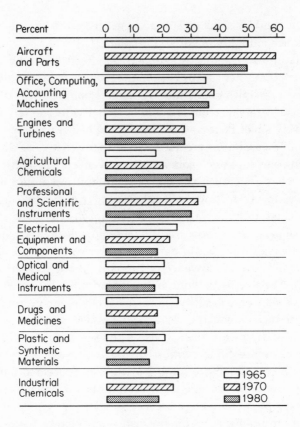

FIGURE 5.5
United States Shares of World High-Technology Exports

Source: Bruce R. Scott, "National Strategies: Key to International Competition," in Bruce R. Scott and George C. Lodge, eds., *U.S. Competitiveness in the World Economy* (Boston: Harvard Business School Press, 1985), p. 29. The Scott table is in turn based on data from U.S. Department of Commerce, International Trade Administration, *An Assessment of U.S. Competitiveness in High-Technology Industries,* February 1983, p. 10.

(CEPII) shows that Japan's actual trade balance in high-technology goods is as high as that of the United States. (See figure 5.7a.) America has a "comparative" advantage in high-technology goods because we have a trade deficit in everything else. (See figure 5.6.) Japan has trade surpluses in medium- and low-technology goods, so its "comparative" advantage in high technology is, by definition, less dependent on high tech than we. Using comparative advantage to say something about the shifting competition among the advanced countries in a way hides the fact that in competitive terms Japan is as strong as the United States in high technology and stronger in the rest of manufacturing. Our position in high technology appears even more fragile as we continue. If we take the high-technology

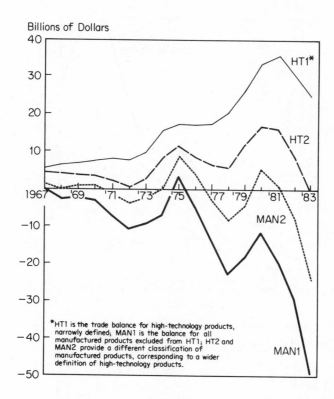

Billions of Dollars

*HT1 is the trade balance for high-technology products, narrowly defined; MAN1 is the balance for all manufactured products excluded from HT1; HT2 and MAN2 provide a different classification of manufactured products, corresponding to a wider definition of high-technology products.

FIGURE 5.6

Compared Trade Balances for High-Technology Products and Other Manufactured Goods in the United States

SOURCE: Elizabeth Kremp and Jacques Mistral, "Commerce exterieur ricain: d'ou vient, ou va le deficit?," *Economie Prospective Internationale* (Paris: 22 1985), Centre d'Etudes Prospectives et d'Informations Internationales (CEPII).

exports and divide them by our trade in manufactures, the American position is roughly equivalent to the German and well behind the Japanese. (See figure 5.8a.) If we try a different statistical tack and set high-tech trade balances against GNP, the American position is equivalent to that of France and Britain and well behind that of Japan and Germany. (See figure 5.8b.)

The very definitions of high technology and medium technology are, as we argue in the next chapter, quite misleading. Figure 5.7a shows the enormous trade surpluses in so-called medium technology goods (autos, electrical equipment) run by Japan, Germany, and even France throughout the 1970s. This is not a phenomenon of the high-valued dollar of the early eighties. Throughout most of the period in question, the dollar was at a

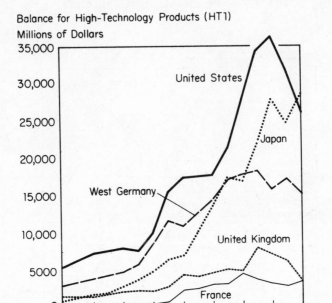

Balance for High-Technology Products (HT1)
Millions of Dollars

(a)

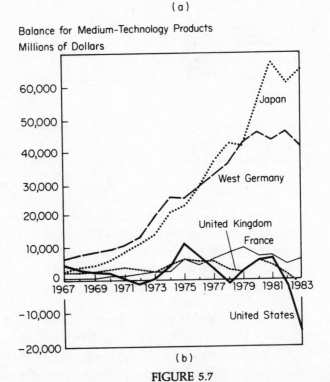

Balance for Medium-Technology Products
Millions of Dollars

(b)

FIGURE 5.7

Compared Trade Balances for Manufactured Products for Five Countries (in millions of dollars)

Source: See figure 5.6.

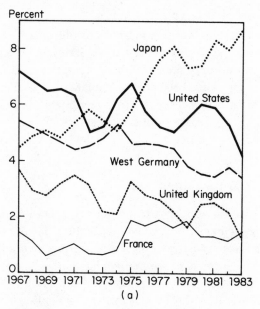

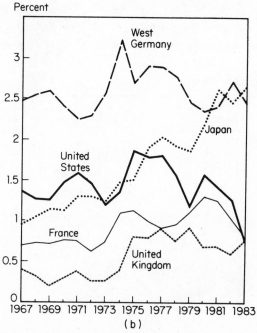

FIGURE 5.8

Trade Balance of High-Technology Products for Five Large Industrialized Countries
(a) Ratio of High-Technology Trade Balance Divided by Half of Manufactured Products Trade
(b) Ratio of High-Technology Trade Balance to Gross Industrial Product

SOURCE: See figure 5.6.

much lower value. Nor was it just labor cost differentials; Japan may still have had lower wage rates than the United States, but German and French labor costs were certainly no lower than U.S. labor costs for the period in question. Japan may have been able to insulate its capital markets and keep its capital costs far below those in the United States, but the Germans and French have had to adjust domestic interest rates to world, especially U.S., rates.

TRADITIONAL MANUFACTURING

Let us turn to non-high-technology goods—ordinary, traditional manufacturing sectors such as shoes and textiles. These are the mainstays of the list of sunset industries, out of which America is supposed to shift. So it comes as no surprise to see that we have indeed been following such council and have ceded position (although the incredible plunge after 1981 may be something of a shock even to the most enthusiastic shifter). But it might be instructive to note that America's two most formidable and most advanced competitors, the Germans and the Japanese, both run substantial surpluses in this category. They have not shifted out, and give no

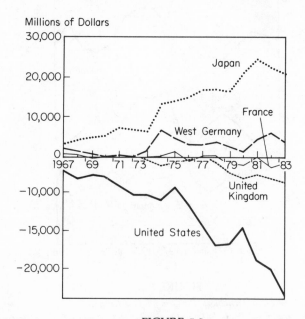

FIGURE 5.9

Trade Balance for Manufactured Goods Excluding High-Technology Products

Source: See figure 5.6.

indication of doing so.[25] While we have moved up and out of traditional manufacturing, and advise ourselves and anyone who will listen to do the same, the Japanese surplus in traditional, sunset manufacturing has been growing steadily since 1973 (see figure 5.9) even as its wage rates have grown both absolutely, relative to rates in the low-wage countries trying to compete in these sectors, and relative to rates in the United States. And the surplus in traditional manufacturing has grown while Japan went from a deficit in high-technology goods to a surplus, and to a surplus in high-technology trade with the United States.

Clearly something is very wrong. And what is wrong is not the performance of the German or Japanese economies. It is the analyses and categories for analysis of conventional economics that make us anticipate different behavior from such economies and prescribe different behavior for our own. What the German and Japanese data on sustained competitiveness in a broad range of production industries reveal is that effective diffusion of production know-how and technology into the production process and even the production of simpler goods can create competitive advantage. For purposes of international competitiveness we must reconsider what we mean by high technology: it is not simply a list of new science-based products—or even a list of industries with high body counts of PhDs—it is also an approach to production.

What our "comparative advantage" in high technology may suggest is not an easy superiority over our competitors in new, knowledge-based goods, but rather a radical inability, relative to them, to apply high technology to the production of traditional goods and to maintain our competitive position by diffusing technology and know-how widely throughout the manufacturing economy. If this is the case—and we believe it to be so not just on the basis of these data but on the basis of sector studies, both the series conducted by BRIE and the research of others—then our trade problem is deep and serious. We note with pessimism that the boom in textile productivity in the United States was the result of introducing imported textile machinery. We were, the optimists tell us, able to draw on the stock of textile technology developed in Europe and Japan. We were able to get productivity growth by buying the machines without investing in the technology. Isn't this what Japan and Europe did when they borrowed technology from the United States, some ask? Not at all, we reply. It would not disturb us if the United States were exchanging production equipment in textiles. The Europeans and Japanese were moving in the other direction, from being borrowers to developers of technology. Can America sustain that productivity growth—or match the growth abroad— if it is dependent on foreign machine developments? Can Americans ever make semiconductors or hubcaps better than the Japanese if most of our production equipment (and vital pieces in particular) has to come from Japan? Certainly, trade in the tools of production is good for us all. However, we note: that the position of American semiconductor production-equipment makers is being seriously undermined; that there are no longer any U.S. merchant producers of photo mask blanks or ceramic packagings; that shuttleless looms are no longer produced in the United States; and that the American machine tool industry, only a few years ago a major exporter, has now lost not just most of its export markets, but has also lost 50 percent of the American market in numerically-controlled (NC) machine tools. We cannot stay ahead competitively if the United States loses its position as a major developer of the equipment that makes increased productivity and competitive advantage possible.

American competitiveness is eroding. Insisting on the developmental potential of a shift to services or on the consolations of a revealed comparative advantage—but a declining competitive advantage—in high technology is irresponsible analysis and perverse policy. A fundamental, underlying competitiveness problem in the dominant economic and political power is always a cause for concern, both for its citizens and for those outside its borders—often its competitors—who rely on its established behavior and leadership to maintain international stability and a given form of world order. America's declining competitiveness is especially troubling at this particular moment in history. Precisely because the fundamental changes in production technologies and in the extent and forms of international competition that we examine in the next part are likely to prove enduring, the outcomes of industrial competition today will matter disproportionately. The international hierarchy of wealth and power is being reshuffled, and it is happening fast and now.

PART II

Managing the Transition

6

Confronting
the Transition

THE WORLD ECONOMY is changing in fundamental ways. The changes add up to a basic transition, a structural shift in international markets and in the production base of the advanced countries. It will change how production is organized, where it occurs, and who plays what role in the process. It will reshuffle the wealth and power of nations.

In retrospect, the consequences of previous transitions are discernible on every level of society, in every aspect of life. Steam technology quickly transformed production and social life. What was made changed; so did where it was made and how it was made. The factory came into being. Cities mushroomed. Goods proliferated, and so, for many, did misery. Old ways of life were destroyed and new ones created. And new technologies such as the railway, that would themselves change production and society, became possible. Today we watch the advent of mass application for a new set of technologies—information technologies—that extends from the semiconductor through digital telecommunication nets and centers around computing. And yet newer technologies—new materials, biotechnology—that they have made possible are coming on fast.

Successive waves of economic transformation were accompanied by a reshuffling of the hierarchy of nations as well as major perturbations of societies. Sometimes these adjustments were neither slow, smooth, nor peaceful. Britain pushed to the head of the list with the original industrial revolution. As the steel and chemical industries developed, Germany emerged as a major power. And American power matured in the early twentieth century along with integrated continental markets and mass production. Now as microelectronics-based technologies alter the very logic and meaning of mass production, Japan enters the ranks of major powers.

Basic Transitions

Basic transitions such as the one we are now witnessing result when firms respond to new market opportunities and conditions with fundamentally new technologies, organizations, and strategies that radically alter the mix of production processes and products. In this as in previous transitions, these two major engines—markets and technology—are motoring the changes. They interrelate in their impacts. The first motor is the relatively rapid and massive exposure of major segments of American manufacturing and some services to international competition.[1] The second is a technological revolution spreading across major segments of manufacturing services. It is based on the advent, for application on a large scale, of new microelectronics-based product, production, and telecommunication technologies. The agents of technological transformations will for the moment be microelectronics and computers. Its emblematics are the semiconductor, the computer, the robot; potent combinations of these are found in such technologies as CAD (computer aided design), CAM (computer aided manufacturing), CIM (computer integrated manufacturing), and a variety of telecommunication acronyms. Biotechnology and "exotic" advanced materials will follow soon. A distinctive feature of this transition is the importance of the diffusion of transformation technologies. Indeed the "modes of intersection between leading-edge technology and traditional industries will be points of great opportunity for profit and productivity."[2] As Frank Press has argued, "The economic impact of advanced technology is all the greater because its benefits will not flow solely from the production and marketing of high tech products. Instead, the greatest benefits may flow from the diffusion of advanced technology throughout the industrial, agricultural and service sectors."[3] By technological development we mean not just the advancing frontier of technical possibilities or the apparatus that embody those possibilities. We include also the organizations in which the machines and the know-how required to use them are embodied and take form. The organizational and social innovations often make it possible to employ new techniques: ". . . to capture the economic possibilities of the new technologies firms might have to move toward vertical disintegration—with activities once combined rigidly within individual firms being recombined in softer, flexible ways."[4] Carlo de Benedetti, president of Olivetti, has noted that "The development and diffusion of new technologies depend not just on the amount of R&D, but above all on the circulation of innovative ideas and information (in the area of 'soft' technologies) and on skilled labor mobility."[5] The transition will come out of the application of advanced technology to products and production processes throughout the economy.

The two forces—market changes and evolving technology—are interconnected. They interrelate and compound. Competition drives the development of the technologies, the rates of their diffusion, and—as importantly—the ways they are used. In turn, the use of these technologies is a major component of new competitive strategies throughout the world economy. Thus, new producers, be they the Japanese companies entering American domains today or the German companies that entered British preserves sixty years ago, compel established producers to reconsider what they produce and how. The new technologies are often the most visible manifestations of change, and consequently the transition itself is often thought to be driven by technological development. However, technology is not simply significant in itself—though new technologies create new opportunities; technology becomes established as it provides an instrument to create opportunities and to respond to radical challenges. In fact, as we shall see later in this chapter, the technology itself is molded within the societies that use it to respond to the problems of shifting markets and social needs.

The transition is an interplay of an advancing frontier of technological possibilities, an evolving set of market problems, and the political choices we make about our priorities and the kind of community and economy we want; the interplay—of market, technology, and politics—produces a broad band of interconnected technological and institutional innovations that ultimately touch an entire society. The combined effect is to propel America smack into the middle of an industrial transition it didn't ask for and may not be prepared to cope with very well.

The advanced countries will make this industrial transition together, but not uniformly. They will confront similar problems, but will have diverse responses. How effectively each nation manages the transformation will determine for the next generation the composition and relative strength of its industrial base. The hierarchy among nations, their relative positions of power and wealth, is already being reshuffled. After World War II few would have believed that France would have moved above Britain in the industrial hierarchy or that Japan would be well on its way to catching and perhaps passing the United States. The transition, though, is not a simple footrace with all the entrants running toward the same goal in parallel lanes. A better metaphor would be backgammon: chance is a substantial factor, and the moves made by each player affect the choices open to all the others. Trade will link together the developments in the several nations. It will not be easy for any advanced nation to escape competition in international markets by withdrawing into protected internal markets. A failure to adapt to the new technologies and market conditions, whether that failure is expressed in protectionism or in trade deficits, will reverberate throughout the national economy. Failure to adapt will slow the pace of productivity increases and adversely affect the nation's relative standard of living. At an extreme it could even result in real declines in wages and living standards. In particular, America must absorb and apply effectively the new possibilities for industrial production— or lose its technological base and hold on its markets.

We will argue in this part that the key to American adjustment to a transforming world economy and an evolving technology may prove to be the capacity to remain or, better still, to become, once again, competitive in manufacturing processes. The implication is that firms will lose control of what they can't manufacture competitively. Product innovation cannot permanently substitute for a country's capacity to competitively manufacture what it can imagine and design. Production skills and manufacturing capacities will be decisive in international competition. At the moment, this is a crucial weakness for American industry. American corporate strategists must make a basic and decisive choice; they can alter existing production structures to incorporate both what American companies have learned about manufacturing from foreign competitors and the possibilities of new programmable automation equipment. This will at least permit them the possibility of neutralizing manufacturing advantages built up by competitors. Or they can try to fit the new equipment into the old structures and continue the slow productivity growth that threatens American competitiveness. Production innovation must be a central strategic concern. They must consider whether fundamental manufacturing innovation required to become competitive can be achieved by running offshore. A decisive advantage in manufacturing that will allow American companies to retain control of what they design can only be built up with skilled labor at home. In our view, American firms must solve their manufacturing problems in the United States. Solving them offshore by substituting inexpensive labor for fundamental production innovations that afford real productivity gains gives temporary, not permanent, advantage. Equally it risks building up strong competitors at the offshore locations. For once, in a reversal of the old GM saw, what is good for America—manufacturing innovation at home—may be good for American corporations.

The consequences of the changes America is experiencing may be exaggerated and their significance pushed out of proportion. Only hindsight will provide clarity, but such clarity may prove a feeble consolation. However, serious analysts—and not just the popular press—are beginning to assert the historical significance of the present period. Frank Press, president of the National Academy of Sciences, suggests that we are indeed at a historic transition.[6] Michael Piore and Charles Sabel talk of the Second Industrial Divide, and while we don't share their vision of what the divide can or ought to look like, we do share a conviction that profound change is accumulating.[7] In France, for example, Thierry Gaudin, head of the Center for Forecasting of the Ministry of Industry and the Ministry of Technology, argues that to "understand the present period, one must look back in history."[8] He contends that it is only recently that a preliminary view of the present period has been established.

> In the past there have been two technological mutations comparable to the one we are now living through. The first was in the middle ages, toward the twelfth century, the second at the end of the eighteenth century, known under the name of the industrial revolution, the beginning of the era of "machines."[9]

CEPII (Centre d'Etudes Prospectives et d'Informations Internationales) sees the current period as the "third" industrial revolution. The first, emerging in the late eighteenth and the nineteenth centuries under British impulsion, was founded on coal, steam engines, railroads, and textiles. The second, the American era, was based on oil, electrical machinery, autos, and chemicals. Now we come to the third.

> In the third industrial revolution, which is coming on us in the next decades, electronics will call into question the modes of production and consumption with which we have lived, electronics will thus play an even more decisive role than that of classical electromechanical equipment, which in its turn, supplanted the steam engine.[10]

Importantly, in their opinion, throughout these next years, industry will remain the agent of growth and development. In the next decades industry will remain the motor of the structural transformation affecting the modes of consumption and production. The service sector will not be able to develop in a healthy fashion unless it rests on a profitable and dynamic industrial base.

We have defined the transition as the interplay of market evolutions and technological developments, with the measure of transition coming from the character of changes in international trade and the significance for the economy and society of the technological developments and industrial reorganization. Other analysts look not just at trade flows, the technologies, or the sociology of production but at the macro-patterns of industrial growth. When they examine macroeconomics dynamics, they also see the emergence of a new era.

One only has to look at the rates of growth in gross national product and productivity and the pace of inflation before and after 1973 to recognize that a change has occurred. (See table 6.1.) The questions, of course, are why it happened and what it means. Here there is little agreement. Some think that the previous period of growth ended because of a series of chance events that happened to strike simultaneously, the huge oil price hikes being the most important or evident. Others see a diminishing capacity of the advanced countries to adjust to increasing pressures for economic change.[11] That diminished capacity is variously attributed to the power of interest groups in capturing government for their own selfish purposes and to the breakdown of the coalitions that had supported postwar growth.[12] The argument has been going on for a decade.[13]

More fundamentally, argue those who see a truly new era, the interconnections in the economy that set the dynamics of growth seem to have shifted. Once, they suggest, there was a virtuous cycle in which increased investment meant greater production efficiencies, lower product costs, and raised sales volumes. It also meant higher wages which increased demand and sparked new investment. The cycle started again as productivity increases meant higher profits and higher wages. That basic pattern seemed the same in all the advanced countries during the 1960s. Industrial modernization was tied to employment increases. The common pattern seems to have broken down. Instead, in the late 1970s there appear to have emerged somewhat different patterns of growth in Japan, Europe, and the United States. In Japan increased volumes in both domestic expansion and international sales have sustained the cycle of investment, productivity increases, increased sales, increased employment, and further investment. In Europe the increases in productivity have come, it seems, at the expense of jobs. In the United States average manufacturing wage rates have dropped and productivity has been slow, but employment has stayed high.

Investment, growth, productivity, and employment do not appear tied together in traditional ways. The common patterns of the past have broken apart and a distinctly new and stable pattern of growth has not yet emerged. In each of the three cases—Japan, Europe, and the United States —the international competitiveness of industry becomes a limit on national growth.[14]

Identifying Transitions

In the chapters that follow we build the case that the United States is experiencing a fundamental change in its industrial economy and that manufacturing skills and a reorganization of traditional production will be decisive in that transition. We believe that the preponderance of evidence supports our position and should persuade the reader that the United States must approach its national economic choices and corporate options from this vantage, and that analysis of the advanced industrial nations must begin there. Yet we cannot demonstrate our position unequivocally. Put more formally, the arguments set forth in this part of the book are not posed as hypotheses that can be tested. The story is too complex. To formalize it prematurely may ultimately prevent us from understanding what we know. Nonetheless, it is worth stating clearly what a test of the argument would involve and why such a test matters. Many popular works build convincing and often provocative cases about forces that have driven the recent past and provide seductive arguments about how the immediate future will evolve. A convincing brief does not constitute evidence in a formal test of an argument. Indeed it is often easy to amass evidence to persuasively argue a position that is in fact quite suspect. How much confidence, though, should you the reader have in the argument and evidence we offer? A "test" is a way of formally posing a problem so that we may decide how confident we can be that an argument is correct. Professionals may quarrel about how the "test" is done, debating about what is called methodology. That methodological argument matters precisely because it affects the credence we give to the results. The formality of the argument required to test a position and the technical character of the evidence often make these debates difficult to penetrate. Yet "tests" matter. A test involves stating an argument in such a manner that it can be denied—that is, in a manner that it can be shown not to be true—and that the evidence required to test it can be spelled out in advance. In other

TABLE 6.1

Patterns of Inflation, Growth, and Employment

Year	Japan			France			West Germany			United States			United Kingdom		
	A	B	C	A	B	C	A	B	C	A	B	C	A	B	C
1954	5.7	6.0	1.5	4.2	0.0	1.7	7.7	0.0	7.0	-2.2	0.0	5.6	3.8	1.9	1.4
1955	8.6	-0.9	1.6	4.7	1.0	1.6	12.0	2.0	5.1	6.9	0.0	4.4	3.3	3.9	1.1
1956	7.5	0.4	1.5	5.9	2.0	1.1	7.2	2.5	4.0	2.2	1.5	4.2	1.6	4.9	1.2
1957	7.3	3.1	1.2	6.0	2.6	0.8	5.6	2.1	3.4	1.9	3.5	4.3	1.9	3.7	1.5
1958	5.8	-0.5	1.3	2.9	15.0	0.9	3.5	2.2	3.5	-0.5	2.7	6.8	0.2	3.0	2.0
1959	9.1	1.1	1.3	3.2	6.1	1.3	7.4	1.0	2.4	6.0	0.8	5.5	4.0	0.6	2.2
1960	13.1	3.5	1.1	7.2	3.6	1.2	8.9	1.3	1.2	2.1	1.6	5.5	5.2	1.0	1.6
1961	14.6	5.3	1.0	5.5	3.2	1.0	5.1	2.3	0.8	2.3	1.1	6.7	3.3	3.4	1.5
1962	7.1	6.9	0.9	6.7	4.8	1.2	4.4	3.1	0.7	5.6	1.1	5.5	1.0	4.3	2.0
1963	10.5	7.5	0.9	5.3	4.8	1.4	3.0	3.0	0.8	4.1	1.2	5.7	3.9	1.8	2.4
1964	13.2	3.9	0.8	6.5	3.4	1.1	6.7	2.3	0.7	5.1	1.4	5.2	5.2	4.0	1.8
1965	5.1	6.5	0.8	4.8	2.5	1.3	5.6	3.5	0.6	6.0	1.6	4.5	2.3	4.8	1.5
1966	10.6	5.1	0.9	5.2	2.6	1.4	2.5	3.4	0.7	6.0	2.9	3.8	2.0	3.6	1.5
1967	10.8	3.9	1.3	4.7	2.8	1.8	-0.2	1.5	2.1	2.7	2.8	3.8	2.6	2.4	2.3
1968	12.8	5.4	1.2	4.3	4.5	2.1	6.3	2.9	1.5	4.5	4.2	3.6	4.1	4.7	2.5
1969	12.3	5.2	1.1	7.0	6.5	2.3	7.8	1.8	0.8	2.6	5.4	3.5	1.5	5.3	2.5
1970	9.8	7.8	0.9	5.7	5.3	2.4	6.0	3.3	0.4	-0.1	6.0	5.6	2.2	6.4	2.4
1971	4.6	6.3	1.2	5.4	5.3	2.6	3.2	5.4	0.8	2.9	4.3	5.9	2.7	9.5	3.5
1972	8.8	5.0	1.4	5.9	6.2	2.7	3.7	5.5	1.1	5.8	3.2	5.6	2.2	6.8	3.8
1973	8.8	11.5	1.3	5.4	7.4	2.6	4.9	6.9	1.2	5.4	6.3	4.9	7.5	8.4	2.7
1974	-1.0	23.3	1.4	3.2	13.7	2.8	0.5	7.0	1.6	-1.3	10.9	5.6	-1.2	15.8	2.6
1975	2.3	11.7	1.9	0.2	11.7	4.1	-1.8	5.9	3.7	-1.0	9.2	8.5	-0.8	24.2	4.1
1976	5.3	9.4	2.0	5.2	9.6	4.4	5.2	4.5	3.6	5.6	5.8	7.7	4.2	15.8	5.7
1977	5.3	8.1	2.0	3.1	9.4	4.7	3.0	3.7	3.6	5.1	6.4	7.0	1.0	16.0	6.2
1978	5.1	4.2	2.2	3.8	9.1	5.2	3.6	2.7	3.5	4.8	7.6	6.0	3.3	9.0	6.1

TABLE 6.1 (Continued)

Year	Japan			France			West Germany			United States			United Kingdom		
	A	B	C	A	B	C	A	B	C	A	B	C	A	B	C
1979	5.2	3.7	2.1	3.3	10.3	5.9	4.4	4.1	3.2	3.2	11.4	5.8	1.3	13.3	5.7
1980	4.2	7.7	2.0	1.1	14.0	6.3	1.8	5.5	3.1	−0.2	13.5	7.1	−1.9	18.4	7.4
1981	2.9	4.9	2.2	0.5	13.4	7.6	−0.3	5.9	4.3	2.0	10.2	7.6	*	11.9	11.3
1982	3.7	3.1	2.4	1.0	14.0	8.1	−1.4	5.9	6.1	−1.9	7.7	9.5	2.0	11.0	11.8
1983	3.5	1.9	2.6	0.7	9.2	8.3	3.2	3.7	8.0	6.5	3.3	9.5	3.4	5.3	12.6
1984	5.7	2.9	2.7	1.4	8.9	9.7	3.1	3.1	8.5	4.6	4.6	7.4	1.9	5.1	13.0
1985	4.0	1.8	2.6	2.1	3.4	10.1	2.4	0.7	8.6	2.9	3.2	7.1	2.8	5.1	13.2

Column A: Annual growth rate of Gross Domestic Product (constant prices)
Column B: Annual percent change consumer price index
Column C: Annual unemployment as percent of total work force
*figure unavailable

SOURCES: For growth rates—Organisation for Economic Cooperation and Development. *National Accounts of the OECD Countries* (Paris: OECD); for inflation—OECD, *Main Economic Indicators* (Paris: OECD); for unemployment—International Labour Organisation. *Yearbook of Labour Statistics* (Geneva: ILO), and OECD, *Main Economic Indicators* (Paris: OECD).

words, we agree in advance what the rules are that we must follow before we accept an argument. Simply, we want to prevent ourselves from being persuaded by what we want to believe. We want to understand clearly how a given body of evidence supports a particular argument. Therefore let us pose our problem clearly.

Formally put, what is a transition? During a period of routine, when behavior seems to follow understandable rules and rest on definable premises, there are parameters that give regularity to behavior. In politics those parameters may be the operations of critical bureaucracies, the nature of the electoral game, or rules about the powers of judiciary and executive. In economics those parameters may be market structure or features of the production processes and technological development. During transitions the parameters that create regularity in routine periods are themselves in flux and unsettled, and consequently behavior becomes unpredictable. Equally important, the evolution of the parameters themselves may be inherently uncertain, with the result that the choices of individual players or the outcomes of particular crises can determine the new rules of the game.

We would define a transition as a period of uncertain and unstable parameters linking two phases with stable parameters; two periods in which routine behavior is predictable are joined by a time of real uncertainty. There is a logic to these times of uncertainty, but the outcomes may not just be unknown, they may be genuinely indeterminate. While the outcomes may be indeterminate, not all things are possible. The range of choices, the possible lines in development will be distinct in each country. In this era of transition the results of political conflicts will reset the parameters that structure social and economic life. A systematic argument about which parameters will be decisive and about the forces that will produce distinct outcomes in each nation's case will not be attempted here. To support the notion of a fundamental transition, we offer evidence both that the market problem confronting the advanced countries in the late 1980s is distinctly different from a decade or two ago and that the technological and organizational materials with which to mold a response are of a distinctly new kind. We examine the revolutions in production and telecommunications as instances of those responses. While we argue in the chapters that follow that the conditions for a basic transition are met, we do not put the position to a formal test.

The present transformation will certainly be a moment of opportunity and risk for the country. Here we agree fully with Thierry Gaudin that "each technological mutation involves a new series of winners and losers," and that the mutation we are now experiencing "is particularly radical."[15]

The manufacturing base, which we have shown to be critical, will not disappear; rather, it will be recast. Even if this shift proves not to be epochal, even if a formal test were to establish that the present period did not meet the criteria of a historical transition, these years will certainly matter powerfully and will decisively affect the position of the United States in the years to come.

7

Market Competition, Technological Development, and Trade

TRANSITION is a word that triggers a reaction—usually bored annoyance. After all, nothing is more permanent than transition, especially in economics. A healthy economy is always in a state of transition. And competitors are constantly struggling for a new product, new processes, and new kinds of efficiency. That's what makes the game so constructive; it keeps us on our toes and busy citing Schumpeter.[1] Economics abhors big and sudden movements. They are simply uncongenial to its way of thinking. Economics's basic formulation of problems, its theoretical base, is carefully tuned to marginal adjustments that sit atop large statistical bases. In conventional economics, change is rather steady and cumulative, compounding at 2, 3, sometimes even 5 percent a year. Big changes dilute in the statistical soup; their impacts on The System as a Whole are barely perceptible.

One can approach economic development differently and focus on disjunctions and dislocations and the conflicts that go along with them. Such an approach would argue that marginal changes often accumulate and then find rather sudden expression. It is rather like the California earth on which we sit while we write. Deep down, about 50,000 feet below the surface, the Pacific and continental plates slide over one another steadily and gradually—at three centimeters per year—in a way that would delight econometricians. But the earth's crust does not move. It holds steady while the marginal changes quietly accumulate until a "readjustment" becomes compelling. Those readjustments—unlike the forces that produced them—are neither gradual and marginal nor smooth. The changes cannot be understood simply as an accumulation of marginal shifts. Basic changes in markets and technologies do produce radical and abrupt changes in the market position of firms, the international position of national industries, and the relative economic strength of nations.

This chapter develops an optic to permit us to conceive America's problem, to allow us to see the issues. We want to convince the reader that radical changes in the patterns of growth and the positions of firms, industries, and nations occur. We wish the reader to understand that how Americans respond to transition will shape this country's future. We try to develop not a formal theory, but a set of analytical tools that will permit us to unravel the significance of the changes we are witnessing.

Technological Change and Market Position

Sharp changes in technology or markets can create abrupt and often irreversible shifts in the market position of firms. The basic notion here is very simple. The corporate skills it took to be a winner in one technology may not meet requirements imposed by new technologies. The strategy that succeeded with one set of competitors and a particular set of technologies may fail radically when the market changes. Thus, American producers of television sets had been very successful, but they were unable to adjust to a new mix of product and production strategies adopted by Japanese producers. Likewise, American producers of electron tubes never became important producers of microelectronics.[2] Let us put what happened a bit formally. Static efficiency, the ability to maximize profits under stable conditions, did not assure dynamic efficiency, the capacity to adapt to rapidly changing circumstances.[3] The national, or corporate, capacity to adjust to the changing demands of markets and technologies will prove to be a central part of our story.

A firm's failure to manage a changed market is usually clear and easily explained after the fact, but there is no simple way to predict when a firm will survive a transformation of technology or a shift in competitors and the terms of competition. This is unfortunate, for theoretical elegance has its own attraction, and in this case it would have practical and profitable applications as well. We can find some partial explanations for success and failure by systematically analyzing the ability of a set of firms to manage change. But we should not be tricked into pursuing complete explanations and absolute certainty—not just because the knowledge required would be costly to obtain or because any theory would be difficult to establish—but because much will always remain inherently unpredictable.[4]

Established firms sometimes slip. New firms based on new technologies are often able to establish for themselves enduring positions in traditional markets or establish entirely new markets. RCA and General Electric (GE) were established producers of electron tubes, but they did not succeed with the replacement technology, semiconductors. A new series of firms —Texas Instruments and Fairchild, to name two—created a place for themselves and became industry leaders. Through a later window of opportunity created by a new round of technological development, Advanced Micro Devices (AMD), Intel, and National Semiconductor, to name a few, entered the industry. Then in the next round of innovation Japan's giants such as NEC (Nippon Electric Company), Hitachi, and Matsushita—along with a newcomer, Sony—made their entrance on the world stage. Unlike the American integrated electronics firms that stumbled along the way, the Japanese companies made the transition from electron tubes to microchips. They built powerful world positions both in consumer electronics and, ultimately, in microelectronics. A British firm introduced the first commercial jet transport, the Comet, but the plane's failures (it crashed with some regularity as a result of early design failures) pushed it out of the market and opened the doors for twenty-five years of American domination of world aircraft markets. At the same time, the Comet's failure helped provide the knowledge for other producers to create safer planes which finally altered air travel.

An established market position does not assure a capacity to react to radical change and can consequently be washed away quite quickly,[5] but established firms often do hold on. The clearest and best example is IBM. IBM, an established U.S. producer of electromechanical equipment, did make the transition to electronic computers. In the present period the question is whether IBM can adapt to an era when the bases of competitive advantage in the computer industry are shifting. Boeing has adjusted effectively to sharp changes in the types of planes demanded, to dramatic rises and falls in the number of planes demanded, and to the emergence of a new kind of competitive threat in the European Airbus consortium.

Market positions can change quickly, and then equally quickly become fixed and difficult to reverse.[6] The opening for radical readjustment can close rapidly. Fluid situations freeze. After a brief moment when drastic shifts are possible, an industry returns to more normal circumstances of progressive or marginal change. Barriers to entry or obstacles to expansion are built up as new dominant technologies and business organizations or strategies are established. It is for this reason that mature industries have stable structures.

As market conditions shift and technology frontiers advance, firms respond by bringing new products to market and new processes to production. To do so, they invest in people and equipment. A body of know-how —the unquantifiable "art" of technology—builds up inside the firm as proprietary knowledge. Many processes are closer to recipes than to formulae. An implicit or explicit strategy then emerges. The collected investment, as well as the strategies and habits needed to use it, entrench the position of the successful firm or nation for the duration of the technology's market importance. Industrial organization becomes settled once again.

Examples abound. U.S. Steel had a dominant position in the 1950s in open-hearth production technologies. In the 1960s, using basic oxygen furnace technology (a production innovation developed in Austria), Japanese producers established themselves as the dominant low-cost producers.[7] In autos, electronics, and aircraft, corporate positions become entrenched as competition involving radical innovation in the nature of the product gives way to incremental innovation. But at the beginning of a market battle for new technologies, the position of the players is usually very fluid. As the investments consolidate, the market positions become more rigid. Positions can erode, but massive investment or another innovation may be required to change them.

Each type of innovation may require distinct specialties for the innovating firm to establish itself, for a follower to capture market position, or for an entrenched firm to respond. We may be able, as David Teece suggests, to define the conditions within which an innovator can establish itself and the type of assets a firm may require to commercialize an innovation.[8] Decisive assets required to complement the innovation are those which cannot simply be bought immediately, but which themselves are a proprietary resource. Sometimes a marketing channel may be required. For pharmaceutical innovations such channels have proven decisive. Indeed, biotechnology firms that are creating new products are now moving to build such channels in anticipation of their products. Techniques of biogenetic engineering permit a range of product innovations. Achieving entry requires establishing the vital complementary assets to support the new products. In other cases distinctive manufacturing capacities may be at issue. Xerox was unable to produce its Star word processor cheaply enough to attack the market outside the office, or rather its production costs were so high that it could only sell to the office. American semiconductor firms, which have innovated a range of products, now find it difficult to capture the gains from innovation in a direct manufacturing competition with Japanese rivals. In one sense this is a narrowly defined business strategy question. Which assets must an innovating firm establish if it hopes to capture the gains from its innovations? Which assets can an established firm use to hold market when attempting to imitate the innovator? In another sense, there is a historical question. In different historical periods different problems had to be resolved. In the late nineteenth and early twentieth centuries the creation of mass production systems and national distribution channels were decisive. Today, once again, manufacturing abilities are decisive. To see even the business strategy problem we must adopt a language that permits us to see historical evolution.

This suggests a first conclusion about how to approach problems of radical change. We cannot use the tools appropriate to more static periods; questions about efficiency give way to issues of effectiveness at perceiving and managing change. The issue in every case—whether the firm uses a radical change to establish itself or conversely whether it is displaced—will be *whether the resources, habits, and strategies that the firm had built up in one period could be applied to the tasks of the next period.* Did a firm's existing capacities match the new tasks it faced, or could it at least develop new capacities fast enough to respond to the tasks at hand and hold position. As we proceed we will see that the same may be true for nations.

Technological Plasticity and National Settings

An important lesson about the nature of technological development lies in the process by which market positions freeze after periods of fluidity. That lesson will matter as this discussion unfolds. The possibilities at the beginning of a technical transition are broad, but they narrow over time. Knowhow accumulates around a particular technology. As the investment builds around the products that are succeeding in the market, alternative technical solutions become economically less attractive. Funds for experimentation in these areas dry up. Continued development therefore tends to follow lines already established.

The development of automobile engines is illustrative. One way of increasing fuel efficiency is to make cars lighter. One of the heavier components of the car is the engine. Engines could be made lighter by substituting aluminum for iron. But aluminum, though lighter, is not as durable, as strong, or as easy to manipulate in engine manufacturing processes. The technological question became whether to try to make aluminum stronger or to reduce the amount of iron in an engine to make it lighter. Iron won out in mass-production cars not because of its inherent properties, but because automobile engineers had much greater knowledge about it and experience with it.[9]

The direction of technological development, then, is not determined by inherent technical characteristics or by any economic advantage that will accrue to all producers.[10] Instead, it is inherently uncertain. It depends in critical ways on chance, social conditions, corporate strategy and choice, and government policy. Take government as a case. Regulations influence the direction of private investment, and public investments shape the economic infrastructure. Because both government policy and corporate strategy will vary in different nations, the direction of technological development will also differ from nation to nation. At any moment the state of science, engineering, and know-how will define a "technical possibility set." But they do not define which options in the set of possibilities are exploited.

Innovations emerge from complex interaction between three factors: market demands as expressed in prices, needs that might be satisfied but are not yet expressed by buyers and sellers in the marketplace, and new additions to the "technical pool." Certainly technology is not plastic, shaped to our will. Not all things are technically possible, but technology has no internal logic that inevitably dictates its evolution or use. Technological development does not drive society as it evolves, rather technology itself is shaped by social development. Moments of radical shifts in technology, periods of transition, are periods when political choice can exert some control over technology. Technological and social development are interactive, shaped by and shaping each other.

This line of reasoning leads us to several conclusions. If technological development is inherently uncertain, then the most conservative national or firm strategy for assuring the success of a development is to spread one's bets.[11] The best analogy is to covering the table at the roulette wheel. Some might see this as a form of redundancy. We would argue that it is not. A spare tire is redundant, but it is essential if there is a flat tire. A second phone line provides a cushion of capacity if the first one is in use. Both are identical to the apparatus they replace. They are quite literally redundant, or extra, during ordinary conditions. Bets on a roulette wheel, however, are not identical; each is valuable precisely because it is different from the others. In terms of static efficiency, the extra or unused efforts would be duplications, wasted effort. In dynamic terms, the extra options are essential to guarantee success.

Technology managers have often recognized this. Indeed, the Polaris submarine development program built multiple bets into the program at critical technological junctures.[12] The biggest technical uncertainty was whether the missiles could be fired from below the surface, and a set of different projects were undertaken to solve the firing problem.

The multiple bets that technological development requires will not be placed evenly around the table. Instead, they will cluster in two areas, according to two principles. First, research and development bets will be historically rooted. They will reflect the past development of the firm and the national economy and tend to follow the direction of past work. The resources available for tackling the next round of technical problems will reflect what comes before. Technology has history. Second, the needs to which the technology is being applied will be different in each national community, and so the technological tasks will vary. The implications of these two principles around which technology bets cluster on the roulette table are significant.

If we accept these two principles, we are led to a range of conclusions. When a technology is in its infancy, and still fluid, the line of its technical evolution is inherently uncertain. This is not to say all things are possible, but rather that more than one direction of development is possible. An emphasis can be put on making steel stronger or lighter. The pace and direction of development is a matter of decision. The direction a technology takes will depend partly on circumstance and individual choices. The directions of effort and evolution are set by the cluster of the technology bets. The outcome, the winners among competing possibilities, emerges when the sunken investment becomes so great that radical alternatives are too pricy. Broad market acceptance of a new technology, for whatever reason—be it public relations or real performance—excludes new possibilities. After positions freeze, a radically new technology will not be developed unless it is so attractive that producers and users are willing to walk away from their investments in earlier technologies. If the gains from new technical approaches look marginal, they will be ignored; if gains look potentially important but slow to develop or very risky, they may never be captured.

Technological development is shaped by the community in which it occurs. It is not, as many analyses suggest, an independent force shaping the economy or the society.[13] During ordinary times, when national differences produce only small branches off the main trunk of technological evolution, the ability of society to shape technology is not nearly as visible as the powerful constraints that mature technologies have set for society. Alternate routes—the roads not taken—are hidden in the past. In periods of transition, however, the direction of technology itself—its branches, not its twigs—is affected by the clustering of bets. The direction in which the investment develops will be heavily influenced by where the bets are placed. That placement will depend on the needs of the national community and the resources built up during its previous development. Thus, the bet "placer"—be it a company or a nation—actively shapes technological development. As the new branches grow, they block others from emerging.

National context, by setting the cluster of bets, shapes technology. Computer technology, for example, could grow along several different lines in the next years. The line that wins out will reflect the historical contours and current needs of its community of origin. By blocking other options, the winning route is imposed by sustained investment on other communities. Because the winning and then dominant technological route reflects, at least in part, the historical roots and national needs of a specific community, it gives at least an initial advantage to the innovating country. The technology emerges from and plays to the national strength of the innovating country. The winning technology always imposes its own constraints, and once set, it can shape the patterns of trade. Technology *becomes* a binding parameter; it does not begin as one.

Winning and Losing in a Set of Industries

Advantage can shift in a set of sectors quite as rapidly as in one sector. Changes in the welfare of a single firm or even a single sector will rarely if ever affect the pace of national development, but if a set of firms in a particular community or a set of industries in a region or nation begin to lose market position, the economic as well as the social and political consequences can be substantial. The present problem facing the United States is that it is losing competitive advantage and market position in a range of manufacturing sectors. These do not appear to be a set of separate stories, each with its own special circumstances. They appear to be related manifestations of the same fundamental problem. The United States seems to be losing the dominance in manufacturing established early in this century with the twin innovations of mass production and the giant firm.

Consequently, America's ability to hold or appropriate the gains from product innovation within this country is weakened. Production technologies developed when the American market was insulated may have been rendered vulnerable to production technologies developed during rapid growth in Asia. The corporate capacities built up during the period of dominance appear inappropriate at best and actual handicaps at worst. New capacities will have to be created to match the tasks confronting America in the present transition.

The basis of competitive advantage in many sectors or industries, each seemingly distinct, often depends on the same thing. That critical element common to a range of sectors may be dependence on the same transportation facilities, or on the price of labor or energy, or on a specific factor of production. Apparel, shoes, and footwear, for example, have traditionally depended heavily on inexpensive labor, so as unit labor costs have grown, the cost of production has risen in these sectors, and all three find it harder to compete internationally. Similarly, aluminum and petrochemicals are both energy-intensive goods, so when energy costs rise, their production costs jump. Each becomes less competitive with alternative materials.

More important for our story, several industries may depend on a common understanding of production and a similar set of skills for sustaining it. Thus, Sweden's export advantage, critical in that small and trade-dependent high-wage country, lay in ending industries in which advantage rested on design, engineering, and efficient production—ship building and auto manufacture, for example. These are all metal-bending industries. Production in these industries rested on a roughly similar set of skills and a similar approach to manufacturing. Indeed, a Swedish national deal between labor and industry rested on the ability to move labor from one similar industry to another when advantage in world markets shifted. This set of Swedish engineering and metal-bending industries were thrown into crisis in the 1970s when similar goods were produced with lower-cost labor and roughly the same production technology in the newly industrializing countries. In other words, when standard production technologies were transferred to nations with cheap labor, Sweden was in trouble.

In the 1970s, it became apparent that the Japanese had made basic innovations in mass production. Their advantage in world manufacturing came to lie with these innovations—not, as was often argued then, simply with lower labor costs. In a range of sectors—best exemplified by durable consumer goods such as television sets, automobiles, and cameras—Japanese production now uses less labor per unit of production than American production.[14] The innovations have been given a variety of labels: "just-in-time production" refers to the management of component flows, and "total quality control" refers to the shift of quality responsibility from staff to the production line. "Flexible manufacturing" suggests the capacity to vary volumes and types of products. As these labels suggest, there is constant tinkering with the production system to strip away unnecessary labor and to adapt, improve, and create new production equipment.[15] The system also rests on and creates a distinct pool of management and labor skills that provide the basis for its further development.

The mass production system that emerged in the United States sixty years ago also produced, in its day, a common approach to manufacturing, a commonly held view of the links between manufacturing and product and price strategy, and a pool of skills and technologies to implement that view. As the system emerged it made America the dominant world producer, capable of supplying the world with war material during World War II.

Such common approaches to manufacturing can often be seen in the machines with which other products are made. Thus the machine tool industry is one "carrier" of knowledge about how to manufacture. As Nathan Rosenberg has written: "because these processes and problems [in machine tool making] became common to the production of a wide range of disparate commodities," industries that were apparently unrelated "became very very closely related (technologically convergent) on a technological basis—for example, firearms, sewing machines, and bicycles."[16] The mass production system, as it developed, generated a conventional wisdom about machines, the uses of machines, and labor organization. Today, many of the traditional skills and organizational techniques are, in fact, obstacles to effective production. To understand the transition we will look carefully at the evolution of production equipment.

Production innovations that influence several industrial sectors can rapidly alter a nation's trade position in international markets. They involve common underlying approaches to manufacturing that cut across whole sets of industries; for that reason, imitating them quickly in large established firms that have built different strategies on massive sunken investment in organization and machines is very difficult. The weakness in the old system must be identified; the direction of production innovation spelled out; the resources to implement a new strategy provided; and the mass of middle management convinced that the company must and can change direction. Accomplishing such changes in one firm is hard; doing it in the fabric of an entire economy can be very slow if possible at all. These innovations become cross-sectoral because they reflect common, widely shared approaches to manufacturing; for the same reason, they are very difficult to imitate immediately in other countries. The consumer durables industry suggests the problem. Its various products, in which production rests on the management of complex processes, provide the high-wage jobs essential to a wealthy economy. But the accumulated mastery of manufacturing can be rendered obsolete. If advantage is lost suddenly in these sectors, as it has been, the problem of adjustment—how to move from declining to expanding sectors—becomes much more serious. The market may not be able to absorb the workers and the capital released, and the result may be a drop in real wages like the one experienced in the United States over the last ten years. America may not have to worry much about the loss of competitiveness in a single sector. However, when we see difficulties in the whole set of sectors in which competitiveness depends heavily on common manufacturing skills, we should be very concerned indeed.

The Interconnections Between Sectors: Change Spreads Throughout the Economy

Radical shifts in the international competitive position of one sector or set of sectors can reverberate throughout the economy. Nothing less than America's position in the international hierarchy of wealth and power can be at stake. Competitive or technical developments in one industry always have effects in the sectors to which that industry is connected. In this period of radical shift, those interconnections become decisive. They affect the level of output in the economy, but even more importantly they shape the process of technological development and diffusion which underlies competitiveness for the firm and productivity growth for the economy.

The most obvious connection is that industries buy from and sell to each other. The expansion of the cotton industry in Britain encouraged investment in industries that produced and sold the machines needed to make textiles.[17] Railroads and, later, interstate highways lowered transportation costs and altered the character of America's national markets. Once Ohio was the Far West, and it was harder to travel from Philadelphia to New York than it is now to travel from San Francisco to Tokyo. The railroad industry bought steel in the form of rails, encouraging the expansion of the steel industry. Some seventy years later the automobile industry played the same role, creating demand for rubber, cement, glass, and more. Today the nation's telecommunications systems are being reorganized so that networks which once carried only voice can begin to carry data as well; that reorganization itself is provoking secondary investment, which will shape the evolution of the computer industry and also alter business management and communications. The expansion of the electronics industries rests on a national pool of skills and knowledge, as the expansion of German chemical industries did nearly a hundred years earlier. Germany forged an advantage in industries that required an educated work force, research, and heavy investment. From a historical perspective, strategic industries whose growth promotes expansion in related sectors—industries such as automobiles or textiles, whose own development at a critical moment generated enough power to move an entire economy forward—stand out. Automobiles, for example, established a scale and form of production that was then imitated in a set of similar and related sectors.

Conversely, the decline of a central industry can unravel the industrial combines built up around it. In Britain, when auto imports rose from 10 percent to 50 percent of domestic demand without any compensating increase in exports, demand dropped for steel, machines, and glass.[18] We can quantify the volumes lost. But the impact on the steel, machine, and glass sectors is greater than the quantities and harder to assess. The drop in sales represents lost profits, lost volumes required for efficient production, potential labor problems, and a failure to sustain investment in machine innovation in the face of declining sales by final users. Certainly the troubles in the auto sector reflected problems throughout the British economy. The market was penetrated by foreign producers because British companies were badly organized and inefficient producers. The troubles in the auto sector, though, contributed to the general erosion. Decline, like expansion, is cumulative. Manufacturing sectors are linked together, just as services are linked to manufacturing.

The sectors that are critical for the continued development of the economy cannot be easily distinguished from those that are not. The French in the early 1980s used the word *filière* to refer to the fact that there are critical interrelations in pieces of the economy. This amounts to conceiving of the economy as a series of vertically integrated strands. An electronics *filière*, [19] for example, refers to the fact that silicon is transformed into microchips which are put into computers, which are used in telecommunications equipment, which serves as a link inside and between companies and communities. But the notion of a *filière* is no more useful than an input-output table in determining the strategic links in an economy, or what their character is. It doesn't answer the question—for a firm or a government—of where to invest. As one French businessman remarked: "It all depends on where you are in the *filière.*" He meant that some pieces of the electronics industry are profitable for a company, but some aren't profitable. The notion of *filière* doesn't answer, for a government or a corporation, the strategic policy question: Which segments are vital and ought to be supported? It doesn't indicate whether a semiconductor chip should be treated like a ball bearing that can easily be imported or like a vital electronic system that might have to be developed at home. Nor does it tell whether the loss of the capacity to produce semiconductor chips competitively blocks the path to more vital electronics capacities. Worst of all, the answers don't stay the same as the industries evolve.

Overemphasizing the sectoral ties—from the view that since all things are connected to each other, all are critical—leads quickly to a defense of autarchy. At the other extreme, ignoring them leads to a view of the economy as a scattering of different industries that have only remote connections with each other. The task, we repeat, is to identify which sectors are strategic, which nodes of interconnection are vital.

What matters to us most are the links that promote ongoing market adaptation and technological innovation. Advanced computers and telecommunications equipment depend on innovation in electronic devices. An expanding telecom industry provides a market for computers and microelectronics components. Japan's early advantage in certain advanced semiconductor products—for example, CMOS (complementary metal on silicon) memory chips[20]—was built on its market position in consumer electronics. This instance suggests a broader conclusion: advantage in a national economy is embodied not simply in the capacities of specific firms but in the web of interconnections that establishes possibilities for all firms.

Technological innovation depends on a series of subtle and complex interconnections. Knowledge of auto manufacturing or airplane manufacturing promotes innovation in machine tools, and advances in machine tools permit production innovation in many other industries. The widespread technological interplay involving small improvements may be even more important than the dazzling breakthroughs. Nathan Rosenberg has summarized the complexity of this interplay well:

> The ways in which technological changes coming from one industry constitute sources of technological progress and productivity growth in other industries defy easy summary or categorization. In some cases the relationships have evolved over a considerable period of time, so that relatively stable relationships have emerged between an industry and its supplier of capital goods. . . .
>
> Often, however, an innovation from outside will not merely reduce the

price of the product in the receiving industry but will make possible wholly new or drastically improved products or processes. . . .

The transmission of technological change from one sector of the economy to another through the sale of intermediate output has important implications for our understanding of the processes of productivity in an economy. *Specifically, a small number of industries may be responsible for generating a vastly disproportionate amount of the total technological change in the economy.* [our italics][21]

Again, the national technology networks represent a resource for all firms. The national position—not just the position of specific firms or sectors or sets of sectors—can shift radically. The object that is sold, whether a machine tool or a refinery, does not embody the whole of the technology. The know-how, the understanding of how it was developed and how it can be used or modified, lies in the network that developed the technology and helps apply it. The know-how is untraded information embodied in people and organized in firms.[22] Access to innovative products is not always sufficient to spread the innovation throughout the economy. The more standard the machine and the more conventional its uses, the less vital are its informal extras. The more advanced and the more innovative the products, the more critical its extras become.

Vital "soft" knowledge comes from a pool of scientific, engineering, and technical know-how. We suggest that those pools, for industrial purposes, are fundamentally national in character and organized differently in each country. While technologies are borrowed, stolen, and licensed from abroad, the national technology pool is a decisive resource for most firms. When vital technical knowledge is sold as a product by specialized service firms or equipment companies, as in the United States, it becomes readily accessible. The pattern of innovation in the American electronics industry has created a variety of market networks and specialized service suppliers so that access to American technology is simple. The technology pools in each country are not equally open. The United States is a fast-diffusing environment that is quite open to outsiders because of the quite special role of university research and the mobility of engineers among companies. Japan, by contrast, is a slow-diffusing setting; and in addition, the diffusion there appears to take place chiefly within the country and only with difficulty spreads outside. The Japanese technology world, focused around corporate research centers and characterized by limited mobility, is more closed. The openness or closure of the national technology pool turns on the organization of the research community.

The United States is left in an unsatisfying position. There can be little doubt that sectoral interconnections are critical to the continued innovation on which a steady growth of productivity rests. Yet an economy is not like a piece of fabric that unravels when one strand is broken, nor is it like a ball of putty that is easily molded back into a whole after one piece is removed. Looking backward, it is always possible to see the lines connecting one technology to the next. But it is hard to identify in advance the critical sectoral nodes where innovation will be induced. Perhaps there are a small number of possible nodes of technological synergy. We cannot know which will be critical until the technology twists along its uncertain course. Sometimes—as now, when a basic change has already begun—we may be aware of the river but still unable to predict its future course. At such times it becomes crucial to know whether public policy can direct the course of the rivers or transform their energy into national development. As we shall argue, the technological choices will depend in substantial measure on the skill levels in the work force and the character of labor conflict in the national economy.

We are arguing that the mix of manufacturing activities shapes the potential for development of the economy. We choose the word "development" intentionally. The notion of growth as used by economists implies a bloodless, smooth, and quite mechanical process. There are shifts and movements, but not disjunctures and dislocations. Development implies transformation. Those looking at the newly industrializing countries today or at the history of the now advanced countries can see clearly the dislocations, can see the fights and struggles that were settled in some countries in a way that permitted the accumulation economists call "growth" to proceed.

We are suggesting that the composition of production matters, contrary to the received wisdom that the mix of production activities does not affect America's economic possibilities. The composition of production ought to be a concern of policy. The present mix and organization of production, we suggest, has various implications for economic expansion and innovation. First, different sectors have different potential for growth or face different degrees of foreign competition and have different capacities to resist that competition. Let us take one simpleminded instance. The apparel industry in the advanced industrial countries will expand slowly. Populations are reasonably well clothed. Additional personal income will be spent on other goods. By contrast, the demand for telecommunications equipment of all kinds has begun to explode. In a world of only two industries with total national specialization, apparel and telecommunications equipment, countries of apparel makers will in this period grow more slowly than nations of telecommunications producers. Second, we have seen how the ability of any given sector to adjust and develop depends, in part, on the mix of other industries in the economy. In some cases the links between sectors may cross national borders. A sophisticated electronics and automated equipment sector permits the textile companies and unions to dream of reorganization of the apparel industry and then act to achieve it. In the U.S. textile industry much of the vital production technology was imported from abroad. However, in other cases, making links within the national economy creates real advantages and speeds the development of the most advanced technologies and the applications of these new possibilities to traditional industries. National economies, each with a different manufacturing base or production profile, differ in their potential for future growth.

Some have argued, as we noted, that at any given moment particular industries are economically strategic[23]—that is, certain sectors are at the center of a web of technical evolutions and developments that will reshape the entire economy. The mastery of steam engines altered the application of energy to manufacturing throughout Europe. Its use in rail transportation altered economic and social distances. The emergence of the modern chemical industries created new products and altered old ones. The expansion of the automobile industries had a similar effect. There are elaborate theories that would argue formally that growth moves in spurts, driven by waves of technological development.[24] But we do not need an entire theory of growth to contend that those countries solidly placed in these strategic industries which symbolize the transition and which have a web of sectoral interconnections that permit the industries that are driving the technological advance to influence more traditional industries are better situated for sustained expansion.

The Japanese Ministry of International Trade and Industry (MITI), of course, is held up as proof that such sectors can be identified and their development supported. When Japan was a backward economy it could see the outlines of its economic future in the structures of its competitors' economies. Many have noted the criteria it chose to spot its future. The primary criteria were: (1) income elasticity—would demand for products grow as Japan got richer; (2) scale and learning curve economies—would the price of the goods drop as the volume produced grew; (3) would their expansion drag the economy along in their wake; and (4) could they become export industries.[25]

Now that Japan is a fully advanced economy, seeing the future in the tea leaves of foreign economies is no longer possible. Yet MITI continues to target or focus attention, investment, and research on particular areas. Those areas now are electronics, biotechnology, and new materials. Do the Japanese know something the Americans do not that allows them to predict the future? Are they simply following the U.S. stock market?[26] If so, their predictions are confirming ours and ours theirs, because importance is assigned by American investors to Japanese policy judgments, and apparently Japanese policy judgments take account of the choices of American investors.

The targeted technologies all have one characteristic in common. They are transformative technologies—that is, they are inputs to the products and production processes of other sectors and consequently transform those industries through their evolution. As a result, they possess the potential of affecting the economy at large. There is substantial evidence that, as the technologies are mastered, production costs will come down and that they will be export sectors. Importantly, they all are likely to reduce imported materials inputs into each increment of GNP. In other words, the Japanese will use less in the way of imported raw materials to grow. For a resource-poor economy that must export to survive, the social gains from following a technology path that reduces import requirements are enormous. Whether the Japanese are right in their judgment that demand for these products will grow—independent of government policy— may not matter. By focusing attention and investment, the Japanese may provoke new technology paths that they can dominate. Simply, the prophecies of technological and industrial centrality can—for transformative industries with real potential—become self-confirming.

We must emphasize this. The so-called high technology industries are in fact transformative sectors. The products and process alter or transform the goods and production arrangements throughout the economy, that is they alter the choices open to firms and the very nature and definition of markets. To put it technically, the interindustry spillovers are enormous and can potentially influence a nation's industrial structure. Hence we use the notion of transformative technologies emerging from transformative sectors.

Precisely because the new technologies involve the emergence of new sectors and reopen and disrupt established competitive patterns in traditional sectors, they make competition a strategic game. It is not simply one in which the clear constraints of competition in perfect markets bound the choices and possibilities of firms. Rather the decisions of particular firms, and often of governments, alter the market by changing the possibilities of other firms in the industry. Competition in emerging and transforming sectors does not follow the model of perfect competition so dear to economic analysis. Markets in these cases are inherently imperfect and the outcomes—what firms produce and where—are powerfully and often in an enduring way shaped by corporate strategic decisions and government policy. Indeed we have argued in this chapter that an initial position by a firm or a nation in these sectors can become enduring. Put technically, the dominant firms as an industry congeals into a more enduring form can control a stream of product and process innovation that makes market entry much harder for followers.*

The national production profile—the distribution of industries in the manufacturing base—describes a country's economic present. It also structures the country's industrial future. The question for the United States is not simply whether it has a manufacturing base, but what its composition will be and what potential for growth it embodies. Since national economies differ in their structures or production profiles, they represent different national futures. The opportunities for economic expansion and innovation tomorrow differ with the sectoral mix of production today. There are fast and slow roads of economic growth. How well America manages today's transition will determine its economic future for a long time to come.

National Shifts, Trade, and Technological Change

The American transition will not take place in isolation. It is taking place as part of an intense international competition. New technologies such as microelectronics open up possibilities; but the speed with which they are adopted and the purposes to which they are put are pressed by international competition—the need for firms to create, defend, and reestablish competitive positions in trade. Corporate reshuffling will take place across national borders, with clear implications for national economic positions.

Trade affects national position during the transition in three main ways. First, the corporate shifts that often attend technological development alter national positions if advantage moves from firms of one nation to those of another. Second, a single innovation—a machine, an electronic device, a way of producing—may affect a range of industries. It may, for example, advance the international position of a set of user industries. The chief trade question in this case is whether the innovation—and the know-

---

*Note that the new trade theorists create the possibility of strategic behavior altering industrial outcomes. However they are far too conservative in their evaluation of the consequences of such strategic behavior. They underestimate interindustry spillovers, discount the possibility that such spillovers will stay within one national community, and assume exogenous technological advance. Limiting the analysis permits a more careful evaluation of each argument, but only the assembly of the pieces emphasizes the importance of a dynamic not static equilibrium approach.

how to use it effectively—can be easily obtained by foreign firms. Can the Japanese obtain critical semiconductor product technology from the United States? Can the Americans obtain production know-how in Japan? Can the Europeans obtain from the United States or Japan vital microelectronics design capacity to implement new electronic systems? Third, the interconnections that permit continued innovation may be unraveled by the loss of a specific firm or set of firms. Does continued innovation in textile manufacture depend on a national textile equipment industry? Can American textile firms obtain needed production equipment and know-how quickly enough to adjust their strategies? The vital question here is whether a nation's firms can innovate in the application of new technology, if not in its direct development. If a sector declines, it may lose its capacity to spark innovation in linked industries. And since trade between the advanced nations rests in part on technological advantages, often quite minor ones, a decline in critical sectors can threaten to unravel the whole web of technological connections that sustain innovation and growth in an economy. Recognition of this risk, however, should not push America to seek self-sufficiency in the development of technology or cut itself off from vital foreign sources of technological development. Technology can be imported; it often is. Japan would not have succeeded if it had not borrowed technology. U.S. policy makers must not be swayed by the narrow profit motives of American producers, who may defend autonomy as a means of obtaining protection for themselves; they must judge which streams of technology can be imported. And technology can be imported in various forms: as product, through licenses, in the form of direct investment, or as services.

There is another dimension of the problem. Governments with distinctly different priorities and capacities for action are involved. There are political asymmetries. Certainly each nation must live with the priorities it chooses, a matter to which we will return in the final chapter. However, there is one issue we wish to note but not develop. Do the efforts of one advanced country to promote its own technological and industrial development limit the ability of its trade partners to achieve theirs? The answer is, it all depends. It depends, in the first place, on the nature of the promotion policies being used to support technological development. The link between domestic support of R&D, on the one hand, and closed markets or limited access to commercial technology, on the other, is crucial. Protection can backfire seriously if the protected firms cannot use it to establish themselves in world markets. However, if they do become important world competitors, then domestic protection has serious international consequences. Domestic markets that are closed to foreigners can certainly deny foreigners some potential sales. More important, the protected home market can serve as a launching pad for new products, a safe haven in which local producers can gain experience in new products or in new sectors before entering international competition. Much evidence now suggests that when an initial position in a domestic market serves to establish producers in world markets, those producers are usually able to defend their home terrain against foreign competitors when protection is lifted. If demand for the new good is promoted in the closed market, the pace of national development is accelerated. When foreign producers are prevented from competing in this launch market, it makes it harder for them to stay in touch with the lines of technological development emerging in the protected country. If the government in the protected country promotes generic technologies of commercial significance—that is, if it helps solve technical problems that appear in a range of products—it may speed the development of its own producers. Whether it succeeds will depend crucially on whether the new research is open to foreign producers as well as to domestic ones. Policy objectives may not be realized; ambition does not translate automatically into reality. But the *potential* for policy to consciously shape technological development is definitely there.

There are no simple rules to apply in guiding policy. The proper choices will differ from sector to sector and will change with the competitive situation and tactical position of the firms involved. And there is real uncertainty about the direction technological development will take. This may be frustrating to policy makers who want clear guidelines; but imposing a pattern where none exists can only lead to continuous policy mistakes.

Premises of the Debate: A Summary of Conclusions

We have now developed six hypotheses that will be used as premises from here on in, so they merit repetition. First, technological developments can provoke rapid market shifts. Second, technologies are shaped by the needs and arrangements that exist in the nations from which they emerge. Third, some critical technologies can affect the competitive position of a whole range of industries; and if one nation uses these technologies to gain a lead in a vital product, it can forge an important trade advantage for itself. These are *strategic transformative industries* characterized by imperfect competition and with powerful interindustry spillovers. Fourth, continued technological development depends heavily on the connections between producing firms, their suppliers, and their customers. A web of structural and operating arrangements supports technological development, and that web can unravel. Fifth, this reshuffling of market position in a period in which important new strategic transformative sectors are emerging is powerfully influenced by government policy. Sixth, the reshuffling can result in new international hierarchies of wealth but also of power.

There are sound reasons to accept that a period of technological transition can resituate an economy and its potential for growth, but equally important to recognize that a nation's position in that transition can be strengthened or unraveled by policy. We argue here, of course, that we are in the midst of one such transition.

8

Production Skills in the Logic of the New Trade Game

T HE FIRST ELEMENT of the transition is the change in the market problem. The advanced countries are pressed on all sides and must make quite fundamental adjustments in what they make and how they produce. There will be no safe havens in which to avoid the force of the market storm. This is even true for a country such as the United States whose domestic industries have been traditionally insulated from foreign competition by the enormous home market and a real competitive advantage in many sectors. Let us look at the changing market problems from the vantage of the United States.

The evidence that a basic change in the structure of world trade in manufactures affecting American industry is occurring is overwhelming. Most obvious is the relatively rapid and massive exposure of major segments of American manufacturing, and services, to international competition. Once this country was relatively insulated from foreign competition. We imported little, and the bulk of our manufacturing could be indifferent to developments abroad. The growing importance of trade in the GNP is the best single measure of the change. It does not, though, express the change in the international position of American steel from a net exporter to a net importer, or of the radical change in the U.S. position in textiles, autos, and televisions. This new exposure is different in extent and kind from anything America has previously experienced.

Of course the United States is not alone. Trade as a portion of the national economy has increased dramatically for all the advanced countries, reaching an average of $131.77 billion for European countries (of which only $56.271 billion is outside the European region).[1] For a country like Japan, manufactured exports are essential to pay for the raw materials it utterly lacks. For Japan trade represents 24.8 percent of its GNP. For the United States the equivalent figure is 15.3 percent.[2] Among the advanced countries, the United States remains the most insulated from trade, though no longer autarkic. This is partly a matter of its relative size. The openness of a nation to international trade is related in an almost geometrical way to the size of the economy. For large nations such as the United States, trade represents a smaller portion of GNP than it does in smaller nations such as Sweden. Roughly, cut the size of the country in half and double the ratio of trade to GNP.[3] Yet in the last decades the exposure of all countries has grown.

Over the past generation America preached, to itself and to others, a doctrine of interdependence. But it was other nations that were interdependent, on each other and on the United States; we were independent. As late as 1970 imports into the United States totaled only $40 billion; by 1980 they had climbed to $245 billion; by 1984, to almost $350 billion.[4] Until only yesterday imports in manufacturing averaged around 4 to 5 percent of sales and were easily balanced by exports; now they are about 25 percent of sales and some 70 percent of U.S. industries are subject to foreign competition.[5] Where industries such as television equipment, steel, and autos have not adjusted, or have done so only partially or slowly, the consequences have been evident in failed firms, lost market share, and lost jobs.

There are many other indications of profound change in America's relation to the world market. The changes are not just ones of scale. Old competitors, located mostly in Western Europe, caught up from an unnatural lag in the kind of production that created the power of the United States: they mastered complex manufacturing in such industries as autos, chemicals, and aircraft. Some evidence, indeed, suggests that in critical ways some European production processes have pushed ahead of those in the United States.[6] The Europeans accumulated, or dug up, capital. And they have never been behind on the fundamentals: education and the ability to create technology. But perhaps more important, new competitors —most obviously Japan—have come on line. Japan's size and the importance of its production innovations make it distinctive. U.S. trade with Japan has grown to $84 billion and the U.S. current account deficit with Japan rose to roughly $50 billion.[7] U.S. trade with Japan alone is now a substantial portion of our trade with Europe.[8] Japan, though, simply heads the list of new competitors, and there is a separate list of established competitors that may emerge stronger and more dangerous. Manufacturing exports from the developing countries, particularly the small number that have come to be called "newly industrializing countries" (NICs), are now important in the markets of the advanced countries. Such exports doubled in the 1970s, growing at a rate nearly twice that of all imports. Although the base is low, such exports now represent 3.4 percent of the consumption of manufactures. In some sectors, such as textiles, exports from less developed countries (LDCs) represent 18 percent of total consumption in the advanced countries.[9] There are a few very visible sectors and countries, but the range of sectors and nations involved should not be underestimated. As Susan Strange argues:

> The new international division of labor appears to be unstoppable. The move of manufacturing industry to the Third World is structural, not cyclical. Though more visible in the export oriented economies of South Korea and Taiwan, it is also happening in India and Brazil where an expanding mass market—for clothes, radios, even computers—is increasingly satisfied by domestic production rather than by imports from the old industrialized countries.[10]

U.S. trade with the NICs has grown from $33 billion in 1980 to over $56 billion in 1984.[11] Even Korean exports to Japan have exploded in recent years, though the Koreans argue—and we tend to agree—that they are being excluded systematically from open competition in that market. And the beginning of Korean and Yugoslav export of autos to the United States simply extends to automobiles a pattern that we have seen before in shoes, textiles, apparel, and consumer electronics. As the Japanese captured nearly a quarter of the American automobile market, a voluntary restraint agreement (VRA) was adopted. The Japanese themselves limited auto exports to the United States when threatened with legislated restraints by the United States. If you limit the number of cars (or shoes, shirts, or televisions) one nation can sell to another, a clear logic is generated. Limited in the number it can sell, the exporter may maximize sales and profits by selling the most expensive, highest value products that it can. America has encouraged Japan to begin moving up market in automobiles (as it encouraged Japan and others to do in shoes and televisions). The American market vulnerability at the bottom end of the market, simple and inexpensive cars, still remains. Consequently, a new round of producers is stepping in. The voluntary restraint agreement with Japan may momentarily slow the pressure of foreign competition, but it will not end the necessity for American firms to adjust. The competitive pressures in the form of new products and firms in the market will spread around the edges of the agreement.

The geographic composition of American trade and world trade has, as a consequence of the new competition, changed as well. Not only has Asia replaced Europe as America's principal trade partner, but more than "one-third of LDC exports now go to other LDCs . . . Over half of South Korea's growing exports of cars and trucks—now nudging the half-million mark go to other LDCs, even though ten years ago the industry did not exist."[12] Yet we must note in passing that Europe remains our principal export market, Asia our dominant and new competitor. Our exports to Europe are three times those to Japan and the Asian NICs.[13] Critically expanded trade among the Asian NICs and the huge expansion of Japanese trade with the United States demonstrate one thing clearly: differences in labor costs do not account for the most basic changes in trade patterns. There is a particular character of the change in U.S. trade with Asia and Europe. Although 29.1 percent of U.S. imports come from Asia, only 19.1 percent of U.S. exports go in that direction. Conversely, Europe, the United States's traditional partner, takes 21.6 percent of U.S. exports and represents only 17.9 percent of U.S. imports. Simply put, the United States *imports* massively from Asia, while it continues to *export* to Europe. This is the case particularly in semiconductors and telecommunications. (See figures 8.1–8.3.)

The Changed Logic of Trade

Most importantly, the logic of trade has changed. In the 1960s it was thought that production costs and production structures in the advanced countries were converging and that the expansion of trade would therefore lead to greater specialization within sectors. Intra-industry trade would grow. In the machine tool industry, for example, Germany would capture a large share of the market for some tools, while the United States would become increasingly dominant in other areas of the tool market. Expanded exchange would lead to increased company specialization and produce higher incomes for both trading nations. International trade, it appeared,

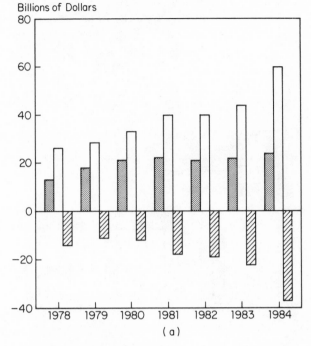

Total U.S. Trade with Japan
Billions of Dollars

(a)

Total U.S. Trade with the E.E.C.
Billions of Dollars

▦ U.S. Total Exports to Japan

☐ U.S. Total Imports from Japan

▧ Trade Balance

(b)

FIGURE 8.1

Total U.S. Imports from Japan and the EEC

Source: The trade figures for figures 8.1–8.3 were compiled from Department of Commerce data, the International Monetary Fund's *Direction of Trade Statistics Yearbook, 1985,* and the OECD's *Statistics of Foreign Trade: Series B, 1979–1984.*

Total Imports from Japan and the EEC
Billions of Dollars

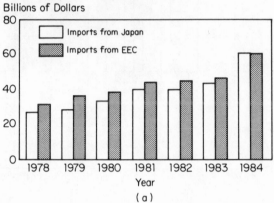

Year
(a)

Total Exports to Japan and the EEC
Billions of Dollars

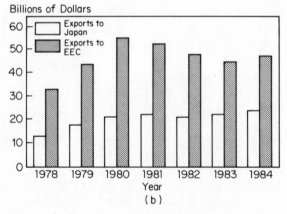

Year
(b)

FIGURE 8.2
U.S. Trade Patterns with Japan and the EEC
SOURCE: See figure 8.1.

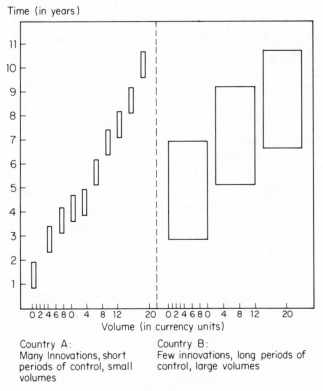

Time (in years)

Volume (in currency units)

Country A:
Many Innovations, short
periods of control, small
volumes

Country B:
Few innovations, long periods of
control, large volumes

FIGURE 8.3

Innovation-Based Export Streams: Volume and Duration of Advantage

Source: See figure 8.1.

could grow without precipitating massive dislocations of workers and firms, and thus the domestic political costs of expanded trade were low. There would only be winners in the trade game.[14]

The analysis of the 1960s hinged on a simplification. That simplification proved to be wrong. Production technologies, given the same levels of capital investment, were assumed to be the same in all countries.[15] Consequently, it was thought that as capital and labor costs converged, so would production costs. The implication, as we said, was that the advanced countries would make similar products in similar ways, and trade among them would hinge on product variety and specialization within industries. However, in the 1980s it has become clear that production technologies are not the same in all firms or nations. The economists' analytic simplification hides the importance of the organization of manufacturing and production skills to economic outcomes. That simplification misleads economists about the nature and results of trade. Rapidly expanding production volumes generate not just the advantages of large-scale production—economies of scale—but the benefits of learning from doing—learning curve economies.[16] Thus we now talk glibly about one firm being further down the learning curve than its competitors, and some extend the notion to talk about a nation's position on the learning curve. What is learned from rapidly expanding production becomes embedded in modified capital equipment, the tools of production. The faster a firm grows the faster it can add tools and innovate in the tools it uses. In other cases, that learning is embedded in the social organization of production, entrenched in the way the machines are used. Together the machines and the organization that employs them evolve to permit ever greater productivity. These new approaches involve changes on the shop floor and in the ties between production units. It means, in some cases, a breakup in production integration, that is, more activities are contracted to independent but related firms and fewer are conducted within the corporation itself.

A critical point was reached when the American automobile industry finally acknowledged that Japanese firms had established a real production advantage based on the more effective use of capital—that is, in the effective organization of labor and equipment—not on low-cost labor. Suddenly the possibility had to be faced that production costs among the advanced countries may diverge as one nation gains a real advantage, an advantage that cannot be rapidly imitated abroad because it has to become embedded in machinery and social organization. The United States has been slower to realize that equally significant changes are occurring in places like Italy.

The market problem is more complex than we might have thought at first. The advanced countries cannot just run away from low-cost competition by moving into high technology. All the advanced countries are trying to squeeze into the same range of businesses: not just computers, but also specialty steels, sophisticated chemicals, and high-fashion garments. All the advanced countries face the need to produce the high-value-added production machinery, indispensable medical equipment, and specialty consumer goods if they are to buy the products made in the NICs by low-cost labor using those machines. Suddenly, specialization among firms of different nations, which was assumed would leave trade a congenial sport not a deadly combat, does not appear inevitable. Not only are the firms of the several nations trying to squeeze into the same product space, but production advantages will give some competitors real and enduring advantages in a wide range of products.

Finally, while U.S. attention was focused in the late seventies and early eighties on the dream of high technology, which seemed to imply a stream of new products, manufacturing skills may have become more important than ever to international competition. There are no sunrise and sunset industries. There will be only those industries or firms that successfully incorporate the new potentials for product and production processes implicit in the new technologies . . . and those firms that do not.

There are really three sets of international market pressures to which American firms, like industries in all the advanced economies, must respond and to which new technologies must be adapted.[17] First, in labor-intensive industries, where goods are sold on the basis of low cost, the low-cost labor of the newly industrializing countries has permitted firms in those nations to penetrate the markets of the advanced countries. Advanced country producers cannot survive without basic shifts in strategy and production organization. As long as shoes and apparel are made by labor-intensive methods, only cheap wages will permit competitive advantage. Firms must either reorganize production, making labor-intensive production into a game of automation, or alter their mix of products and, at the same time, their marketing and corporate strategies. Those products produced with standard designs and technology will be made at low-cost labor locations. Second, in consumer durables industries such as autos and televisions, competitive advantage rests on the mastery of *complex manufacturing processes,* as well as on distinct product and marketing strategies. Those productive processes are being revolutionized by microelectronics. Plants are being radically reorganized, and the links between steps in the production process are being reshuffled. The ability to produce a wide variety of products, to bring new products to market quickly, and, of course, to produce with low cost at high quality is the object of the production innovations. Finally, in advanced technology sectors such as computers, semiconductors, and sophisticated communications, the ability to competitively implement new engineering and scientific knowledge in products and production is critical. The basic science and much of the generic engineering concepts used in these industries are in the public domain or can be sold for only limited gain. The ability to successfully commercialize these ideas is the basis of enduring market advantage.

The Importance of Production Skills

Common to these three categories of industrial competition is the importance of manufacturing processes, of production skills, to retaining industrial competitiveness.[18] The ability to produce competitively stands out decisively. The impending revolution in manufacturing is as important as the often touted acceleration in the pace of product innovation. Indeed, rapid product innovation depends on the ability to bring product from lab to factory to market. When pressed by producers using cheap labor to achieve low costs, American companies can sometimes transform a labor-intensive production process into one that is capital and technology intensive. This, of course, involves substantial displacement of labor, a reorganization of the labor that remains, and changes in corporate habits. Sharp dislocations of workers and communities have generally produced political trouble that disrupts the adjustment process. Evidence from around the world suggests such dislocations can be avoided in three ways: diffusing the pressures; outright suppression of the losers when they complain, which is altogether improper and quite unpleasant; and negotiating the terms of change so that there are not winners and losers in the process of adjustment.[19] At any rate, competitive position over time, in a broad range of products, such as consumer durables, rests squarely on the ability to master the most advanced manufacturing techniques. Even in the so-called haven of high technology, the long-run competitiveness of firms and the national economy will rest on translating product advantage into enduring market position through manufacturing expertise.

Let us consider this in concrete cases. In the 1980s American semiconductor manufacturers found themselves caught in a competition with Japan. The American firms had virtually created the industry, indeed proprietors of many of the firms had been involved in the basic product innovations, and dominated the markets. The manufacturing skills of Japanese firms allowed them to enter the industry during a phase of product innovation—the move to 16K memory chips. They entered these new markets rapidly, even though there were product areas where they had design weaknesses. The Japanese domestic market provided the leverage to step into world markets. Sales by foreign firms in Japan were limited—in our view, policy and corporate structure contained the market share gains of foreign firms and diminished the profits from product innovation of the American firms. Since profits from each round of innovations were limited, it then became harder for American firms to reinvest in innovation and indeed in manufacturing processes. In order to remain competitive in 1987, American firms, which have a clear design and innovation advantage, have had to dramatically improve their manufacturing skills.[20]

Production weakness undermining product advantage is not a new story. Indeed, the inability to implement new designs contributed to American failure in technically advanced but commonly produced products. Twenty years ago, American color television manufacturers were beaten by Japanese producers for a mix of reasons.[21] Important among those reasons was the Japanese manufacturing costs advantage, partly a product of wage differentials, but primarily the result of real innovation in production processes. Indeed, the Japanese entered the market through a niche. Small black-and-white sets could be built inexpensively using the then radically new transistors instead of tubes. Transistor components also facilitated manufacturing innovation, and the Japanese invested in auto-mated equipment. The American producers focused on the wage differentials between themselves and the Japanese. They believed cheap wages were at the core of Japanese advantage. They did not recognize that funda-mental manufacturing innovation was really at the heart of the Japanese cost position. The American producers were replaced—even in the U.S. market—as the dominant force in consumer electronics.

There were at least two major consequences of the consumer electron-ics story. One was that the American consumer electronic goods companies lost a base from which to innovate in the next generation of products. Manufacturing skills trumped product design. The Japanese became design leaders from a manufacturing base. A second result was that the semicon-ductor industry was denied experience with products that were important in consumer electronics but which contained technologies critical to more sophisticated final products. Manufacturing production mattered directly to the ability to sustain innovation. A strong product position and a strong market position were eroded by a manufacturing weakness.

Whether or not government policies mattered in originally establish-ing market position, in the end the Japanese entrenched themselves through innovation in the production system. We are concerned, conse-quently, when American firms move offshore without reflecting on how to maintain, over the years, a competitive production position. Locating abroad to obtain lower labor costs or to avoid an exchange rate that makes American-produced goods expensive can prove costly over time. The short-term palliative has been tried. We believe it can provide only tempo-rary relief. If the move offshore is a substitute for production innovation, it may represent a long-term disaster, both for the firms and the nation.

Let us look more closely at a second industry story. In the late 1970s the semiconductor division of a major electronics producer tried to figure out why they were always late—relative to their competitors—in the re-lease of integrated circuits that they themselves had designed.[22] The story was told to us this way: "What we discovered was that we were actually doing *better* designs than our competitors, but our manufacturing technol-ogy was *old.*"[23] The company had not invested in manufacturing technol-ogy because it did not have the volume of product to make manufacturing investment pay off. Design advantage was undermined by manufacturing weakness. The story should stop here, but there is another fascinating chapter. The firm decided to invest in manufacturing technology, though they did not then have the volume to show a financial payback that would, in conventional terms, justify the investment. "The gamble paid off. Now we have one of the best integrated circuit (IC) design teams in the world. In fact, the design team got so good that they did enough to eventually make the manufacturing investment pay off."[24] Improved manufacturing permitted a design advantage to *create* the volume needed to support the production investment.

Indeed, manufacturing expertise permitted the Japanese to establish a substantial position in the semiconductor industry in the first place and is now the basis of their advantage in many product lines. Michael Borrus at BRIE has done a number of studies on U.S.-Japanese competition in the semiconductor industry that show clearly how American advantage in design and product innovation, and in making markets for new products, has been and continues to be the basis of the market position of many American firms. The Americans have a relative advantage in the design and market-making end of the business. The Japanese firms have established a relative advantage in manufacturing, both in the organization of production and in the actual equipment, that threatens to become a decisive advantage in the industry.[25] The American producers' strengths in design are evident in products such as microprocessors, logic devices in general, and custom products. The design advantages cannot be defended, however, without competitive production skills and equipment. The Japanese strengths in production are evident in their dominant position in the industry's commodity products such as random access memory (RAM) devices. They have captured the advanced RAM business, controlling 86 percent of the world market in 256K RAMs at the end of 1985.[26] These products serve as "technology drivers," permitting firms to master production of chips with ever-increasing densities—that is, numbers of transistors on a chip. Design advantage matters only if all producers are at equivalent levels of density. The Japanese threaten to pull away.

The Japanese manufacturing advantage in semiconductors was not, in our view, a product of management style and strategy or cultural propensities that led to a more cooperative approach to manufacturing. Rather it was a product of rapid expansion in a closed domestic market. The Japanese caught up with the original American advantage in semiconductors by a combination of: (1) licensing technology from American firms that were denied direct access to the Japanese market, (2) government investment in and organization of development and diffusion of the licensed technology, and (3) low-cost capital for Japanese firms to expand in a market from which the dominant foreign producer was excluded. The government played the role of doorkeeper to the Japanese economy and promoter of domestic development.[27] However, whatever the role of the government or of closed markets, the outcome of the Japanese corporate strategies was real production advantage.

The semiconductor story is a critical case for our argument. This is a high-tech industry par excellence. The industry itself was created by a series of fundamental product innovations—the transistor, the integrated circuit, the microprocessor. Continuous product innovation based on design and software skills is a fundamental feature of competition. Yet, in this quintessential high-tech industry, dependent on its laboratories and innovations, manufacturing proves decisive. A second such high-tech sector is the commercial aircraft business. Firms like Boeing spend billions on research and development. Product characteristics, such as differences in the operating costs of the airplane, are crucial to airline purchase decisions. Nonetheless Boeing's competitiveness, profitability, and even its survival have turned on its production skills, including overhead and inventory control. If software, design, and product innovation are not sufficient to compensate for weakened manufacturing skills in semiconductors and are critical in aircraft, then such production skills will be all the more critical in consumer durable industries and other sectors in which production rests on complex manufacturing processes.

If innovation is not sufficient in high technology, then manufacturing skills are vital in each of the categories of industrial competition—high technology, products depending on complex manufacturing processes, and those where low-cost labor has been the basis of foreign competition. We have told only a few stories about the consumer electronics and semiconductor industries, but we could add many more from our own research and that of others.[28] In the dismal decline of the American steel industry lies the story of a missed revolution in production technology, the basic oxygen furnace. As the Japanese industry matured, it did so with a more modern plant that represented an entire generation of production. The difficulties of the American automobile producers was partly the result of dramatic changes in the kind of car demanded in the market as oil prices rose and fell—that is, small cars became more attractive, and the Japanese made them. However, it slowly became clear that the Japanese had a decisive production cost advantage that rested not on differences in wages, but on distinct abilities to organize production. In labor-intensive industries, such as textiles, apparel, and footwear, portions of production cannot be competitive in the advanced countries without protection. Those firms that are able to compete have done so by adjusting their product mix and marketing strategies to take advantage of more sophisticated production strategies that permit, for example, real product diversity. Throughout this chapter we show instances of how production skills create advantage and how production weaknesses undermine firms.

Only real manufacturing innovation, using America's superior innovative skills to leapfrog competitors in manufacturing, can assure American firms an enduring competitive position in the international marketplace. Once we recognize the importance of manufacturing in establishing competitive position and shaping trade flows even in high-technology or R&D-based industries, we must reinterpret our understanding of trade data. The reinterpretation will indicate that America's position in world markets is much weaker than we might otherwise have thought. A distinction is usually made between R&D-based high-technology sectors, middle-level technology sectors, and low-technology sectors, with Americans often taking comfort because their high-technology exports have grown while exports in other sectors have declined. Seemingly, the data show that all is as it should be; the United States is moving out of the blue-collar past to a high-tech future. But is it? We have already noted that the so-called American comparative advantage in high tech rests not so much on distinctive high-tech abilities as on distinctive weaknesses in other sectors.

The notion of "high-tech comparative advantage" is misleading in another way. The measure of "high techness" is the percentage of a firm's revenue spent on R&D. Thus, the semiconductor and aircraft industries are high R&D spenders, while the VCR and automobile sectors are middle spenders. What these quantitative measures disguise is the *importance* of innovation or R&D to a firm's competitive position. Thus, R&D created the VCR and digital disc as products, while production innovation allows the Japanese to establish and sustain dominant market positions in these goods. In other words, advances in product and production technology underlie competitive position and trade flows in the consumer durable sectors. The relatively low ratio of R&D to sales in something like VCRs does not indicate that R&D is not essential to that industry or that this is not an industry in which competitive advantage is deeply affected by R&D-based innovations. The proper measure, but not one convenient for the data collectors, would be the competitive leverage of R&D.

The importance of innovation in consumer durables involving complex manufacturing is disguised by traditional measures. It is disguised in two ways. First, production innovation may depend on shop-floor reorganization. R&D takes place in equipment industries that sell to the final producers. Those R&D expenditures in equipment firms will not appear in the accounts of the firm that buys the innovative products. Thus, for example, GM is sparking innovation in manufacturing equipment and imposing a new communications standard for production equipment, but the research will be conducted by its suppliers. (True, some suppliers are subsidiaries, such as EDS, but the basic point holds.)[29] Second, in consumer durables, commodity R&D is essential to the creation of the products, but again part of the R&D will be done in supplier firms, such as the semiconductor houses who supply the components. More generally, these volume production sectors turn on the effective diffusion of fundamental technological advance in other sectors; competitive advantage rests on the implementation of transformative technologies. In all these sectors, though, realizing the gains from innovation—that is, selling a product at a profit—depends on a competitive capacity to manufacture and sell the products. Thus, to take the case of the semiconductor industry, we note with trepidation that America retains a technological advantage in design while the Japanese have established an advantage in processing.

Rethinking the Role of Product Innovation and Production in Shaping the Patterns of Trade

The importance of manufacturing skills in industrial competition requires that we advance our understanding of technological development and product innovation in creating competitive advantage. We must reformulate our understanding of the influence of product innovation in trade to incorporate the importance of manufacturing advantage. Product cycle theory has been the way most analysts conceive the role of technology and innovation in the dynamics of trade.[30] According to this theory, trade in manufactured goods typically follows a set pattern: a country that introduces a good will at first become a net exporter of it but will eventually lose its net export position when production of the good becomes standardized and moves to those countries that have the capacity to produce it and the mix of resources that make such production of standard products attractive. (See figure 8.3.) The innovating company may use its initial position in export markets to open manufacturing facilities in countries to which it sells. It may hold market position or foreign rivals may challenge it, but in any case, the location of manufacturing will change. Americans should not, in this view, worry about the move offshore of the production of goods originally produced in the United States or about the emergence of foreign producers. This suggests that industry in an innovative country can make its living by initiating a series of new products and ceding production of established goods. The limits of this theory result in misleading clues to corporate strategy and government policy.

A new twist to this theory is needed. The benefit to the nation of a product innovation depends on the *volume of exports* and the *length of time* that the innovators hold an advantage, if not a monopoly. Let us imagine a national innovation-based export stream. We might therefore imagine each innovation as beginning a stream of production, an arrow. We need be concerned not just with the speed of innovation or the number of innovations—represented in the chart by the number and size of the arrows—but with the total innovation-based export stream. Such an export stream can be described by the length and width of the export arrow generated by an innovation. The longer a producer can hold onto an advantage and the greater the volume during that period, the greater the national innovation-based export stream. Obviously a few big export winners can make up for a great number of short-term successes, though the broad portfolio of successes will give stability to the export stream. Simply, the pace of the product cycle matters.

The speed with which a competitor establishes a strong position in its national market previously dominated by a foreign firm that moved abroad on the basis of product innovation—and thereby limits the gains to product innovation—is crucial. The pace at which the rents of innovation are eaten away clearly depends on two things. First, and obviously, it depends on the speed with which the product itself can be imitated. Second, and crucially, it hinges on the speed with which a competitive manufacturing position can be built. There are some obvious conclusions. If an innovator's manufacturing skills are weaker than those of its competitors, then it will lose part of the potential gain from its innovation. A manufacturing disadvantage can ultimately undermine a product advantage and block continued product innovation.

Factory and Laboratory: Losing Control of What You Can't Make

America cannot maintain its high-wage economy by trying to play the role of laboratory for the world, producing the ideas and prototypes while others make the products. First, if America can't make the products, its technology edge will erode. In the first part of this book, we remarked that after several rounds of product innovation, the innovative initiative will pass to the firms that make the products. They end up understanding the market and the product in a way that permits them to become the technology leaders. The United States's sad experience in steel and consumer electronics ought to convince us of this. Even if American firms could keep up technically without manufacturing, there is another problem, equally serious. The rents from innovation—that is, the exceptional gains on which high profits and high value-added are based—are realized in producing the goods, not in selling the technology.

To explain the problem, let us ask a simple question: How do you value a technology if you want to buy or sell it?[31] If you want to buy a car to drive to work or a modem to hook your home computer up to your office network, you probably have an idea of what the product can do and what the value is to you of various gizmos on the car or extra features for the modem. But neither the function nor the value is obvious when new high-technology products are first being sold. The value of raw technological knowledge is even less clear. Fixing a price can then be extremely difficult. The seller will value the hopes for the new product or knowledge, while the buyer will emphasize the uncertainties and risks. What kind of bargain will they reach?

There are three types of uncertainty, or risk to the buyer, that reduce the sale value of the technology, that reduce the gains made by the laboratory not the manufacturer. First, even if a developer of a technology may have a fully working product and production process, the buyer may still not be able to assess its value in the marketplace. Of course, the buyer will intentionally emphasize the risk and uncertainty. Indeed, a standard problem is that if the developer and the marketer are in different organizations, market need and technology will not be meshed. The buyer will not be committed to a product or component that was developed elsewhere or will suspect or resist what was not invented internally within its own organization. Most importantly, in any radically new product, as was the case with the microprocessor, the final users may have trouble understanding the use of the product and its value. Intel Corporation had enormous difficulty explaining the use and value of the new product to highly sophisticated engineers who are its customers. Intel had to *create* a market for its new product.[32] Indeed, the great talent of many American innovators is not just making a product that works, but making a market for it. A manufacturer buying a technology from a prototype laboratory cannot assess the market gain—and in fact faces real market risks. If the manufacturer buys or produces a series of technologies and creates a portfolio of product technology investments, the risk of a market flop for any innovation can be absorbed. That portfolio of technology investments may translate into real gain, as it in a sense has for venture capital investors putting money into new companies. The risk of market flop for any product means that the seller technologist[33] is in a weakened bargaining position on each deal and will find it harder to capture the full gains of any substantial market success. Second, if the technologist has only a prototype, there is a substantial risk that the product cannot be manufactured at a price at which it can be sold. This, similarly, reduces the price for the technologist seller. Third, if the technology for sale is not a prototype, but a stream of research—say work on advanced semiconductor materials such as galium arsenide—the risk for the buyer that a marketable product will emerge is even greater. Consequently, the value of the technology is reduced again.

There is a fourth, and even more serious, problem for the technologist. It lies in the problem of selling knowledge not a product or service. If the technologist is unwilling to explain the fundamental base of the technology, the buyer has even greater trouble agreeing to a price. An effect may be generated in the laboratory, but unless the buyer knows why and how it occurs, it is hard to decide how valuable that effect is. However, if the technologist does reveal the core of the technology, then the essential knowledge is already gone, and the technologist is left with nothing to sell. We recall the problem of a Berkeley faculty member who had devised a sophisticated financial hedging operation that permitted certain financial risks to be insured. The model could be demonstrated to work. It could provide a valuable financial service. A deal, backed by a major venture capital company, was worked out with a major insurance company to provide an exchange rate insurance based on the operation of the model. The deal fell through. The staff of the insurance company wanted the model equations and experience using the model. They felt that if anything happened to the developer, they would have been exposed to enormous risk. The Berkeley professor, the model's developer, was unwilling to part with the equations on the grounds that, having given them away and explained their use, he would no longer have anything of value to sell. Moreover, he argued, and this is a fifth difficulty, those to whom he explained the model would then have the technical foundation to become his competitors. There was no contractual arrangement to avoid these difficulties. Eventually the project went forward as part of a complicated partnership that produced substantially less gain to the financial technologist than the original form of actual production arrangement that was originally attempted. Indeed, part of the reason for multinational corporations is to permit a solution to the transfer of technology by doing it within a single organization.[34]

A firm or a nation's industry cannot survive at a substantial production disadvantage to its major competitors. It has often been said that a company must maintain its hold on its final market, even if that means pumping through those channels products produced or designed by others. Perhaps so. But this can be only a temporary solution, for in this era of fundamental production innovation, other firms that can build manufacturing advantage will develop alternative distribution channels. The decisive corporate asset required to realize technology is likely to be production skills. Let us summarize our position as a simple proposition. *Lose control of the manufacturing or production process of your product and you risk losing control of both the technology and the final markets.*

9

Manufacturing Flexibility: The Slogan of the Transition

FLEXIBILITY has become the slogan of the current transition, and with good reason. For the last decade or more the economy has twisted and turned while it rolled over some very steep hills. The *level of demand* has risen and fallen quite steeply, with the two oil shocks provoking downturns and the effort to control inflation in the early eighties provoking a deep recession, a near depression.[1] Moreover, the *composition of demand* changed over these years. Goods that took lots of energy to make or use—such as aluminum, steel, and autos—rose sharply in price with the oil hikes. Producers and consumers alike made serious efforts to conserve energy. The change was real. Each increment in output took less additional energy than before. However, oil prices first jumped around 1973, then declined in real terms only to rise sharply again.[2] The mix of products demanded fluctuated as well. Consumers wanted small cars that used less gas, then, as the cost of driving dropped, began to shift back to large cars, only to go through the whole cycle again.[3] Between 1973 and 1985, large cars got smaller and small cars became more luxurious and went up in price. Hit simultaneously by radical shifts in the products demanded and by the arrival of Japanese in force in the market, Detroit got whiplash. Throughout the economy, companies had to adapt, and those which were more flexible had an advantage.

The distinction between *static* and *dynamic* flexibility is critical to us, not the differences in techniques used to achieve flexibility.[4] *Static flexibility* means the ability of a firm to adjust its operations at any moment to shifting conditions in the market—to the rise and fall of demand or the changes in the mix of products the market is asking for. It implies adjustment within a fixed product and production structure. Flexibility has come to mean a whole variety of ways of adjusting company operations to the shifting conditions of the market. The term is used to refer to the ability of a firm to vary efficiently its strategic direction, level of production, composition of goods, length of the work day or week, level of wages, organization of work, or any of a variety of other elements of operations.

The techniques to achieve static flexibility can thus be technological, political, or organizational. Firms may employ new programmable machine tools to increase the efficiency of batch production, reach an agreement with unions to reduce the number of job categories, or develop a network of subcontractors. The reduction in the number of job categories in the New United Motors (the GM-Toyota venture in Fremont, California) permits easier changes on the shop floor.[5] American Airlines announces it is reducing the number of full-time employees in many airports, shifting to part-time personnel in order to increase its operational flexibility. A worker buy-out of a steel plant in Weirton, West Virginia, permits a wage reduction, the workers accepting "wage flexibility" because they have a stake in the company profits.[6] In static terms—that is, at any given moment —increased flexibility means greater capacity to adjust to short-term market changes. Continental Airlines used Chapter 11 bankruptcy proceedings to break union contracts and lower wages. Static flexibility, consequently, decreases the risk that the firm won't be able to adapt to changes in the number and types of goods demanded in the market; it increases the ability to adapt quickly to changed conditions.

Dynamic flexibility, by contrast, means the ability to increase productivity steadily through improvements in production processes and innovation in product. Burton Klein presents the notion well. He argues that Japanese firms, and auto firms originally,

. . . evolved a practice that can be described as dynamic flexibility. . . . contrasted with static flexibility, dynamic flexibility is not concerned with producing more than one product (e.g. cars and light trucks) on a single production line—although the Japanese do this too. Rather it is concerned with designing production lines in a way that they can quickly evolve in response to changes in either the product or production technology. In other words, the central pre-occupation is to get ideas into action quickly. . . . [In practice in Japan] the main purpose of dynamic flexibility is to make rapid changes in production technology for the purpose of lowering costs and thereby improving productivity.[7]

We agree with Klein that "continuing productivity gains presuppose advances in relevant technologies and a keen desire to make good use of this progress."[8] All studies of postwar economic growth in the advanced countries highlight that technological advance, not the simple increase in the number of machines or the amount of capital or labor employed, is at the core of sustained increases in productivity and economic development.[9] Indeed many economists argue that, where R&D expenditures have dropped, productivity increases have fallen years after the drops in R&D expenditures.[10] Increased productivity permits lowered costs or, depending on the response of competitors, higher wages and profits.

Dynamic flexibility is the corporate capacity to develop and introduce these technological advances. A commitment to such flexibility in Japan is reflected in the structure of the market for computer-controlled manufacturing equipment. In Japan many firms develop internally their own production equipment. "Almost every Japanese auto company has a large machine tool operation in which 200 to 400 people do nothing but create new tools, which are quickly introduced into the production process."[11] When successful, these machines are often then sold on the market. In Japan, as a consequence, the machine tool market is highly fragmented, shared among many producers who are developing equipment for their own internal purposes and then selling it on the open market. In the United States, where less production equipment development occurs internally, the market for programmable machine tools is highly concentrated—that is, it is shared among a few big producers. The result is that American firms tend to introduce production innovations periodically, moving from one plateau of best practice to another. The Japanese, studies suggest, move through continuous and iterative production innovation, steadily improving the production process.[12] In fact, the Japanese system, with its greater dynamic flexibility, has achieved greater productivity gains over the last years than the more rigid American one.

Technological advance inherently involves risk; new ideas may not work in practice or may not work as well as hoped. Consequently, dynamic flexibility involves a management of levels of risk sufficient to match what competitors are doing. Levels of risk, Klein argues, vary from industry to industry.[13] A norm emerges within a given sector. Partly, this is a product of the possibilities inherent in the technologies of the moment. If the potential returns are very high and the risk relatively low, one or another firm in a sector may take the risk of product development. Partly, the risk norm—the propensity to engage in risk—depends on the intensity of competition in the industry. In the United States, in our view, firms in many oligopolistic sectors had established a low norm of technological risk that was part of a competitive truce or at least a corporate Geneva convention about the terms of civilized combat that reduced the need to take risks. American firms in a variety of sectors suddenly confronted foreign competitors who assumed higher norms of risk—partly a reflection of the pace of national development in the home market. American firms were caught off balance, and the results are evident.

Static and dynamic flexibility are inextricably linked. Static flexibility to short-term shifts in market conditions can be achieved in a variety of ways; how it is achieved will affect the long-term capacity of the firm to introduce the evolving technology on which its product and production position depend. A decision to move production offshore may be taken because it will allow lower wages and/or because it will make it easier to shut plants during downturns. The move offshore, it seems to us, makes it harder to steadily improve the production process itself. Similarly, decisions to reduce skill levels in domestic plants to reduce resistance by skilled workers to technological development may eliminate the very skilled workers required to effectively implement new production technologies. Indeed, increased skill levels may permit flexible strategies, with both static and dynamic economies. Extensive investment in hard automation technologies may simply be a slow and expensive alternative to shop-floor skills. In a similar vein, firms may have to choose between short-term economies of scale, which may involve large fixed costs in the form of investment in equipment, and the long-term necessity of responding to evolving technologies, which may involve smaller and less efficient plants. Japanese and American firms have made different choices. "Japanese plants for producing cars are only about one-third as large as comparable American plants," ostensibly to permit greater dynamic flexibility.[14] The technological strategy is not simply a matter of efficiency narrowly defined; it is, rather, a product of the political environment in which firms operate. Our suspicion is that strategies to reduce costs through cheap labor or to gain greater control of the shop floor by displacing skills ultimately result in rigidity in an era that requires flexibility.

A period of economic transition is a time when "dynamic flexibility" is of predominant importance. Our contention is that the crucial change now taking place is the transformation of manufacturing and service, not the replacement of industry by service. The transformation of manufacturing does not simply mean that a few "sunrise" manufacturing sectors, such as personal computers, are assuming the importance once held by certain traditional manufacturing sectors, such as automobiles. Rather, as we shall see in a moment, computers and microprocessors have begun to alter the production process throughout industry. The transformation is occurring because the new high-technology sectors are agents of change, sources of innovation, within the traditional sectors. Much of "high technology" really consists of producer goods—goods used to make other products. As individual consumers we do not buy a bag of silicon chips; we buy the products that incorporate semiconductors, and some of these products that incorporate semiconductors have been made by machines that also incorporate those omnipresent chips. We do not buy high-speed computers or mainframe computers; we buy products that are developed or processed on those machines. Supercomputers are purchased for aircraft design and automobile design. The insurance industry long ago became a dominant buyer of mainframe computers and even minicomputers.[15] *The proper object of American concern should be how the new technologies will spread throughout the economy as part of a national response to changing competition. The United States must have a national economy that can absorb and apply the new technologies.*

As we consider the problem of assuring continuous production and product innovation—dynamic flexibility—in American firms, two sets of choices strike us as critical: *First,* Will American firms innovate and automate at home, building a capacity for continuous development, or will they emigrate abroad in order to produce with cheaper labor? To find short-term advantage with cheap labor will, in our view, undermine the capacity of firms to develop and apply the possibilities of the new production technologies at a competitive pace over the years.[16] *Second,* Will the new technologies be used to assure management control of an essentially unskilled and ill-paid work force resulting inevitably in a reinforcement of a pattern of successive plateaus of production development decided and developed centrally and imposed on the shop floor or will the technologies be used in collaboration with a skilled and well-paid work force to assure continuous innovation. In our view, eliminating skilled labor from the shop floor to allow management to gain control may leave management in control of firms that lack the flexibility to sustain competitive production development, firms whose rigidity will soon lead them to a corporate rigor mortis. In our view, neither markets nor technology dictate the decision. The path of technological development will be molded by political choice. What kind of community do we want to live in? What kind of world will we build?

To begin to answer those questions, we must consider the last great industrial transition, the one that brought America to the fore. The structures and habits that Americans built up in that era have now become the country's legacy, or handicap, in responding to this new transition.

America's Rise to Dominance and the Last Great Transition

America's emergence as an internationally dominant industrial power in the twentieth century hinged on the particular character of its industrialization in the nineteenth century.[17] Initially, in the nineteenth century, a new technology—the railroads—integrated the resources of a continent into a national economy. Indeed, railroads opened the flow of grain from the American hinterland—places like Ohio—to world markets. Recall that the South in the Civil War had assumed that its supply of cotton would prove so critical that England would support its secession. Of course, the South's objectives were frustrated. Because grain had become equally critical to Britain, Britain's interest in the conflict was balanced between the North and the South. As the flow of grain from the United States grew, Europe was rocked. In the 1880s, less than twenty years after the American Civil War, the flood of cheap grain provoked profound political shocks across Europe among European peasants, who could not compete with the American farmers.[18]

America's power and its industrial position have rested, for more than half a century, on two fundamental innovations that emerged in the course of U.S. industrialization: mass production and the giant corporation. The continental economy established in the nineteenth century was based heavily on small family farmers and a high-wage working class, which together created a far-flung homogeneous market—a large number of buyers were spread out across a broad geographic area. Mass production, which meant manufacture in large volume at low prices using interchangeable parts, replaced the artisanal fabrication of individual items. The mass production system was innovated, as the story goes, in gun manufacture and was given its form and identity by Henry Ford with the making of his Model T. Thus, the large homogeneous market of an emerging middle class with common tastes induced mass production in the United States. A virtuous cycle, as they say, was set in place. Heavy investment allowed volume production, which meant lower prices. Lower prices increased demand, which required increased investment and created more jobs. Increased investment and productivity meant more jobs and higher wages. A high-wage work force could afford all those new low-priced products. At the same time, the early development and elaboration in this country of mass production gave American producers a substantial competitive edge in the wide range of industries where a demand existed for standard but low-cost products and in which that demand could be met by these production techniques.

The second innovation on which American economic power rested was the giant hierarchical corporation. Americans now take for granted the market power of giant firms such as IBM, with its worldwide sales of $45.9 billion. In 1985, two computer firms, Burroughs and DEC, with sales of $4.9 billion and $5.6 billion, together employ 150,600 workers, but are referred to as the dwarfs of the industry.[19] The fifty largest corporations, representing 24 percent of production, dominate the American manufacturing sector.[20] Commonplace now, these economic bureaucracies were, when they were created at the turn of the century, radically new forms of economic organization.

These giant corporations emerged in two steps, as Alfred Chandler has so brilliantly shown.[21] The first step came in the late nineteenth century, much at the same time as mass production. Until then the image of a firm as an entrepreneurial small-scale entity was a reasonable representation of the economy. Bureaucracies belonged to government, not to the marketplace. Hierarchy within companies as a means of controlling their activity emerged to solve specific and now seemingly straightforward marketplace problems. One such problem was the need for the scheduling of railroads in order to avoid accidents. One couldn't just send trains down the track. With one track and two directions, scheduling to avoid collisions was essential. An organization was needed to manage the process. Another such problem was the need to provide continuing service after the sale of agricultural machinery. Without such after-sales service, the value of the machinery would be much less. As soon as the farmer could not repair the machine himself, the machine would simply lie in disrepair. Indeed, one enduring feature of underdevelopment is the absence of indigenous capacity to repair a wide variety of machines. One might imagine a set of small service firms springing up, creating a market for servicing of equipment. However, such service companies had to follow, not precede, the emergence of mechanized agriculture. The machines had to penetrate the farms before an industry servicing them could emerge. Moreover, in the geographically dispersed American market, such service business was slow to emerge. Consequently, to promote sales, such a manufacturing company had to provide the service through its own organization. Such organization required hierarchy to function effectively.

The next step in the emergence of the giant corporation came in the early twentieth century. Simply, the early large corporations were hierarchical organizations divided roughly into functional divisions such as sales, production, and service.[22] Steel production, mass production of cars, and rail traffic could be organized this way. A single hierarchy could manage one or a few related products. However, a set of quite different products would create serious strains in the organization. The skills needed to make paints might not be the skills needed to produce industrial chemicals, or market them for that matter. Moreover, effective coordination of, say, sales and production became difficult when there was a single sales organization. Product variety could not be effectively managed in this centralized functional structure. Losses forced companies like duPont to find a new structure that would reflect the new product and market strategies they had adopted, that would allow them to manage what were, in essence, a multitude of businesses within a single structure. The divisionalized corporation, which is so familiar to us, was the result. It is, simplified, a series of hierarchically arranged businesses with synergism tied together and directed from a corporate headquarters. (When the businesses are unrelated or distantly related and are held together only by financial ties the firm is generally called a "conglomerate" or "holding company.")

The advantage created by these two innovations—mass production and the hierarchical and then divisionalized corporation—was consolidated in the first decades of this century. A dominant pattern of work organization and competition in major industries emerged. A stable model of production was developed. Named after one of the early successful practitioners, it has been labeled as the "Fordist" model of production—standard products made on highly rigid assembly lines from components produced in enormous volumes. The objective was to gain maximum economies of scale. There was no effort to capture either static or dynamic flexibilities. Work was organized along what came to be called "Taylorist" principles, after Frederick Taylor, who formalized the ideas. Work should be divided into tiny manageable tasks, workers turned into the counterparts of machines and merged into the machines and assembly lines that characterized mass production. Required skill could be reduced to permit interchangeable workers along with interchangeable parts.[23]

As competition stabilized, a pattern of oligopolistic competition in national markets emerged. Oligopolistic competition meant that a limited number of very large firms dominated the market and could adjust their behavior to each other. The result was that the need for innovation and pressure for risky choice was reduced. Because American firms had real production advantages and were operating in a market insulated by distance from foreign firms, these domestic oligopolies in industries such as steel and autos did not have to concern themselves with foreign competitors. Automobile firms ceased to compete on the basis of either price or product innovation, but rather competed with marketing and styling.[24] Elimination of price pressure eliminated the need for radical product and process innovation. Consequently, the automobile companies paid premiums for worker quiescence in the form of very high wages. The firms then passed on the additional labor costs to the consumers in the form of higher prices. This limited the need for flexibility either among their work force and management or in the structure of their organization.[25] Managers bought control of the workplace and agreed to a set of union rules that allowed management to have authority over a rule-bound work organization.

In the 1950s world of rising and managed consumer demand, the need for flexibility was thus limited. Moreover, technology had matured and American producers were insulated from foreign pressures to develop and implement new *production* technologies. Some would argue that the triumph of Keynsian policy reflected the political dominance of the large "Fordist" producers. In an era of steady growth a strategy of investment in automated equipment for volume production could thrive, so that such investments were more attractive when the business cycle was smoothed out.[26] During the Great Depression, firms, such as the French auto producer Peugeot, that had invested heavily in capital-intensive but inflexible production equipment were severely damaged. Indeed, sharp downturns and radical fluctuations in demand have often pushed for less capital-intensive, less "modern," less automated equipment.[27] There is, we should add, evidence tying this logical sequence to the political position of social groups and parties, but it is not decisive.

The Fordist model—what Andrew Sayer calls the "Just in Case" system—which is said to be typical of American manufacture, has been characterized and caricatured by many.[28] Yet there is substantial agreement on several of its characteristics. Sayer provides the basis for this summary. (1) It is geared to uniform and standard products, and is inflexible and unresponsive to changes in the market. (2) When used for the manufacture of complex products like cars or TVs, it creates difficulty in balancing the flow of various parts and subassemblies into the main assembly process without causing gluts and shortages. Introducing greater product diversity only aggravates the problems. (3) Rejected parts and other problems are concealed in buffer stocks. Buffer stocks also disguise the interdependencies in production and hide from workers the way their actions affect the system as a whole. (4) Buffer stocks, which reduce the incentive to resolve the source of problems, are expensive to carry. This has contributed to higher overhead costs that have begun to seriously penalize American firms. (5) Because problems are not caught as they emerge but are, by choice, buried in buffer stocks, extensive "testing" is required to assure quality. That testing is only partly successful, resulting in a high rate of rejections. The testing is also expensive. (6) Fragmenting work into detailed single tasks underuses the ability of workers. Many believe that this reduces their motivation and increases boredom and fatigue, absenteeism, and resistance. (7) The rigidity of the system, which disguises problems and is combined with a commitment to sustaining production volumes, inhibits both process and product development. (8) Finally, there is evidence that pushing specialization and fragmentation increases the need for formal central control to assure coordination. Once the possibility of adjustment on the shop floor by workers who understand how the system is interconnected is eliminated, this need for central control is almost certain to result. In sum, a rigid system of large volume production was established. The buffer stocks it used to balance flow hid quality problems and resulted in higher overhead. This production strategy, which destroyed skills and initiative, eroded the capacity to adjust. These weaknesses in the standard American system were hidden until foreign competition displayed them with stark clarity.

Although problems with Fordist "mass production" were discovered later, by the mid-twentieth century a real manufacturing advantage based on mass production and a divisionalized structure was the foundation on which American firms became global companies. The multinational corporations that manufactured around the world had real product and production advantages as well as the organizational strength to use those advantages in a range of markets. In the years after World War II, the American industrial advantage became a European political issue. In England and France during the 1960s, government policies to encourage firms to imitate the American structure were adopted. Now twenty years later in the United States, the debate about Japan is a response to the emergence of a substantial newcomer during an equally important, if not more significant, economic transition. The United States should never forget that American advantage, like that of the Japanese today, rested on innovations in manufacturing and corporate control, and that Americans also were borrowers of technology.

Are Advantages of Flexibility Implicit in the Course of Industrial Development Abroad?

American industries whose innovations in production and organization had created the advantage eventually became rigid and vulnerable to innovation elsewhere. The course of development elsewhere, in Japan and Italy in particular, left those countries with a legacy that may provide their firms with advantages in the market competition during this transition.

Let us take the case of Japan. The question is how did Japan create a distinctive manufacturing advantage, an advantage that, in our view, rests in part on organizations set up to capture dynamic flexibility. Much has been made in the serious and popular literature of the fluidity and flexibility of management and labor arrangements within Japanese companies. It is less often recognized that such arrangements were responses to real political and economic conditions, not some inherent cultural bent. The Japanese pattern of giant companies offering lifetime employment has unquestionably allowed closer ties between management and the shop floor and great adaptability on the shop floor. Lifetime employment and company unions were not some element of the traditional world carried over to the present, but a twentieth-century creation and, in part, a corporate and political response to the emergence of radical trade union movements in the 1950s. Moreover, it operates as a type of worker insurance policy in which worker investment in the form of wage restraint is repaid through this form of private unemployment insurance. Similarly, the Japanese companies' pursuit of market share is often presented as a long-term alternative to the short-term pursuit of profit. In Japan during the 1950s and 1960s, the long-term goal of market share and the short-term pursuit of profit became the same, and the organizations developed to pursue these objectives facilitated dynamic adjustment.

The Japanese economy must be understood and explained as a function of three interconnected elements: (1) government policy structured market dynamics, (2) market dynamics drove corporate strategy, and (3) corporate strategy—particularly production strategy—drove the organization of the shop floor. The first step concerns the creation of the market dynamics that are distinctive to Japan, and in part III we will comment on the pattern of policy that structured the way market dynamics worked. Here we want to examine the next two steps briefly: how market dynamics shaped corporate strategy and how corporate strategy affected the shop floor in a way that generated enduring production innovation.

Intense domestic competition in a protected and rapidly growing internal market among firms that had access to international product and production technologies had predictable results. As long as the Japanese were aggressive and systematic technology borrowers in a rapidly expanding domestic market, they faced a fundamentally different economic situation than that of foreign companies. The differences in their situations produced the Japanese emphasis on market share and production innovation so often remarked on. With apologies to the general reader more interested in conclusions than how they are reached, we set forth here the outlines of a formal argument; such readers may skip the next page and rejoin us after figure 9.1. This issue is too decisive to our overall position to be hurried. Murakami and Yamamura have developed an intriguing analysis of the consequences, more precisely the advantages, of Japanese efforts to overcome technological backwardness.[29] Put formally, Japanese firms faced long-run declining cost curves, rather than concave cost curves. Or to use Burton Klein's analysis, the Japanese have a style of continuous production innovation that compels firms to maximize dynamic flexibility.[30] Assuming a concave cost curve, a firm will eventually face rising production costs as volume rises. This is a central principle of microeconomic analysis. To avoid rising costs it must innovate and jump to another production cost curve. That new production curve represents a new technology. (See figure 9.1.) A firm may make that jump if it can anticipate that an increase in demand will justify the investment, if rivals are making or likely to make that jump imposing competitive pressure to do so, and if the cost of innovation is low and success predictability high.

Figure 9.1 suggests the difference between a firm with fixed production technology and one in which the production technology is constantly being revised. In the first case, the firm has a concave production curve which may change from time to time. However for extended periods the production technology and consequently the cost curve are fixed. In the second case the technology is constantly evolving. At any moment there is a concave cost curve, but the real choices facing the firm, and the options on which the firm acts, are expressed by the long-term curve connecting several static curves. This dynamic curve is downward sloping, fundamentally altering the logic of the market dynamic.

Operating in a mature market with relatively advanced technologies, the difficulties and risk of that jump to the next curve are high. Markets will not expand rapidly, so a new production technology must replace the old. New production technologies often have bugs, which make their introduction unpredictable. The firm must maximize profits in the short term. In contrast with American companies, Japanese firms faced rapidly expanding demand and a stream of replacement production technologies

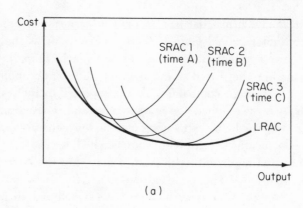

(a)

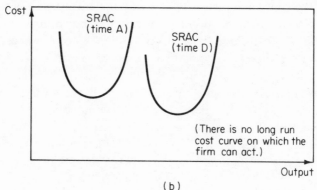

(b)

FIGURE 9.1

Production Innovation and the Evolution of Costs
(a) Continuous Production Innovation and Corporate Choice
(b) Discontinuous Production Innovation

available abroad. Therefore the jump to new technology was easier. One consequence was that profit-maximizing firms attempted to maximize market share in order to have the volumes required to introduce new technologies. (New technologies require that they both capture economies of scale and learning curve economies.)

Similarly, when firms are operating on the decreasing long-run average cost curve (i.e., decreasing long-run AC, thus also decreasing long-run MAC), we can also show that the aggregate industry supply consists of long-run MAC curves of individual firms pursuing the MSM strategy. However, a crucial fact to be noted is that an equilibrium reached can be an unstable one.

Furthermore, it is not difficult to see that this is the case, *both the firms following MSM strategy and those pursuing profit maximization strategy will behave in the same manner.* This is so simply because, when average cost is falling and the market price of output is given, an individual firm can increase its profit by increasing output. A result is that all firms are anxious to supply output that is greater than the quantity they are now producing, provided that an increase in output can be obtained anywhere above the AC curve. This is to say, when AC curves are "added" up, we obtain the amount that all the firms in the industry wish to produce collectively. This simply means that *when faced with decreasing long-run average cost, both the profit-maximizer and the MSM firms behave in virtually identical fashion and there is no need to distinguish the difference in their respective motivations. In both cases, the equilibrium reached will be unstable,* as expected of any decreasing cost industries. The point we wish to emphasize here is that profit-maximizing firm behavior is indistinguishable from MSM behavior. *Italics in original.* [31]

We can predict much of the behavior of Japanese firms with this analysis. We need make only one assumption—easily supported—that Japanese markets were closed to foreigners. There is no need to resort to arguments about the art of Japanese management or the character of the Japanese work force.

Those Japanese firms that could organize themselves flexibly to capture the gains of introducing successive waves of borrowed technology would be the winners. The style developed during the years of borrowing continued as a pattern of success as the Japanese began independent production innovation.[32] The history of Honda Motors, for example, shows this story clearly. Honda borrowed and invented technology after technology as it moved from a marginal position in the motorcycle industry to an established player.[33]

This logic of Japanese growth—the distinct market dynamics—we remind the reader, rests on a distinct pattern of policy. Protected domestic markets, policies to promote an expansion of demand, policies that provide finance to facilitate that expansion all sustain the competition for market share. Indeed, the policy arrangements in the rapid growth years and the altered version of a developmental strategy that drive this logic of investment and growth go a long way to explaining Japan's pattern of trade and the character of its trade problems with the United States. Critically, the market dynamics produced distinct corporate strategies. From those corporate strategies emphasizing market share and production innovation emerged new approaches to manufacturing.

Something very real did happen on the shop floor. Sayer summarizes it well:

> . . . the Just in Time (JIT) system is a learning system which generates economies by making fabrication and assembly more closely approximate a continuous flow line, by reducing the amounts of machinery, materials or labor power which are at any time inactive or not contributing to the production of saleable output. . . . Economies do not follow simply from major technolog-

ical developments, though that is likely to occur too, but from a different way of organizing the labour process coupled with piecemeal changes to the machinery.[34]

The revolution on the Japanese shop floor is at the heart of the continued rapid increases in industrial productivity.

This system did not emerge from the mists of Japanese history nor was it adopted full blown. It was a logical extension of corporate responses to the market dynamics of Japanese economic growth and the emergence of internationally competitive firms. As with the American system which became known as Fordist, the Japanese production revolution is thought to have begun in the automobile sector with Toyota. The *first phase* in the postwar development of Japan was based on light labor-intensive industry. Low-cost labor gave Japanese firms advantage in world markets in sectors such as textiles. In a *second phase,* heavy investment in equipment allowed Japan to enter capital-intensive industries such as steel and ship building. New world-scale facilities based on advanced technologies created economies of scale. Labor productivity jumped, giving the Japanese higher output per man hour and increasing cost advantage over their American competitors in these sectors. Indeed, the disadvantage of a lack of raw materials and a destroyed steel industry was turned into a substantial advantage. The differential in the cost of steel alone is estimated by some to give Japanese producers of products such as forklift trucks and construction equipment a 5 to 8 percent cost advantage.

The *third phase,* in the late 1960s and 1970s, was a strategy of focused manufacturing. Although Japanese groups are known for their size and financial muscle and despite the world-scale facilities in some capital-intensive industries, many Japanese firms in these years were smaller than their foreign competitors. When attempting to compete with much larger European and American companies, the Japanese found they could not efficiently produce as wide a range of products. This disadvantage was turned into a virtue. The Japanese focused "all their available resources on those portions of the product line where market demand was the greatest and access to the customers was the easiest."[35] The focus created substantial cost advantages. It also is thought to have begun the process of shop floor reorganization that culminated in the full just-in-time system. A wide variety of products adds enormous complexity to the production process. That complexity generates substantial overhead costs needed to manage the physical flow of materials and to maintain control of the process. Having first reduced cost by limiting complexity, the Japanese then learned to *manage* the complexity more effectively, with the result that they could increase product variety and the rate of product introduction while continuing to reduce overhead and increase labor productivity.

Product variety means complexity in production. That complexity in production adds costs in two important ways: the time it takes to shift from one task to another is one cost, while handling and storing the multitude of parts required to make a diversity of products is a second.

Innovative Japanese producers were determined to reduce changeover times. They did so by designing machines and locating them to accomplish this:

> In the 1950s the production engineers at Toyota concentrated on significantly reducing changeover times and run lengths in Toyota's factories. Toyota set one minute as a goal for the changeover of a machine from one part to any other part the machine was intended to produce. For machining operations, changeover times were reduced by investing in extra tooling and related equipment rather than in inventories. Extra machine components were purchased so that tools could be left set up to make specific parts. Jigs were fabricated so that the tools could be placed in or removed from machines quickly. The extra tools and jigs were moved . . . to locations beside the machines. . . .[36]

The success has been staggering. James Abegglen and George Stalk report drops in turnaround times from eight hours to one minute in some cases. (See table 9.1.)

TABLE 9.1

Representative Reductions in Changeover Times

	Machine	Initial Setup Time (Hours)	New Setup Time (Minutes)	Implementation Time (Years)*
Toyota	Bolt maker	8	1	1
Mazda	Ring gear cutter	6.5	15	4
	Die casting machine	1.5	4	2
MHI	8-arbor boring machine	24	3	1
Yanmar	Aluminum die caster	2.1	8	2
	Cylinder block line	9.3	9	4
	Connecting rod line	2	9	4
	Crank shaft line	2	5	4

*The time required in some cases is overstated. Yanmar achieved reduction in setup times of 75 to 90 percent in less than two years for many of its processes.
SOURCE: James C. Abegglen and George Stalk, Jr., *Kaisha: The Japanese Corporation* (New York: Basic Books, 1985), p. 97. Based on Shigeo Shingo, *Study of Toyota's Production System from Industrial Engineering Viewpoint* (Tokyo: Japan Management Association, 1981), p. 64.

Machines were arranged so that workers could move between them. Because many machines or a variety of tools for a specific machine would be employed at any workstation, the machine tools were made lighter and less expensive. Consciously, scale economies were sacrificed for the economies of flexibility. As we well know, the Japanese did not raise costs to gain flexibility, they simply went about lowering costs in a different way than American producers. We underline here that these shop-floor reorganizations left Japanese companies and production lines well arranged to absorb the new computer-based production technologies that we discuss in the next chapter.

A reduction in turnaround time is the first step in an interconnected set of steps, each producing pressure to adopt the others. It permits the most efficient production runs to be reduced in length—that is, it becomes efficient to produce any given component in smaller quantities because the machines can immediately be put to use making something else. However, reducing production runs puts pressure on materials handling. The right materials must arrive at the right spot exactly at the right moment. Otherwise, the advantages of small batch production—manufacturing in small quantities—are lost because the machines sit idle. Production lines that permitted a simpler flow of parts from one step to the next without need for intermediate storage were created. "Departments based on manufacturing technologies were dismantled and their machines were moved to newly created product departments."[37] If limited production with quick turnarounds is applied throughout the manufacturing system, then machines at one step produce the pieces required for the next step in the line. Assembly and fabrication were tied together. This permitted the entire production process—the mechanisms by which flows through the factory are regulated and in which production schedules are set—to be controlled differently than in Western factories. The elaborate kanban, or just-in-time, system—thought to have begun with Toyota—was the result.

The advantages of the full-blown system are substantial and run from the ability to produce a greater variety of products to the ability to introduce new products more quickly without cost disadvantages. Having begun reform of the production system to gain cost advantage by focusing on product strategies that limited variety, many Japanese firms ended up able to create even greater variety at ever lower costs. It was in fact a production revolution.

We need to emphasize three things about the Japanese experience. First, the system is based on concrete choices about how to organize production. The structure of the labor market and labor-management relations are crucial elements in shop-floor decisions. The distinctive features rest more on the particular postwar politics of Japan than on Japanese culture.[38] Indeed, woven into the pattern of increased worker responsibility is diminished protection for many workers and what some consider an outright increase in the pace of work.[39]

Second, the system has not resulted in a pattern of extended flexibility in all directions. For example, there is evidence that the number of basic product types in the Japanese industry—measured in terms of such things as chassis and motor sizes—is greater than in the United States.[40] This makes sense, since there are more firms. There is also evidence that the Japanese have more flexible production lines; for example, several types of cars or cars and light trucks often can be produced on the same line.[41] This may result from a need to compensate for the economies of scale lost through market fragmentation. However, Japanese producers are—by other evidence—able to tolerate fewer changes in design than American producers, and as anyone who has bought a Japanese car knows, they come in tightly defined packages of options, which clearly reduces the number of model types on the assembly line.[42] Others suggest that the elaborate network of suppliers and the stratified work force tightly tuned to just-in-time delivery is less able to absorb radical fluctuations in demand than the American system.[43] That inability is, in their view, translated into a downpouring of exports and radical price-cutting. While substantial production innovation has occurred in Japan, it does America as little good to glorify it as to deny it.

Third, much of the production innovation has rested on the reorganization of skilled workers, *not* on heavy capital investment or on technological innovation. Indeed, the reorganization of skilled workers has created the possibility for technological development.

Japan is not our only competitor or model. The Italian case represents a second and distinct logic of growth and flexibility that has begun to capture attention. The logic here is different; but the innovations in Italy, as in Japan, rest in a pattern of industrial development.

The Italians created flexibility in a different way and among very different types of firms than the Japanese. Economic development in Italy in the postwar years was also very fast, producing talk of an Italian miracle. Firms like Fiat combined standard technologies with low-cost labor to establish themselves. Expansion of the mass and large-scale process production sectors of the economy proved rigid and ran up against serious limits. The large factories were manned with southern Italian workers, many moving directly from farms to factories. As those workers, who approached industrial life with traditional rural values, were drawn into labor-management conflicts, the union movement in Italy was transformed. Plant-level conflicts became intense. The result of these battles were legal restrictions that limited the ability of management to reduce the work force during downturns or to effectively control change in production processes as well as an elaborate system of social security protection.

Manufacturers, facing increased labor costs and restricted ability to manage flexibly inside their plants, took to subcontracting production of some components. In some cases the producers even provided the subcontractors with equipment. The subcontractors, being small, used less capital-intensive technology and processes than those employed within the large firms, and also, for reasons particular to Italian politics, fell outside the regulations that affected the giant companies. Frequently, when family firms sprang up, one member of the family would continue to work in a giant company in order to provide protection through the benefits package.

These subcontractors often began to innovate themselves and to produce new production equipment and products. An entire sector made up of smaller firms sprang up. Public policy supported these developments by creating institutions to support these small entrepreneurial operations and to encourage the vertical disintegration of production. In sum, rigidity in the large firms such as Fiat spawned a series of small subcontractors. The large firms subcontracted to avoid legislated social costs and labor rules. Eventually, these small producers broke loose from their subcontracting role to begin a different pattern of dynamic flexibility.[44] They have become innovative suppliers in world markets. Institutions and rules to support their activities have been established. While the Japanese story can be told by looking at Honda or Toyota, the Italian story draws attention to Benetton, the apparel producer.[45]

Interestingly, large firms such as Fiat have pursued flexibility by aggressively automating their assembly lines. The automation, it is reported, is intended to free them from the binds of conflicts on the shop floor. The new automation provides, at the same time, considerable flexibility. Because the reorganization is intended both to provide flexibility *and* to free the shop floor from worker conflict by eliminating the workers, the capital investment is greater than if the new production systems had been organized primarily around worker skill.

We don't need a series of other foreign examples to establish that other national strategies of labor and production organization may now have distinct advantages. As radically different as manufacturing in Japan and Italy may seem at first glance, there are very important common features. They can be seen in the organization of work and in the ties between production units. First, activities that in the United States might be combined into a vertically integrated firm—for example, at the extreme, an auto company that produces its own coal, steel, and components—are spread out into a multitude of firms. The ties between production units are often blurred in a haze of semimarket and semiorganizational links between firms involved in different parts of the production process. In Italy, a single entrepreneur may contract to deliver a fashion product, then look for a source of textiles and a producer to manufacture the good. The risk and marketing are here completely separated from the production. This Italian entrepreneur acts as a product manager with no production facility. In Japan, groups of companies with intertangled ownerships allow semi-markets—buying components or services, for example—to substitute for the rigidities of fully bureaucratic production or the uncertainties of a pure market. Toyota, for example, is much less vertically integrated than GM. American firms such as Ford, many would note, have often shucked off some of their operating units, buying what they used to make. Even IBM has established a series of partial ownerships in firms such as Intel, the semiconductor producer. This is precisely the point. There are great advantages in arrangements that have components of both market and ownership. Second, in both the Japanese and Italian cases—as well as the German, we might note—production work is organized around broadly defined job responsibilities.[46] Consequently, a worker's task is not limited to specific activities and his job does not depend on sustaining those particular activities. Corporate flexibility lies in strategy and the pattern of labor relations that has been bred over the years. The Taylorist approach to labor management in the United States has led to very narrow and rigidly defined job categories, categories that now make firms inflexible. The basis of job definitions lies in the politics of labor relations and is very different in the several nations examined. Third, and most important, distinct political as well as economic conditions in Japan and Italy produced their distinct approaches to production.

In sum, American firms may not have the high hand in the next years. Once dominant, we now face not just one but several alternative approaches to production organization. We have situated in this discussion the story of production flexibility narrowly, delimiting its basic features. Understanding and interpreting its several types of national developments requires that we situate the evolution and development of each production system in its social and political setting. The American production tradition—with its rigidities, its inattention to quality, and its high overhead—is not well situated for competition in this transition, which will depend so critically on maneuverability and flexibility. In its rise to preeminence America may have lost the flexibility to respond to an industrial challenge that rests on flexibility.

10

Dimensions of the Transition: The Revolution in Manufacturing

WE HAVE CHOSEN to examine the industrial transition by considering two manifestations of it. Any discussion of manufacturing and social change that does not consider concrete developments risks drifting into abstract blather. The meaning and need for dynamic flexibility and the significance of the new technologies are clearer if we look at them closely. Here we examine the emergence of microelectronics-based automation equipment and of digital telecommunications systems that merge data and voice transmission. Together, these new nodes of technological development will be central to the growth of productivity and the location and strategies of production as well as to the organization of work and community. Their development will profoundly alter production and distribution, and thus the types of jobs available in the economy and the character of the national community. In discussing these technological developments, we shall not try to sketch the dimensions of the U.S. industrial future. Our objective is simply to show that they present fundamental opportunities, and that any widespread failure by firms to take advantage of these opportunities will create market vulnerabilities that can undermine not just a few companies but America's national position.

Concrete developments, though, risk being taken for the larger transformation. We emphasize that new automation and digital telecommunications do not constitute the transition, but a look at them allows us to grasp its scope and significance. Indeed, the organizational recasting of production will prove of equal significance in determining what use will, in the end, be made of the new technical possibilities.

We do not need to show that the new technologies produce a break with past patterns of productivity growth—that there is a disjuncture in the growth equations. A disjuncture of growth equations would depend not just on the possibilities the technologies represent, but rather on how effectively they are used. In fact, the technologies do not exist apart from the strategies to use them. Indeed, the key issue is whether the United States can absorb the new technologies at a competitive pace, and apply them in a competitive manner.

The Manufacturing Revolution

There is enormous pressure from foreign competition to reorganize production to accelerate productivity. Seen from the perspective of particular firms and particular sectors, American companies have been beaten on the shop floor and must now respond. Seen from the vantage of the national economy as a whole, the slow growth in U.S. productivity risks leaving America in a diminished position in the international economy, and reversing that decline is crucial. Rather than trying to discuss all the elements of this manufacturing problem, we will focus on the emergence of distinctive issues in programmable automation as a means of making concrete our concerns.

Of course, and we have said this so often because it is so often misunderstood, the manufacturing problem does not reduce to issues in mechanical engineering, but requires that attention be given to how new machinery is used. Nonetheless, the new set of technologies permits a radical increase in static flexibility because automated machines can be applied to a variety of tasks. To capture those possibilities will require dynamic flexibility. We believe that unless the possibilities of static flexibility are seized, the competitive position of industry will be compromised.

Put differently, if manufacturing innovation is shunned in an effort to reduce costs or achieve flexibility by moving offshore or by reducing skill levels in domestic factories, then the spectacular promise of long-term increases in productivity will never be seized.

A new era in manufacturing organized around programmable automation seems to be beginning. Its symbol is the robot. Its mythology is being built around stories such as that of the machinery-component producer who made frying pans when demand was slack for its primary product. One central concept is flexibility. Other notions that will congeal as a new orthodoxy will likely prove to be vertical disintegration and reorganization.

How deep and significant are the changes? One risks exaggerating the economic advantages in order to highlight or clarify the evolution in manufacturing practice. Put blandly, programmable automation increases the advantages of batch production over mass production. It has implications for both static flexibility and dynamic flexibility.* In essence, programmable automation equipment can be used to increase static flexibility. However, to capture those static possibilities a firm must have the flexibility to develop and introduce the new equipment. If it does, it will also reap great gains in the form of increased productivity from the new technology.

The price of static production flexibility—the ability to make a variety of different products in the same facility and with the same machines—has gone down.[1] Although one can't speak in terms of specific quantities, because the actual numbers vary from product to product, it is becoming increasingly feasible for a manufacturer to make some of one thing and some of another rather than a greater amount of a single product. At the extreme, Allan Bradley, the American producer of small engines and components, has introduced a system that is reported to allow it to produce a single one-of-a-kind item and ship it within twenty-four hours of an order receipt.

From one vantage, the new equipment might be seen as simply new machines fitting into an otherwise unchanged system. The technical advances may be important, but marginal. From a second vantage, it would seem that there is a new set of choices and trade-offs in manufacturing. Batch production, and the flexibility it permits, becomes feasible in situations where costs had previously required the volumes and rigidities of mass production. Consequently, work organization and factory location,

---

*These terms were defined in chapter 9, where we said that static flexibility means the ability of a firm to adjust its operations at any moment to shifting conditions in the market —to the rise and fall of demand or the changes in the mix of products that the market is asking for. It implies adjustment within a fixed product and production structure. Dynamic flexibility means, by contrast, the ability to increase productivity steadily through improvements in production processes and innovation in product.

which reflect the requirements of large-scale production, will be altered to reflect the work organization more typical of small batch production. The changes in production will lead to fundamental shifts in corporate strategy as firms try to take advantage of the production changes. That the need is to reconsider the production system and not just talk about the machines is the lesson of the Italian and Japanese stories.

There are those who go further and contend that the advanced countries face a fundamental industrial divide, a break in industrial organization and production, a break that will be at the core of basic political choices.[2] To separate fact from fiction we must begin with a basic understanding of production technology itself.

The New Production Technology[3]

The new production technology brings changes both in how goods are made and how they are designed.[4] The application of advanced electronics and computer techniques changes how machines can be controlled and how they sense their environment. Computer controls, for example, allow machines to be directed by electronic instruction and, consequently, permit a machine to change from one task to another. Computer vision, and particularly the more sophisticated artificial intelligence applications, permit robot arms to put walnuts on cheese. The consequences are that automation can be used where it was not possible before, both because now automated machines can be changed from one task to another and because automated machines can be applied to new types of tasks. Again, we emphasize that our story focuses on only one element—albeit an important one—of the manufacturing revolution. Our intent is to convince the reader of the significance of the break, not to present a full discussion of the manufacturing revolution.

"Programmable automation" (PA), the label given to the new manufacturing technologies, is ". . . a family of technologies that lie at the intersection of computer science and manufacturing engineering. 'Programmable' means that they can be switched from one task to another with relative ease by changing the (usually) automated instructions; automation means that they perform a significant part of their functions without direct human intervention."[5] Programmable automation equipment blurs the traditionally sharp distinction between equipment used in small batch production and the dedicated machines used in mass production.

Traditionally, automated equipment had to be dedicated to a specific task. It could, to put it differently, be used only for one very specific purpose. A traditional, dedicated machine tool doesn't just cut metal, it cuts metal to make a specific part and no other. To alter its application is a slow and expensive process. In some cases, it simply is not possible to alter the application once a machine is in place. Consequently, to justify the cost of the machines, one must use them to make a great number of one thing. Plants that made automobile engines in the 1960s were most efficient when they produced at least 400,000 engines annually.[6] The fixed cost of the machines and plants was high, but their capacity to make many units was also high. The unit cost of production, the cost of making a single item, fell with increasing volume. These efficiencies—unit costs declining with increasing volume—are called "economies of scale."

Dedicated machines and fixed assembly lines with substantial economies of scale have been the basis of mass manufacturing in this century. Volume production called for product standardization and marketing strategies to sell large numbers of a single product. The prototype was, of course, Ford's Model T, in which a single company produced a single product in a single color. General Motors introduced some real and some superficial product variety, but the core of the system was unchanged. The system was, to repeat, volume production of standard products sold to a mass market on the basis of price. The label of "Fordist" production has been hung on the whole system. The necessities of such production seemed to dictate particular ways of organizing factories and labor. Management of the work force was, in fact, geared to fitting men to the requirements of machines. The efficient use of labor in this system became a pseudoscience, Taylorism.

Production variety could still be achieved, of course, but at a substantial price. Items not sold in great volume could be made, but they had to be made differently. It was simply more expensive to make a few of an item.

The price of variety has been very steep. As an earlier BRIE study argued:

> The different economics of batch and mass production have traditionally been obvious. With very small batch or custom production, general purpose machines, usually hand operated by skilled workers, produce at most a few items. Capital costs may be low but UNIT production costs are high because set-up time can be considerable, individual machining is a demanding and time consuming task, and all the costs must be spread over a very small number of units produced. Dedicated automation stands at the other extreme. Here initial fixed capital costs are quite high but total unit costs are typically very low because the automation of production increases speed and insures

constant quality. Specialized equipment is set up once and from then on production proceeds in an almost continuous flow. . . .[7]

Productivity in manufacturing is directly related to the extent to which work is mechanized and automated. The limits on automation and mechanization of small batch production have consequences for productivity levels throughout the economy. For example, with a routine materials-handling task the difference in output can be ten times greater using the most mechanized rather than the least mechanized means of doing the task.

> The cost difference between conventional batch manufacturing and mass production was on the order of ten to thirty times per product. In part this was due to the cost of setting up the machinery between batches, which can result in the machine only cutting for an average of 15 to 20% of the time the part is on the machine table. Moreover parts moved in a byzantine pattern from work station to work station, leading to very high levels of work in progress.[8]

Mechanization, of course, is not new. Steam driven machinery was at the core of the industrial revolution. The new element is the introduction of cheap microprocessors, computers on a chip. "Since approximately 75% of all machined parts are produced in batches of fewer than 50, in which capital equipment utilization rates are abysmal, the potential uses of [such] mechanization are widespread."[9] Small batch production, using traditional equipment, could not be automated or mechanized. Using the new equipment, small batch production can be mechanized. The mechanization of small batch manufacture changes the economics of production. The potential for increased productivity made possible throughout the economy by programmable automation is thus enormous.

Programmable automation equipment makes flexible automation possible, or put differently, it shrinks the cost difference between flexible production in batches and dedicated automation. The sharp trade-off between automation and flexibility rested, we have argued, on the need to dedicate automated equipment to specific tasks. Economies of scale could be achieved with dedicated automation, but if the tasks to be performed were to be rapidly varied, they could not (cost-effectively) be automated. The GM plant at Lordstown is an excellent example of the old automation.[10] It was built to manufacture one product and could not be adapted to another. Certainly the automated equipment could often, though not always, be adapted to new tasks. The shift of equipment between tasks, when it is possible, can be boiled down to the difficulty of setting up the equipment.

The difficulty of setting up plant and equipment for new tasks can be measured in cost and time. Programmable automation can reduce the set-up time and cost of shifting equipment between uses. It does so, to over-simplify, because the equipment is controlled by an electronic program. Changing the program, which at a fantastic extreme is a quick set of computer instructions, changes the function of the machine. Of course, it isn't generally that simple; machines may have to be repositioned and parts- or materials-feeding reorganized. As we have seen, though, turn-around time can be reduced from hours to minutes. In any case, the new equipment can be far more cost effective than traditional automated machines. Note, though, how reconfiguration of traditional equipment can create flexibility (table 9.1).

A programmable robot or machine tool cannot be told to do just anything; however, there remains a range of tasks that it can perform, moving between them with limited cost.[11] Clearly the ability to cut, to lift, to weld—and the range of application of these abilities—is still limited at the time of the manufacture of the machine tool. An automobile assembly line cannot be converted to produce aircraft engines, but it may be used to make both cars and light trucks.

The breadth of the range of applications is critical. The range of applications may be a set of parts that a machine can cut, the places that welds can be placed, the types of parts a robot can handle and place. To make our point, let us assume that set-up costs and time are eliminated (although, in actual practice, they are only reduced). In that case, the equipment could be used for a range of tasks as efficiently as for a single one. Consequently, there would be low-cost flexibility in both component production and product assembly.[12]

A new vocabulary has emerged. Programmable automation permits an automated machine to perform a range of tasks. This permits a single arrangement of equipment to produce a variety of components or to assemble a variety of products. *Economies of scope* stand alongside economies of scale.[13] Economies of scope are gained not in the volume production of a single good, but in the volume production of a set of goods. Economies of scope—the economies gained in the volume production of a set of goods—is to the new manufacturing what economies of scale—the economies gained from the production of a single good—are to traditional production. Programmable automation gives the production system the capacity to produce, at very low cost, a variety of products and components. It creates flexibility.

We must not exaggerate. The cost trade-off between volume production and flexibility is not, as a general matter, eliminated by technology. It is simply dramatically lowered, permitting a new category of goods that, in cost, fit between standard production and handmade production.[14] To illustrate, let us take men's suits as an example. For years, there has been a sharp distinction between luxury, tailormade suits and standard, off-the-rack suits. Even the best manufactured suits are substantially less expensive than tailored equivalents. A tailored suit (bespoke tailoring) is both hand cut to the measure of the client and hand finished. Standard suits are both cut to standard sizes and machine sewn and finished. A new category seems to be coming into existence of cut-to-measure by machine and machine sewn and finished clothing.[15] The price is, not unexpectedly, between that of hand-tailored and off-the-rack suits. When cutting machines are controlled by computer, they can be set up to cut a variety of goods. Similarly, custom or semicustom semiconductor design and production-foundry semiconductor operations become possible with new computer-aided design techniques. Semicustom men's suits and semicustom microchips can carry a price premium to the client. However, the new automation has reduced the cost of both custom suits and circuits. When radical cost reductions for variety occur, they result from a reorganization of production.

For the most part, programmable automation applications, no matter how creative, are not likely directly to yield lower unit costs than dedicated automation for two reasons. First, programmable automation isn't a free good. The cost of the programmable equipment is, at least for now, higher than that of equivalent dedicated machines. Consequently, the difference in cost between programmable machines and dedicated machines will be reflected in the average cost of making any product or part. Second, PA equipment is generally not designed for high-volume operation. The impression is that such equipment will usually produce fewer pieces per hour than a dedicated machine. Case studies suggest that these capital cost factors—the lower output and higher cost of PA machines—will, for the coming years, outweigh any savings from inventory reductions achieved by producing smaller quantities just in time for their use or by attaining higher yield rates through better quality.[16] For the moment, flexibility will still carry a price tag, albeit a lower one than before.

Nonetheless, the economies of flexible manufacturing are sometimes quite unexpected.[17] While faster set-up times do lower the costs of variety, there is still some penalty for variety. But there are some circumstances in which flexibility (or variety) and lower unit costs are reported to go together. For example, when the production volumes required to operate dedicated machines at maximum efficiency are not needed, the machine sits idle for extended periods. In that case, several dedicated machines can be replaced by one programmable machine. Consequently, there is a real savings in three forms. First, inventory costs can be lowered, since several parts can each be made in smaller volumes for each production run. Second, the materials-handling costs are reduced as well. Third, the cost of the one programmable machine may be dramatically less than that of several dedicated machines. The utilization rates of the programmable machine will be higher. Together, the lower capital costs and lower inventory costs compensate for the greater efficiency at peak operating rates of the dedicated machines. In such cases, variety and lower unit cost can be achieved together.

The need for production flexibility may be created by demand for product variety or variability in sales. In either case, production flexibility traditionally required technologies and manufacturing organizations that produced goods at higher unit costs than fully automated mass production. Thus traditional manufacturing left a trade-off between production flexibility (the capacity to vary what was made and in what volumes) and minimum-cost automation that pushed toward standardization.

We must avoid exaggeration and unwarranted dreams of a utopia of flexible production, and the new technologies are susceptible to both. First of all, production flexibility can be achieved in a variety of ways. Programmable automation is one technique that addresses one element of the problem. Layoffs, the right to lower wages in downturns, and paying by the piece also give firms flexibility in their operations. Sometimes companies mix production technologies to achieve some flexibility in volume in order to operate efficiently—that is, they adopt a mix of the most efficient automated capital-intensive facilities and less automated, less efficient but more flexible plant. Or as Michael Piore notes, they contract out part of the production to smaller producers.[18] In upturns, the contracts can be signed, and in downturns, canceled or not renewed.[19] The small subcontractor then bears the costs of demand swings, rather than the large firm. The mix of production strategies allows firms to purchase flexibility. The price of flexibility is the difference between the cost of a product produced in the most efficient plant (at the plant's most efficient volume) and the cost of the same product produced in a different factory or bought from a subcontractor. Why use less efficient facilities? Because they provide capacity that can be closed off when demand drops. Unused capacity in the most efficient plants is very expensive. Say you build a plant to make 400,000 car door handles, but demand varies from 300,000 to 425,000 per year. When the plant is running full out, it makes very cheap door handles.

However, when it operates at 75 percent capacity to make 300,000 handles, the unit cost rises. The firm may therefore build a plant to manufacture most efficiently at its most probable sales volume, say 350,000 door handles. During booms it may make the remaining 75,000 with less highly automated, less efficient technologies. The firm produces the stable portion of its sales volume with the most efficient mass technologies and the variable portion with less capital-intensive techniques that make door handles at a higher price. The less efficient facility has the advantage of flexibility. It has lower fixed costs and can be turned on or off more easily. Because equipment is less dedicated, the facilities can be closed or turned to new uses. The firm is able to minimize production costs over time across a range of production volumes.

Next, and equally important, the new electronics technology does not have the inevitable consequence of transforming mass-produced goods into batch production, permitting the possibility of product variety and production flexibility along the way. Sometimes the implications push the other way. For example, telecommunications and computer gear, which once required distinct production facilities, can now share parts of assembly because they are increasingly similar products. Once each good required distinctly separate wiring, while now the circuits are embedded on integrated circuits which in turn are connected on circuit boards. The final assembly task in the making of both goods therefore becomes stuffing circuit boards into plastic boxes; although the circuit boards and boxes are different, they are sufficiently similar for common facilities to be possible. Indeed, wiring itself becomes a matter of assembling the circuit boards. These changes have stripped labor out of the production process, permitting automation. Electromechanical telephone switches required 2,000 workers, SPC-analog switches required 900, and fully digital switches require 50 to assemble.[20] Labor has not been reduced; it has been shifted, importantly, to the development process. With advanced computers and telecommunications switches, the development and software cost become so great that the economies of scale have risen, not dropped. For example, development costs for digital central office telephone switches handling 500,000 telephone lines are $500 million to a billion dollars, while equivalent costs for electromechanical switches were $50 million. Development costs have risen tenfold.[21]

The telecommunications example emphasizes that production should be treated by the *producer* like mass manufacture but appear to the *user* like custom design and fabrication.

The second great consequence of the new electronics (the first being programmable automation equipment which alters the trade-off between

automation and flexibility) is that machines can perform more sophisticated tasks than before because more advanced sensory techniques are
possible. Sometimes that means that the machines can be used in dramatically new ways. Thus, for example, computer aided design equipment,
which is only now emerging, will alter the process of product design, just
as robots and NC machine tasks are altering manufacturing. CAD equipment amounts to a computer with graphic display capacity and software
to process and display solutions to design problems. The technology is
indispensable for some tasks, such as the design of advanced integrated
circuits.[22] Furthermore, it speeds and sophisticates the process of design
and design testing in other products. Finally, it reduces the cost of design
and speeds the shift from design to manufacture. The design data is in the
computer and can be processed to produce computer instructions for the
machine. Introducing new products or designing a range of related products becomes faster and cheaper.[23]

Sophisticated fabrication and assembly machines can be used to replace people in the most dangerous production tasks. These new capacities
rest on computer control systems as well as on sophisticated mechanics
and, often, on sensory systems. The Japanese call this "combination me-
chatronics." The new sophistication allows an extension of automation
and permits production with ever less manpower.

There is reason to believe, however, that if the new equipment is used
simply to strip labor out of production, to directly substitute capital for
labor in the existing production organization, then PA equipment is likely
to be ineffectively used and its potential missed. Many believe that PA will
only produce competitive advantage if it is operated by skilled workers to
achieve new ends.[24]

The new sophistication does not come for free. Indeed, while programmable automation generates flexibility, the increased capital costs of
some of the new equipment creates new rigidities. Consider, from still
another vantage, the semiconductor industry. The key to the industry has
been the integrated circuit, the thumbnail-sized silicon chip that contains
thousands of individual transistors wired to form complex circuits. Putting
ever more circuits on a chip requires shrinking the transistors and the
"wiring" that connects them. Early integrated circuits put hundreds of
transistors on one chip. Current circuits put hundreds of thousands of
circuits on a chip. Circuits anticipated for the early 1990s will put millions
of circuits on a single chip.

Producing those chips requires ever more sophisticated and costly
equipment. A fabrication line in 1977 for the most sophisticated chips cost
$4 million. Today the most sophisticated lines cost in the neighborhood of

$100 million. The ever denser chips command a price premium for a time, but then drop to literally pennies. The memory chip that was the cutting-edge product in 1976, the 16K DRAM (16,000-circuit dynamic random access memory chip) had an average selling price of $30.00 then, but sold for $2.25 in 1981, and now sells for $.95. The chip that is two product generations later, the 256K DRAM, contains sixteen times as many circuits and in 1986 sold for between $2.00 and $2.50[25] with future prices to be set at fair market value under the trade agreement between the U.S. and Japan. Higher volumes than ever before are required to pay for these fabulously expensive lines, because the price of the chips does not reflect their vast increase in power.

The consequence is that higher production volumes can mean—even in an era of flexibility—ever greater production rigidities. Once the assembly line is built the company must pay for the fixed cost of plant and equipment, even if nothing is sold. There are some possibilities of sharing production facilities across a range of products and even companies—that is, there are some possibilities of creating flexibility in the volumes of products that must be sold or the mix of products that must be sold. However, this is only possible once the most sophisticated production equipment is honed on the simplest chip architectures. The possibilities of a steady progression in production rests on the ability to finance the equipment and find huge and stable markets for the product. In the semiconductor industry, the new production equipment has meant ever greater rigidities for many firms. The possibilities of greater flexibility for some firms, such as those making custom chips and using economies of scope, is balanced by greater rigidity for those firms making more standard chips, where these new investments are crucial. Which matters more? Simply, the basic advances in the production technology—from which the custom producers draw their production expertise—are driven by the evolution of the more standard chips. The flexibility can survive only if the most advanced production technology is readily available on the market. If not, the custom producers will—in our view—wither. Under any circumstances, there is increased capital intensity and, consequently, rigidity for all, even though some producers are more seriously affected by that than others.

The real potential of the new production equipment comes from its integration.[26] Imagine a fully integrated system linking design to manufacturing, permitting an automatic shift from one product to the next. The United States is still a long way from any widespread use of such computer integrated manufacturing (CIM) systems. It is even further from the shared data base that will integrate manufacturing into business strategy.

Numerically controlled machine tools are now widely used.[27] The robotics industry is still in its infancy. Only 51,600 robots were in use in the United States and Japan together in 1983. In 1983 worldwide investment in robots was about $800 million–$900 million.[28] However, IBM announced in 1983 a robotics R&D program for 1984 that exceeded the sales volume of the industry in 1982. A return on that R&D investment for IBM alone will require a market that is more than 10 times that of today.

Wassily Leontief and Faye Duchin have emphasized that the world is in the early days of the application of the new production technology.[29] Though this technology is just in its infancy, manufacturing practice and the use of programmable automation are evolving rapidly. The pace of diffusion represents competitive potential for the economy. It will permit a burst in productivity as small batch production is automated. Recall that small batch production is still a dominant part of total production, representing 75 percent of machine parts.

The American competitive problem—we have argued—rests centrally on a loss of competitive advantage in the manufacturing process. The introduction of the new equipment will serve either to remedy that decline or to entrench it. Unfortunately, there are real signs of trouble. While the the number of NC machine tools has doubled to 103,000 in the United States since 1978, the number of robots in Japan (using the strict industry definition) is roughly four times the number in the United States (14,000 versus 3,500 in 1982).[30] Equally, the Japanese seem to be moving more rapidly to establish integrated programmable facilities. "As early as 1978 a full 85 percent of all Japanese robots were being built for integration into flexible machining cells. At the same time, the major U.S. builders of both machine tools and robots had not written a single order that [included both]."[31] In all countries the auto industry has been a major initial user. In the United States large companies producing for the Defense Department were important early users. Indeed, government programs were aimed at developing equipment for their needs. In Japan the range of industries adopting the new technology has been wider sooner. For example, in Japan 10 percent of robots are in the plastics molding industry, an application that American producers have not made.[32] More than half of the numerically controlled robots in Japan were installed in plants with fewer than 1,000 employees in 1979, and by the end of 1984 smaller factories still accounted for as much as 40 percent of total robot installation. As the *Wall Street Journal* noted:

> What robots do is help smaller companies enter precision machinery, from
> which they had previously been barred because of a shortage of skilled work-

ers. . . . thus a small entrepreneurial corporation can now challenge the status quo and labor intensive approaches of old fashion incumbents that have built up a skilled workforce over the years.[33]

We need not focus on Japan. The Swedish and the German stories contain similar messages.

Precisely because the new production technology is in its early days, the capacity to introduce the technology—dynamic capacity or flexibility —is crucial. We are worried that the dynamic advantage does not rest with the United States.

The early Japanese advantage in introducing the new manufacturing equipment may be difficult to reverse. The dynamics in Japan, as we already argued, seem to more readily favor adoption of the new technologies and their possibilities. Large companies accustomed to continuous shop-floor innovation have begun to produce for internal use equipment they can't buy on the market. They then, in turn, become vendors of their internally developed machines. The internal use assures that development is tightly attuned to user needs and provides a "launch" market. As a result, the numerous sellers and types of equipment in Japan are more diverse than in the United States. Japanese government programs have been aimed at promoting the development, application, and widespread diffusion of commercial equipment, particularly in smaller firms.[34] Labor organization, which defines job responsibilities broadly, is well suited to adopting new technologies. The labor force is being educated to understand both the technologies and their applications. Rapidly rising wage rates and low interest rates make the companies even more willing to invest in machines to reduce labor input.[35]

We must emphasize that the fundamental changes in production strategy and organization in Japan discussed earlier are an important basis of the rapid introduction of programmable equipment—NC machine tools, robots, and the like. At crucial moments, when equipment was selected and installed, economies of scale were sacrificed for flexibility—that is, the advantage of using equipment dedicated to one task while providing low-unit costs at volume production were given up. Equipment was put in place that could be moved between tasks. Flexibility allowed savings in overhead, reductions in wasted production, and lower direct labor cost. The organization needed to achieve that flexibility emphasized production in smaller batches to avoid buffer stocks. Cutting production costs through the flexibility of small batches in essence prepared the organization to adopt the new programmable equipment when it became available.

In the United States, manufacturing risks entering a vicious downward spiral. The first element of the problem is that high interest rates and declining wage rates push industry to substitute labor for machines. In the past, beginning in the nineteenth century, skill shortages and rising wage rates encouraged investment in manufacturing equipment. Now the relative prices are reversing themselves:

> From 1915 to 1950 labor's hourly earnings in manufacturing increased five fold, while the prices of metal products only doubled. From 1965 to 1977, however, the average prices of metal working machines produced in the United States increased by 116 percent, matching the 115 percent rise of hourly earnings of manufacturing workers. Since 1965 the index of capital costs rose more each year than the index of unit labor costs. The high price of capital compared to labor cut firms' willingness and ability to invest in productivity enhancing capital-deepening strategies. Labor intensive methods simply appeared more cost effective under a regime of expensive capital.[36]

In fact, since 1973 real wages in manufacturing in the United States have declined, reducing the pressure to invest in machinery.[37] Studies of the diffusion of NC machine tools in Europe and the United States have found that high wage rates promoted diffusion.[38] Ironically, corporate strategies to retain profit margins by reducing labor costs rather than by reorganizing production simply slow the adaptation to an international market in which foreign competitors have lower wages than the United States and in which the U.S. advantage or that of any advanced country must rest on mastery of complex manufacturing. A second element is that government policy has promoted the development of machines for sophisticated defense use. Indeed, the pattern of use in the United States and the market positions of American equipment producers reflects this early government emphasis on sophisticated defense applications.[39] The pattern of labor relations, created as much by management intent as union strategy, emphasizes narrow job definitions and adversarial confrontation on the shop floor. This is thoroughly unsuited to the effective use of PA. Finally, America has a corporate tradition of advancing production technology through a set of plateaus, each reached by a discrete jump, that remain frozen until the next jump is taken. The United States has tended not to engage in continuous production innovation—the constant interactive improvement of a system in place. This slows the move to new production systems and the mastery of them. The jump in manufacturing now being taken is a substantial one. Until the bugs are out of not only individual factories or machines, but a whole range of new machines, constant tinkering and interactive production innovation will be needed. Slow introduction of the new equipment slows productivity, which in turn slows wage increases, making labor-intensive production strategies more attractive. Let there be no doubt. Steadily declining wages will undo both macroeconomic policy and the incentives that encouraged mechanization in the first place.

The implications of programmable automation can be seen today; the economic and political consequences will be felt in the next decade. As the technology spreads, it will alter manufacturing competition and labor organization. Unfortunately, at least at a quick glance, it would appear that the organizational habits of American companies, which are the basis of both shop-floor organization and the evaluation of particular investment decisions, would tend to impede the rapid implementation of the possibilities of the new technologies. Production strategies have been based on notions of economies of scale. Shop-floor organization and equipment decisions reflect this. Consequently, implementing the new technologies in the United States seems to require basic changes in organization, which are often quite difficult. Thus, both the way American firms go about keeping production costs down—creating rigid large-scale systems with a commitment to rigid volume equipment—and their bias for periodic wholesale production changes and against continuous production innovation impede the introduction of the new equipment.

The New Manufacturing Competition: The Strategic Possibilities of Programmable Automation

The new automation will profoundly affect corporate strategies. Its implications are broader than cost efficiencies today or even steadily progressing manufacturing productivity. It is not simply a matter of concern to the vice president for manufacturing who is responsible for assuring competitive cost and quality. It is a more basic choice that must concern the chief executive officer and the strategists.

The best way into this story is to begin with the decision to adopt the technology. Adopting any new technology has direct, indirect, and hidden costs. The direct costs include the price of the primary machine and the supporting equipment. The indirect costs include the retraining of personnel or the reorganization of jobs and responsibilities. The hidden costs include the organizational conflicts over responsibility (as certainty shifts and reshuffles organizational power) and the downtime (time when the system doesn't work) that comes with unexpected glitches. The question for any potential user is how to assess the gains.

Two different lenses, as we have noted before, can be used to evaluate the potential gains. In the first lens, the new equipment is seen as a replacement for current equipment or labor in an existing production system. The potential gains are those marginal reductions in cost or marginal improvements in quality that are produced by using new equipment in an old system. The changes in the production equipment will affect the price at which products are made and sold, but they will not influence the link between manufacturing and corporate strategy. As with all other equipment decisions, a rise in interest rates effectively increases the cost of the investment. Put differently, it reduces the present value of possible future benefits from the equipment and thus requires a faster payback from the investment. In this optic, programmable automation is a simple substitution of one machine for another or of capital for labor. The question is efficiency in an *existing* production system.

The second lens shows the gains differently and correctly. The new equipment is seen as part of the introduction of a new production system. That new production system permits flexibility in the manufacture of components and product. It may also permit and provoke changes in the connections between production units. With some equipment, a range of products, previously made at high cost, can now be produced more cheaply by grouping their production together. A milling machine that has been used to make only one part can now be used to make several. Consequently, components can be made in smaller volumes at a cost that approaches and, on occasion, matches that once achieved only at high volume. While mass-produced parts have to be stocked until needed, requiring both storage space and financing costs, small batch production matches component production to the assembly needs. Efficient small batch production makes just-in-time production easier; the result is that general inventory costs are reduced. The just-in-time system permits a shift of quality control from a staff function to the line manufacturing operation. An assembly line once used for a single product or shifted at great cost from one product to the next is now used interchangeably for several products. Again, production flexibility and product variety are not free, but the trade-off between specialized production and standard mass production is radically altered. Seen through this second lens, the production system itself will be *changed*. The question here is how to capture dynamic gains.

The measures used to evaluate decisions must change in order to see gains from shifting from one production system to another. Companies can no longer compare the cost of the single machine to the marginal gains it can bring to production. They must see the machine as one step toward a new manufacturing system with entirely different economics. The future gains are not those of substituting one machine for another within an existing system, but the future benefits from the new production system. Firms must set the costs and benefits of moving toward a new system of production against what they might achieve within the constraints of the existing fashion of organizing production. The benefits from the new PA machine will be greater if production is reorganized to take advantage of its capabilities. The future benefits of the investment in the same machine will be higher if that investment is evaluated through the second optic, which focuses on reorganized production, than if it is evaluated through the first optic. A rise in interest rates will always discourage investment, but if the benefits from an investment are high enough, the investment may be made even if interest rates rise. A shift in the production system is a basic choice. Some now suggest three measures for evaluating the benefits of such a change: return on assets, cycle time, and quality. Return on assets—that is, return on investment in plant materials and the like—suggests that the production system be evaluated as a whole, that the impact of shifting systems be evaluated. Cycle time represents the ability to bring product on-line, the ability to respond quickly to orders, and the ability to reduce inventories of inputs and inventory stocks. The inventory issue is central to real gain from manufacturing innovation. Reducing inputs inventories directly reduces unit production costs. Reducing stock inventories reduces the cost of delivering the product to the customer. The relation of inventory to sales is often measured by inventory *turns*—how many times total inventory is sold out in a year. The more turns, the shorter the "holding time" and the less the financing costs. One firm went from two to sixty-five annual turns. It paid for its manufacturing innovations from the savings. There are measures of quality. Higher quality not only improves a company's image, it also reduces servicing costs. When the manufacturing system is working well it adds flexibility in product mix as well. Certainly, substantial investment is required to implement new manufacturing organization, but ironically it may result in *lower cost* and in strategic advantage.

The question becomes whether firms want to make that change—to cross that divide. Part of the decision is a matter of manufacturing tactics: how to achieve increased productivity and lower-cost production. Part, though, is an issue of broader corporate strategy. The new economics of production have to be judged against the old. The crucial choice is whether the new technology will be used to automate existing practices or to permit new ones. Electric motors, for example, were used directly to replace steam motors until the factory system was reorganized to gain the benefits of using multiple sources of power from small electric motors.[40] Process innovation does not always depend on major technological breakthroughs. Toyota has been able to reduce set-up times for presses from one hour to twelve minutes, while the equivalent time in the United States was reported to be six hours.[41] The techniques did not require extensive automation. A fascination with the technology, rather than with its purposes, can undermine its potentials.

We have focused so far on costs. However, even more importantly, the new manufacturing system can open up new possible strategies. Manufacturing flexibility creates and requires corporate flexibility. Corporate strategies can be influenced by production flexibility in several ways. First, PA permits a fragmentation of the mass market. *Business Week* announced the end of the mass market in a front cover story in the fall of 1983.[42] Increased personal income and the widespread diffusion of basic consumer durables means consumers will pay premiums for distinct products.[43] Traditionally, the variety available to mass markets was superficial because real variety was too expensive to produce. Real product variety can now be achieved at more limited cost than before and is occasionally a free consequence of production reorganization. As a result, while previously one standard product had to be situated in the market to capture consumers with varied preferences, now several products can be aimed at different niches within the market. Real product variety means fundamentally different performance characteristics in a product, not simply superficial characteristics. General Motors, for example, produces a series of cars that are sold in all of its divisions with only minor modifications. The X body car is sold as the Chevy Citation and the Buick Skylark. The A body is sold as the Chevy Celebrity and by Oldsmobile as the Cutlass Ciera. The Chevy Cavalier and the Cadillac Cimarron are cousins. The X car series, the J series, and the A series represent three car types. Defining real variety in autos as the number of different engine and chassis types per 100,000 cars, the Japanese by contrast have roughly three times as much real variety in their product lines as have American firms.[44] The capacity to produce real product variety, to benefit from the economies of scope, means that a manufacturer in an advanced country faced with low-cost products coming from the NICs can now respond by offering, at only a small price premium, a series of products better aimed at the market. It is, as Charles Sabel has noted, the end of the age of Fordism.[45] We must be careful not to exaggerate the move toward batch production. Microelectronics technology, which permits programmable automation, also permits a second approach to flexibility. In telephone switching equipment, electric motors, and home appliances, for example, much of the hardware can be produced on common assembly lines, since the production task is to insert circuit boards into boxes. In many cases the product is adapted with customized software. IBM reports fundamental product interchangeability in its new North Carolina production lines.

Second, new products can be designed and introduced more quickly. Faced with imitation products, companies can quickly introduce next generation products or at least offer improved versions of existing ones. Indeed, rapid product introduction can be a strategic weapon. Honda responded to a challenge from Yamaha in motorcycles by accelerating the pace of model change to win back market.[46] Rapid product introduction reduces the gains from scale—since the total volume of each product will be limited. Rather, dynamic efficiencies of changing the product line are vital. Third, as the mix of products demanded by the public shifts, companies can move more quickly between different products and product lines.

Production flexibility and rapid product development and change is unquestionably one means by which producers in advanced countries are able to respond to the entrance of NIC manufacturers using more traditional technologies to make more standard products. It represents both the possibility of increased productivity and the means of implementing—at the same time and with the same equipment—distinct market strategies. The rapid diffusion of the new technologies depends on an understanding of their strategic uses in reorganizing new production. Firms that grasp the new possibilities adopt the new technologies more quickly. The corporate capacity to absorb and implement the new technologies and their possibilities will be decisive for long-run competitiveness.

The capacity of a firm to envision and capture the evolving strategic possibilities of new manufacturing also appears to depend on how production innovation is organized within the firm. Interestingly, there is a clear distinction at the manufacturing level between firms that have moved quickly to introduce PA and those that have not. Some firms build a manufacturing facility and then operate it, without real change, until a new generation system is built. They move one step at a time from plateau to plateau. These firms do not have experience integrating new equipment or manufacturing ideas into existing facilities. Such firms have been slow to introduce the new technologies or to exploit their revolutionary potential. Other firms continuously make minor improvements and adjustments in their production organization. Those firms, the evidence shows, integrate new equipment, discovering and exploiting its potential, and move to new manufacturing.[47] American firms might be thought to fall into the first category. Importantly, most Japanese firms fall into the second category. Japan's more rapid introduction of robots would seem to have its roots here. The continuous innovation in the manufacturing process induces further innovation and eases adaptation. The difference between Japanese and American firms does not, in our view, rest on the cultures of the two countries. Rather, as we saw earlier, producers in the two countries have faced distinctly separate problems since the war and have adopted two quite different approaches to manufacturing.[48] Japanese producers borrowed foreign technology and expanded production in a protected domestic market. They were faced with rapidly expanding demand and pursued market share. They learned about production as they expanded it rapidly and captured learning-curve economies. They discovered the now widely popular notion that the more a producer makes, the more efficient it becomes. It is a sophisticated and formal version of practice makes perfect. The conditions of expansion and competition induced a pattern and a habit of continuous manufacturing innovation. American producers were internationally dominant. Consequently, there was little foreign technology to borrow and little need to borrow it. The domestic market in most consumer durables was quite mature; expansion was slow. Control of the shop floor and labor peace were purchased by high wages. Price, and consequently production innovation, was rarely a basis of competition among American producers. Thus, habits of step function production innovation emerged and became entrenched. The difficulty for American producers is that Japan's capacities and habits of continuous innovation—or dynamic flexibility—are well suited to the industrial tasks the market and technological transition impose.

As advanced countries are pressed by the NICs into each other's markets, firms that exploit the strategic and tactical possibilities of PA will establish real advantages. Those that do not capture the possibilities, or who are slow to do so, will lose. The competitive markets will drive toward adoption. Those who move first will build up expertise and supporting technologies to push ahead faster through this fundamental transition. Markets will drive the process, but market outcomes tomorrow will be shaped by corporate and government choices today.

One or Several Futures? The Uncertain Consequences of the New Production Technologies

Programmable automation and the other new production technologies will bring with it a reshuffling of industrial competition and the location of market advantage. Corporate strategies will change. Job requirements and work organization will be altered. The location of industrial production will shift.

Some economists believe the technology itself will drive the organization of production. They contend that there are constraints, technological dictates that sharply constrain how the production process is organized. Since firms must solve the same problem because they are competing in the same markets, one should expect that, whatever their national origins, they will adopt similar production structures and look for labor with similar skills to facilitate similar production strategies. Work organization and the mix of labor skills would be derived from the strategies and the technologies.

We take an alternative position, though we have not yet completed work to test the argument. We suspect and, furthermore, we see strong evidence that the existing system of labor relations, the shop-floor organization of labor, and the level of skills in the work force itself constrains and shapes the production organization and hence the strategy of a firm. In this case, we should observe that firms in different countries adopt production strategies which reflect the distinct conditions of their nations. Direct comparisons of French and German plants producing equivalent goods within the same firm in the 1970s show clearly the wide range of possible work and job arrangements within the constraints of a single technology.[49] Early case studies of labor organization in plants in the United States using PA show that efforts to control production lead to centralization and an elimination of critical, but powerful, skilled jobs. While the drive to centralization solves organizational problems, it does not derive from technical necessity. Where different links between the shop floor and management exist, technology will be used to solve different problems.

For now, the new technologies define a set of possibilities. They have not yet frozen into a pattern of established products and defined technologies that will be improved only marginally. Sustained investment by firms and government along a given technological path will tend to exclude efforts to advance along others. As we have argued earlier, the costs of backtracking to technological paths that have been ignored are too costly to make commercial sense. Consequently, as a technology matures it changes from representing a set of possibilities and is transformed into a set of constraints. Programmable automation equipment can reflect the needs of large firms only or serve to displace skilled workers as management attempts to use a technological transition to change power relations on the plant floor. Alternatively, it can develop to provide products for a range of firms and be used to employ worker skills in collaborative production strategies. Because the new technologies have not yet become constraints, the consequences of PA are yet to be determined.

The real answer to the question of how the new production technologies will affect the structure of the economy, the location of jobs, and the organization of work is ". . . it depends." The consequences of the new production technologies are ambiguous.

Let us take the case of programmable automation, which we have focused on already. New production possibilities have been opened. A new set of technology opportunities has been established. Yet, more than one outcome is possible. Small Italian firms are currently building highly sophisticated equipment for sale on world markets.[50] At the same time, Matsushita, the huge Japanese consumer electronics firm, is combining the flexibility to vary product designs and volumes with market power; it is aiming at product variety and rapid turnover and using its massive networks to achieve new market penetration and market share gain. This is a moment of technological fluidity; not all things are possible, but in the range of possibilities one line of development has not yet congealed.

The new technologies can fit into a series of distinctly different economic and social settings. Stated more strongly, the technologies will be shaped by the social context in which they emerge. The new technologies will be used to solve market, management, and labor problems, and those needs will be different in each country. Policy, market structure, and labor arrangements will shape the development of the technology. Let us see why.

The contrast between American and Japanese policy is, again, significant. American policy in programmable automation has been conducted by the Defense Department and has been aimed primarily at the manufacture of weapons from aircraft to tanks. Japanese policy has been aimed at the development and diffusion of commercially applicable technologies. The policy of diffusion was in part aimed at ensuring that small firms could learn about the new technologies, find and develop machines appropriate to their needs, and lease them on favorable terms. The consequences are quite clear. American machine tool manufacturers dominate production of larger machines used for the most complex purposes. Japanese producers dominate production of smaller machines—the machines used for the broadest range of industrial purposes—and thereby control the mass market. They now control about half of the American market for numerically controlled machine tools. The Japanese control precisely that portion of the market that their policy addressed. The segment of the market retained by American producers reflects the development and diffusion policies of the U.S. government, which put its emphasis on applications for military use.

The available evidence suggests that the diffusion of both the new machines and the technology on which their advance rests is more widespread
in the Japanese economy. The diffusion process is apparently quite different in the two countries, the result of conscious public policy as much as
of corporate organization and strategy. Equally importantly, diffusion policy became policy that promoted the competitive development of distinct
segments of the NC machine tool industry.

The present mix of large and small firms in industries—what economists call "market structure"—will likewise shape how the new technologies will be used and, consequently, the way they will evolve. Technology
will not dictate market structure. As we have seen, economies of scale—
the volumes needed for efficient mass production—created a technological
advantage for large firms. Now automated production technologies permit
shorter production runs. Shorter production runs should permit small
firms, whether subcontractors or producers of final products, to design and
develop products that can be manufactured in competition with large
firms. Small companies may, in fact, adjust to an ever-shifting set of
market niches more rapidly than the slower moving giants. But evidence
suggests that scale economies in production are often relatively unimpor-
tant in determining the prominence of small or large firms in an industry.
Fixed costs in marketing, distribution, and finance are often more important barriers to new producers than production economies.

Thus, for small firms to capture the potential for competitiveness
implicit in the new production technologies, institutional supports—be
they public or private—are necessary. Italian small producers may be innovative and entrepreneurial, but they are vulnerable. For example, to continue with our case of programmable automation equipment, there must
first be manufacturers of PA equipment suited for use in small firms. In
America, as we just pointed out, the most technologically advanced equipment is generally developed for large users, and small users may suffer.
Second, there must be a network of service companies to maintain equipment. Large companies can provide service in-house. Small firms may not
be able to do so. Again, institutions to support small firms must exist.
There must be marketing channels and access to credit for small firms as
well as equipment producers aiming to meet their needs. Japan's policy of
financing the diffusion of programmable automation equipment (such as
robots and NC machine tools) to small producers is aimed at creating such
an environment. Similarly, studies of Italy's small producers show a particular institutional fabric that permits these firms to prosper. Once again we
come back to policy.

In nations where large firms are dominant or, better, where small firms are absent as major market or political forces, the giants will shape the emergence of programmable automation by defining initial markets for launching the sale of new production equipment and creating product standards that are best suited to their needs. Large firms may use these technologies simply to replace labor or to reduce component and product inventories. They may not use the potential for shorter production runs to build smaller plants. Rather, they may build plants that extend the range of products offered, and then defend their dominance by finding additional advantage in grouping related products together for distribution.

Another factor in how the new equipment will be used is the existing patterns of labor relations, the arrangements between labor and management, and the skills of the work force.[51] There is evidence that where skill levels are higher and there is labor peace, the new technologies can be implemented with less capital-intensive machines.

The risk for the United States is that the elimination of the skilled workers may have reduced the dynamic flexibility of the firms—their ability to continuously develop, absorb, and apply new production technology. Equally important, the kind and number of skills that the economy will require will not be determined unilaterally by the distant and disembodied force of technological development driven by competitive pressures. Skill requirements—the market's demands for labor—will also be significantly shaped by skill availabilities, but not in the tautological sense of markets always clearing at some price. Rather, the availability or scarcity of skills may shape competitive strategies as well as the development and application of particular technologies. Historical evidence suggests this to have been the case. We can see it as far back in the American past as in the origins of the mass production of muskets, which was an organizational and technological response to perceived shortages of craft skills. Today, and more so tomorrow, new degrees of flexibility in application are inherent in the new microelectronics-based technologies. But which of those new technologies are applied—and how—is, in part, a function of available skills. America appears to be investing far less than some of its competitors in factory floor robotics, in part because average U.S. manufacturing wages have been declining over the past dozen years, while they have been rising very rapidly for America's foreign competitors. Those nations, like Japan, are consequently among the fastest installers of robots. By contrast, America has been making massive efforts to develop and apply technologies that drastically lower engineering time in the design of microcircuits. Part of the reason for the interest in computer aided design for semiconductors is the U.S. shortage of design engineers. In each case, the technology is (or is not) being developed and introduced as a strategic response to skill availabilities and prices, real and perceived. Only careful empirical studies will suggest how binding technological constraints are, and how and when the technology is reshaped by its social setting.

While the economy is changing in substantial ways that will have profound impacts on skill requirements, *skill availabilities* and the relations between labor and management will influence which technical possibilities are in fact employed.[52] They will play a major role in shaping the *direction* of that economic change—that is, in determining the sectoral composition of GNP and the contents of economic activities. If the United States has a skilled work force and management strategies prepared to use that work force to create advantage, it will find technologies emerging to employ those skilled workers rather than replace them. Our conviction, moreover, is that a skilled and involved work force helps firms create the *dynamic flexibilities* required to sustain productivity increases.

Recent analyses of European competitiveness support this view.[53] Neither Sweden nor Germany were at the forefront of the development of computer aided design. But "their general level of skill training was such that they were quickly able to pick up and modify the new technologies to suit their domestic conditions."[54] In the United Kingdom a lack of adequate skills was a major constraint on the ability of firms to adopt new technologies. What is evident is that the ability to diffuse the new technologies in traditional sectors is as vital as the ability to develop them in the first place. Importantly, advanced technological development requires an elite of scientists and engineers. The diffusion of advanced technology, which is critical to national development, turns on a broadly educated and skilled population.

The consequences of the new production technologies, we repeat, are ambiguous. They will depend on the social context in which the technologies evolve. This has some very significant implications.

There are likely to be several simultaneous evolutions, several distinct national transitions. If so, the consequence will be a heterogeneous industrial world. Over the last years America has treated heterogeneity as different degrees of modernity or development and has tended to view development as progression on a single line. Thus, communities of small firms were thought to be anachronistic, politically protected leftovers that would one day erode to permit fully modern economies to emerge.[55] Another image that dominated thinking in the 1950s and 1960s was "convergence"—the several advanced nations would shake off their diverse pasts and converge toward a common future. We suggest that it is more likely that despite increasingly integrated international markets, the specific national conditions will encourage separate technological evolutions. It is an important premise of the overall argument in this book that a national industrial community still provides the central locus of technological innovation and diffusion. This is *not* to argue that these national developments will be entirely separate and distinct. Technologies and strategies emerging in one country will *diffuse* to others. Licensing and joint ventures, for example, are instruments of diffusion. In many industries, such as automobiles, joint ventures for development, component production, and even assembly are becoming important. Offshore production and contracting—manufacture by an American or Japanese firm in Korea or Taiwan for sale to the home market—serves to spread manufacturing know-how. Rather, there may be several distinct sources of production and product innovation.

Consequently, the question is not simply which national industrial economy will move most quickly into the electronics age, but also what form the innovation will take on in a given country, as well as what the pace of innovation and diffusion will be. There are, we repeat, two possibilities. First, one national evolution or innovation may prove dominant in international competition. This would not be simply a product of the inherent advantage of one production strategy over others. It would also be a function of the intensity of investment by one set of producers that pushes one technological line of development faster than others. Merely by dint of national market size and investment, a dominant development is most likely to emerge from Japan or the United States. In that case, other nations will have to move quickly to copy the new dominant production strategy or lose advantage and position in a range of manufacturing sectors. The power of the Fordist idea was an example of a dominant manufacturing strategy imposing itself internationally. American producers in the early twentieth century gained a substantial advantage for reasons that are not likely to reoccur. America's continental economy and its homogeneous population created a mass market and a need for the hierarchical management of giant corporations. Its antitrust policies accelerated the move to large integrated firms. Meanwhile, France, Italy, Japan, and even Germany were still throwing off their historical pasts. Now, the several advanced countries have managed the economic, political, and social transformations necessary for industrial development. Each can become the agent of autonomous development.

The second possibility is that several distinct evolutions will leave the world with a series of alternative uses of PA technologies. Each evolution may be suited best to particular market strategies and patterns of work organization. One standard paradigm, the dominant approach to manufacture, may give way to a variety of viable approaches. This may result in fundamental industrial variety.

Programmable automation is one element of the production changes occurring within the factory. The importance of the whole set of new production technologies will likely turn on the way they are interconnected, which leads us to the telecommunications story.

11

Dimensions of the Transition: The New Telecommunications Revolution[1]

E ACH INDUSTRIAL ERA has its own distinctive infrastructure. Mass production emerged in the United States together with the railroad, the highway, and the telegraph, and soon after came the telephone. These communications and transportation technologies generated the national market that mass production required, and formed an infrastructure that was the underpinning of the transition that brought America to industrial preeminence. Goods had to be ordered and then shipped in volume and raw material had to be transported throughout a continent. Without this infrastructure—the roads and bridges of the economy—it would not have been possible to build a continental economy.

In a world built on information technologies and microelectronics, the new infrastructure will be formed from the web of emerging telecommunications networks combining voice and data transmission. Today these new webs simply link computers; tomorrow they will make videoconferences— once fantasies and costly experiments—everyday matters. Corporate strategy and competitiveness in world markets will turn on a company's ability to implement the possibilities the new telecommunications technology represent. The location of factories and offices are already affected: back office operations can now be located in South Dakota, Arizona, or even Jamaica, entirely separated from corporate headquarters in San Francisco or New York.[2] The organization of production and production innovation will turn on the possibilities of the new telecommunications. The information network has become "one of the world's most effective productivity raisers."[3] This will prove true both in the factory and in the office.

Indeed, the pace of the diffusion and integration of programmable automation, which we discussed in chapter 10, may turn as much on the introduction and capabilities of these new networks than on innovation in and development of the particular equipment that compose the systems. Koji Kobayashi, the chairman of NEC, argues for the link between manufacturing and telecommunications:

> Consider for example the modern manufacturing plant. In order to respond to the shift from mass-orientation toward product diversity and individuality, and to meet a wider variety of customer needs, very large amounts of information will have to be generated. The transfer and processing of this information, moreover, will be done at the plant. And if sudden changes in the market occur, it will be necessary to rapidly adjust the design and manufacture of products accordingly. But for all this to occur, the flow of information at all levels, from the plant floor to the customer, will have to be coordinated. *C and C technology (Computer and Communication technology) has already begun to be the basis of such manufacturing and as it evolves the sophistication of manufacturing will grow.*
>
> It will be essential that such production systems be "distributed"—that they be close to their markets—and that information processing systems, both technical and administrative, be decentralized as well. Such systems will have to be "intelligent" and "friendly" in order to accommodate a wide variety of users so that broad participation in the manufacturing process and the quality of its products is assured. *At this stage, therefore, great advances in the technology of information processing are far more necessary than improvements in production technology.* [our italics][4]

It will take more than a traditional phone line to establish the distributed information processing networks in office and factory that Koji Kobayashi refers to.

Telecommunications decisions, like factory decisions, have taken on a broad significance they did not have before. "Corporate telecommunications is moving out of the controller's hands and into the chief executive's. What used to be a cost of doing business is becoming a source of competitive advantage."[5]

For all but the largest corporations, the possibilities will depend on how quickly the networks are implemented and what they are configured to do. While technical developments make possible these new national telecommunications networks, the character and configurations of each national network will be a product of market forces and policy choices. Once again the question arises: What does America want the technology to do? America's choices will heavily influence the economic consequences of the new technology. To understand how this country's choices about the new telecommunications technology will affect the American economy, let us take the case of small firms and programmable automation. PA, we noted, makes it possible to automate batch production in new ways. It makes possible substantial increases in productivity in batch production, which represents 75 percent of actual manufacturing operations. One implication is that large firms can now fragment markets for standard products, because they can achieve variety at substantially lower costs than before. A second implication is that since batch production is the domain of small and medium-sized firms it opens the possibility of radical increases in productivity. For such firms to enter the world of programmable automation, machines appropriate to their requirements need to be built —that is, a network of specialized suppliers has to exist or develop—and a telecommunication network to tie them into clients must be established. That network involves more than a phone line. It will require, in the end, that the production equipment in one small firm be able to speak to the design and production equipment in client firms.

So where is the difficulty? At the moment the United States is allowing the next generation network to be built to suit the needs of the largest firms, with the risk that the possibilities of productivity increases from the smaller batch production firms may be lost. It becomes tiresome to say this, but the Japanese have made substantially different choices. It appears they will weave a more homogeneous network that will entangle small and medium-sized firms in it. They are using public policy in telecommunications—as they have in robotics and machine tools—to permit small firms, not just large ones, to capture the productivity gains implicit in the new technologies.

New transportation and communication networks act as powerful agents of development because they open dramatically new sets of possibilities. They do so for several simple reasons. Initially, the network has to be built. Once the network is built, the corporate calculus of where to locate operations changes, provoking a broad wave of investment and producing real changes in economic geography. Corporate strategies and production organization are equally altered because the new telecommunications provide new ways of gaining market advantage. Those firms that implement these possibilities from the shop floor through the marketing division will be advantaged. Those that do not will lose out. Corporate choices, to come full circle, depend on the network that has been established or is emerging. The character of the network depends on America's policy choices.

Three issues must be addressed here: First, the convergence of computers and telecommunications technologies is creating a new infrastructure for the economy.[6] The erection of this infrastructure is as important to the contemporary world as the building of roads, bridges, railroads, electric grids, and telephone lines was to earlier periods. The character and configuration of the new telecommunications system—as much as the pace at which it is created—will structure opportunities for national profit and growth, as well as influence who can capture those opportunities. Policy will decide the question of whether—and in what combination—markets, monopolies, or regulated competition will generate the new infrastructure. Policy will determine the shape of the new system. Second, the telecommunications equipment and services industries (which are the communications components of the "information industry" in MITI's terminology) are now strategic industrial sectors. The expansion of these sectors will drive the whole economy through the current transition, provoking and employing technological evolution as well as simply absorbing additional production, in much the same way that automobiles did sixty-five years ago. Producing the equipment for the new system and delivering the myriad new services the technology makes possible will be a lucrative and expanding set of businesses. Equally important, these telecommunications industries will be a powerful, perhaps dominant, force in shaping the development of the computer and microelectronics industries in the coming years. A major question is whether policy makers will use the potentials of the telecommunications network to create a competitive advantage in those related areas. Third, the new telecommunications will alter the terms of competition among firms in sectors throughout the economy. It will reshape the way corporate users of the new technology create advantage in their markets. It will change the products sold, the way they are produced, and the fashion in which firms are administered. In sum, the new telecommunications will prod domestic growth, sponsor the evolution of electronics, alter corporate strategies and the competitive position of a range of user industries, and act as a vital component in trade. The emergence of this new economic infrastructure will itself transform the economy. Economic life will not be the same after it is in place. A fourth issue, which we do not confront in this essay, is the question of how standards are set that permit equipment in the industry to constitute one network. The new equipment must be constructed so that it can "talk" together. Either it must speak the same "language" or technical mechanisms to "translate" must be established. The standards are not neutral. They will influence whose equipment is purchased and what kind of services are made available to users in each country. The value of technologies that fit into networks depends on who else uses the technologies. The possibilities of the new technologies will depend on the configuration of the networks. Network standards emerge from a mix of market dynamics and policy decisions. Standards will be an intensely political issue domestically and internationally.

The New Communications Technology

There is a basic and radical technological change taking place in telecommunications. As with production technology, we need at least a passing glance at that change to understand its implications for the industrial transition. Two interrelated elements are at the center of the new telecommunications technology.

First, communications and computing have merged as the technologies underlying telecommunications and data processing have converged. The French refer to the convergence as *télématique;* the Japanese call it "computers and communications" (C&C). Digitization and distributed networks represent the basic shifts:

> During the 1970s the communications industry moved away from the pure provision of communication pathways for analog voice transmission toward the provision of enhanced communications (voice, data, video and facsimile) using computer technology. This change depended on the digitization of information, be it voice or data. Simultaneously the computer industry moved away from stand-alone computers toward networks of geographically separate computers interconnected through communications pathways for data transmission.[7]

These represent distributed communication and data networks. Consequently, the relatively distinct boundary lines between the two industries were blurred by the decade's end:

> Indeed, telecommunications in the 1980s and beyond will be characterized by the digitization of both national public-switched telephone networks and

private communications networks, and by the increasing linkage of data processing systems to both the public and private networks. Network integration, both within firms and externally in the public and private networks, is the overriding orientation of the current upheaval in telecommunications. Today, the telecommunications industry must be broadly understood to encompass the provision—for information networking—of terminal, transmission, and switching equipment, and voice, data, facsimile and video services.[8]

The convergence changes the character of competition and alters the services and products offered. The transformation will take place in two steps: an initial move toward integrated equipment and networks now, and a profound shift toward *broadband* networks and services later. The distinction between present integration and broadband nets depends on how much information can be carried along a transmission line. Broadband services, such as videoconferencing and bulk data transmissions, require different transmission facilities than more limited services. Consequently, a long phase of experimentation is just beginning, although the direction of evolution is clear.[9]

Second, innovative transmission and distributed switching technologies have proliferated. Technically and commercially viable alternative transmission techniques have undermined the traditional belief that transmission is a natural monopoly. Microwaves, fiber optics, cellular mobile radio, coaxial cables, and communications satellites all challenge the traditional copper wire. These alternative technologies retain the capacity to be interlinked, and consequently can constitute one telecommunications system. However, when combined with highly flexible and distributed digital switching systems, the alternatives represent competitive product packages offering a wide range of different services at different prices.[10] The end to a technological justification for monopoly in communications is critical.

A new telecommunications system will emerge in each country, built on and incorporating the new technologies, but not determined by them. As Borrus argues:

A frontier of new possibilities has been defined: a frontier which identifies the types of new products and services that can be made available. That frontier is itself a product of past choices about research and development to meet, create, or control user needs for communications in the market. Specific choices within the frontier of technological possibilities are not the product of technological change; they are, rather, the product of those who make the choices within the frontier of possibilities. Technology does not drive choice, choice drives technology. Grasping this point is critical, for there is nothing determinative, nothing inevitable about the ways in which the new technological possibilities of telecommunications will be implemented.[11]

In America, the technological possibilities were first released into the market by regulatory decisions to permit alternative transmission and networking products to hook up to the public telecommunications network, and by the legal decision to divest American Telephone and Telegraph (AT&T) of its local monopoly-operating companies and to permit that former monopoly supplier of telecommunications equipment and services to enter any other market. Underlying these regulatory and judicial decisions in the United States is the strongly held belief that the deregulated marketplace should decide how the new telecommunications changes will occur. The market is responding to the particular needs of the largest users of information in America—large businesses and government. We will return to this issue in the following pages.

Building the Telecommunications Network

Building railroads required steel, construction crews, locomotives, station houses, and telegraph (now fiber-optic transmission) systems. Similarly, the equipment and service industries that supply, create, and operate the new telecommunications networks will in themselves be an important focus of growth. Taken in the aggregate, the U.S. market for telecommunications equipment and services reached approximately $116 billion in 1983. This broke down roughly into: $100 billion in telecommunications network services and equipment, $14 billion in data communications equipment, and $2 billion in business communications applications.[12] Optimistic projections of growth suggest that the sector could reach to 10 percent of GNP. Such linear projections are usually silly extrapolations. This one may not be. At any rate, this enormous market is both an expression and product of the major changes occurring in telecommunications.

Equipping the digital telecommunications net will be essential to the development of each nation's electronics industry. Telecommunications, as Michael Borrus has shown, is crucial to the continuing development of the microelectronics and computer industries. In the 1950s military demand drove the development of transistors and computers. In the 1960s and 1970s business uses drove the computer industry, and computers and consumer products were the expanding demand that induced development of microelectronics. Telecommunications will play that leading role now. Demand for home computers may level off, but demand for computers to control telecommunications, central office switches, and private branch exchanges will steadily grow.

The reason lies in the convergence of computing and communications technologies. The sophisticated new services offered over the phone network rest on the abilities of digital, computer-controlled switches to separate control information from the communication and to process the respective digital information separately. The switches differ in purpose and capacity from PBXs [private branch exchanges] to a variety of local central office and toll switches. Since information is transmitted in digital form, it is also possible to encode video images or even documents in digital form and transmit them over phone lines. That also requires more sophisticated computers, a variety of new terminal equipment, from facsimile machines to video monitors and new wide-band transmission media like optical fiber linking the switches and terminals, to carry the enormous amount of data involved. It isn't simple, but many companies in America already offer computer mail services commercially. And in Japan they are already considering replacing first class mail service with the new, Japanese-pioneered facsimile services. In all of these cases, one computer is transmitting data to another computer. The telephone system is becoming a distributed computer network. Conversely, computers are being tied into data networks. It now becomes a choice of how much power and memory to put on the desk, how much to put off the desk, i.e. in a mainframe or mini, and how to link several computers together. The choice depends on the purpose of the system, the tasks of the various participants, their needs for common data and common applications. The computers are linked by telecommunications networking products like local area networks (LAN) or PBXs, and are linked into the public phone network as well. The convergence between the industries is real, not metaphorical. AT&T and IBM, NEC and Fujitsu are dominant in different parts of the same business, and would like to capture part of the others' markets.[13]

As telecommunications and computer networks are created they become a vast market for the computers that are the switches and for the microchips from which the computers are built.

Equally important the new networks will spark a secondary wave of investments. Each firm experiences new infrastructure—be it roads and bridges or broadband telecommunications—in the prices for land, transportation, and communication that it faces in the market. As the parameters of choice change, radical shifts in industrial location occur. It is evident that the cost of moving goods to markets or shipping raw materials to factories shapes choices about what is produced and where. In the United States in the nineteenth century, as rails replaced rivers as the dominant continental transport system, cities that had sprung up because they linked river traffic to inland farms lost advantage to communities that invested in the railroads. The North's control of the rail technology after the American Civil War, we might add, established the economic consequences of the rails.[14] The regulation of the nation's railroads in the mid-nineteenth century established prices to favor the shipment from northern to southern states of manufactured goods and from the South to the North of raw materials and agricultural goods. This directly slowed the industrial development of the southern states while spurring that of the North. The regulatory discrimination served to build the equivalent of a tariff wall around the North. When, after World War II, the interstate highway system was constructed, trucks began to compete more effectively with trains for freight transport. Businesses that depended on such transport, moreover, no longer needed to be tied to the railroad network. The highways and trucks, which permitted much greater decentralization, were sufficient. The freeway pulled firms and their workers out to the suburbs. In sum, as prices change to reflect new costs and new possibilities, locations adjust.

The new telecommunications infrastructure similarly alters the prices and possibilities for transportation and communication, and consequently it affects the location of all activity in an economy. The ramifications are only just beginning to be understood, but early hints are evident. A company's operations can be widely dispersed to different locations with all parts linked over private corporate or public communications networks. For example, insurance companies or financial enterprises that must process large volumes of data and paper can now locate the most labor-intensive parts of the activity away from the home office. Once the information is computer-stored, all parts of the operation can have immediate access to it from terminals located almost anywhere. IBM's internal Corporate Consolidated Data Network now links together about 16,000 terminals and 40,000 users throughout the United States with mainframe data bases in 18 different U.S. cities. The system is largely unattended and is remotely managed from IBM's Network Control System in New York. The savings in rent and labor costs and the increases in productivity make the cost of the new equipment and buildings worthwhile.

Using the Telecommunications Network

Those firms that understand, invent, and implement the new possibilities of the emerging telecommunications technology will gain advantage. Critically, corporate strategies at home and abroad will use the possibilities of the new technology to capture competitive advantage. We cannot, of course, demonstrate how technologies that are only now emerging will alter strategies in ways yet to be imagined. We can only speculate. But there are three kinds of evidence: analogy to other infrastructures that provoked strategy changes, the clear consequences of early uses of the convergence of computers and telephone to form the new telecommunications, and anecdotes suggesting the direction that the emerging technologies can go.

Part of the conviction about the strategic significance of the new technologies is by historical analogy. Railroads, then highways, recast both the location of production and the very conception of company strategies. The jet aircraft changed, again, the conception of distance and further blurred regional markets together to form a single national market. The telephone and telegraph, likewise, served to permit national and international markets. Vast numbers of buyers and sellers spread out over enormous distances could be connected together.

What, though, does the new telecommunications do, and how does the convergence of computer and telephone and the emergence of national data networks matter to company strategies?[15] Examples abound. National and international car rental reservation networks, which depend on the linkage between computers and communications, create enormous advantage for those firms that have them, relegating others to cut-rate strategies in local markets. Airline reservation systems, and the way they suggest flight options to travel agents, have already become hotly contested by those airlines, such as Braniff, whose seats are sold through the networks of their competitors. Pan Am has initiated a national network for flight arrival and departure information that can be accessed through touch tone phones. The first wave of automation in the insurance industry served to cut processing costs of traditional policies. The second wave of automation altered the mix of insurance products and how they were sold.[16] Indeed, electronic financial networks have shattered the institutional walls between different elements of the financial system in each nation. American Express, confronted with rival credit cards, has created a range of computer network-based services to provide new services and hold its customers. The list of service industries dependent on computer nets could continue almost endlessly. In many cases, users are now so dependent on telecommunication nets that they establish wholly controlled private lines, and in the case of the largest users, they establish wholly controlled nets that bypass the public channels. Internal control of telecommunications does not simply save money; rather it permits a firm to establish its own network, assure the system works, and arrange the configuration to its own needs. In sales and distribution industries—be they retail, catalog, or wholesale—the information nets are essential.

In manufacturing, data networks are becoming equally critical. Computer integrated manufacturing has begun to be discussed and attempted in limited ways. The hopes are ambitious: computer aided design linked to computers that control the configuration and operation of production and inventory control systems tied to the actual operation of factories. Networks linking the various computers on production equipment, in design centers, in inventory offices, and in strategy offices must be established. Indeed, the various computers need to be able to share information and talk to each other. The problem of linking them is being addressed by local area networks and private branch exchanges. The central importance of the problem is suggested by General Motors's pronouncement that all suppliers of programmable automation equipment must assure that the controlling computers are compatible with a standard MAP (manufacturing automation protocol) being set by GM.[17] Certainly the reorganization of production itself will depend on communicating computers.

Flexible manufacturing strategies that allow rapid response to market changes will also depend on these new data communication nets. In the apparel industry, as we saw in an earlier chapter, the made-to-order custom-cut machine-manufactured garment and the linking of store data to variable production in volume suppliers such as Benetton have emerged. The latter phenomenon is becoming widespread. Product code scanners at check-out counters in grocery and department stores are now generating an incredible sea of information. Whereas once a company such as Johnson and Johnson would be supplied with market information by Nielsen surveys done every two weeks, they can now receive a weekly sales report broken down by store showing where each sale took place.[18] Without the automatic digital collection and assembly of data, dependent on the networks, this would not be possible. That data and the capacity to analyze it are becoming weapons in market struggles. Indeed, computer companies like Metaphor have developed specially configured microcomputers, data banks, and analytic software to permit firms to address these mountains of data. Finally, in the semiconductor industry, firms are emerging that produce packages consisting of CAD equipment, software, and design data that permit their customers to design their own circuits. Those designs are then transmitted to the producer firm, which then feeds the data into its production nets and manufactures the design.

The uses we have sketched have been based on the earliest versions of integrated data/voice nets. Traditional copper phone lines, for instance, have limited capacity to carry information. The networks now envisioned —and currently being experimentally built, around optical fiber, for instance—will permit a fundamentally new range of services because they will be able to carry radically larger amounts of data. The services the new networks permit will emerge as the infrastructure to provide them is established. As suggested before, the Japanese talk of replacing the first-class letter with a linked net of facsimile machines, for example. The costs of the facsimile machines would be held down by the volumes produced and perhaps subsidized with savings from wages of unneeded letter carriers. For now only satellites can carry the volume of data needed to experiment with these services. Some experiments suggest their implications for business strategy and location. IBM, for example, has reported that by using videoconferencing, product development was speeded 30 percent. More conversations using less travel time permitted groups at different locations to work together effectively.[19] Even with today's primitive equipment, the costs of the conferencing were recovered in time and travel costs not spent. In a business where early product development is essential and where large-scale projects can take years, such a cut in development time can become a truly important competitive weapon.

Slowly, telecommunications is changing from being an aid to business in conducting old strategies to an element in formulating and implementing completely new strategies. We cannot review the full range of developments in strategy and location. We need only recognize that the characteristics and possibilities of the new networks will induce and compel a wave of investment and adjustment.

Regulation, Industrial Development, and Trade

In sum, the transformation of the telecommunications infrastructure in each country will have four powerful effects on the national economy: (1) The network will have to be built, which is an enormous investment. (2) Building that network will require substantial volumes of sophisticated computers, microchips, and software. Telecommunications firms will powerfully shape the development of the entire electronics sector and, through it, the sectors that use electronics. (3) The profit opportunities created by the new equipment will provoke a secondary wave of investment as firms and individuals move to adjust to the changed costs and new possibilities. (4) Firms in all sectors will seek market advantage through the telecommunications services the transformed infrastructure will make possible.

In each country the telecommunications transformation will be shaped by government policy and the dynamics of international trade, albeit differently in the several cases. There will be intense domestic and international political conflict. The choice of policy will have broad consequences. It will affect the international competitive position of the electronics industries in each country. It will influence the ability of firms in each country to invent and implement new corporate strategies dependent on the new networks as well as their ability to achieve new production efficiencies through internal reorganization and relocation. There are three distinct public strategies for managing the emergence of the new infrastructure.[20] The United States has *deregulated*—that is, it has left market competition to shape the basics of the public infrastructure. Japan has *developmentally reregulated*—that is, it has changed the terms of regulation both to provoke competition as a means of assuring rapid diffusion and product development and to retain public control over the nature of the system as a whole. European countries, with the debatable exception of Britain, have *retained a traditional utility structure of regulation.* The United States, Japan, and Europe represent contrasting approaches to the trade and development elements of the telecommunications transition. The several strategies will have critical national consequences. Moreover, the domestic choices of one nation will critically affect the development of all other nations. This is particularly true of the United States and Japan.

From our perspective, the question is whether those policies will lay down and promote the use of an infrastructure that will allow the national economy to capture the benefits of the new telecommunications. American policy hopes to capture the benefits as a result of market competition. Japan intends to direct the process of developing the new telecommunications to capture the "externalities" of the new network. Europe hopes that marginally modified traditional approaches will suffice to leave it competitive in telecommunications equipment and services.

Traditionally, telephones were thought to be a bit like electricity, an undifferentiated product best provided by a monopolist. The new telecommunications permits real competition among providers and real differences in the nature of the services that they provide. In the United States a market driven system is being substituted for the regulated monopoly of AT&T. The choice to deregulate is "a choice to let competition in the market meeting major user needs drive the evolution of communications."[21] U.S. policy assumes that the proper network will be generated by a series of regional companies, a set of competing long-distance companies, and a bevy of firms providing specialized services. In fact, the United States risks developing a system aimed at large users, but not necessarily designed to facilitate the adaptation of the economy as a whole.

Policy choices matter because technical interrelations and economies of system scale mean that the user of any piece of equipment depends on the links to other users. Not only do casual users recognize that IBM and

Apple machines can talk to each other only with translators, if at all, but major users such as GM impose standards on its suppliers of factory equipment. A network can evolve in a variety of ways: (1) by establishing a monopoly (such as AT&T in the "old days") and regulating it; (2) by imposing standards on all equipment makers; or (3) by allowing market forces to establish a standard. The value of an IBM machine is greater because there are so many other users. Apple is compelled to make its machines talk to IBM. Consequently, one standard may emerge, de facto, as the industry standard. The network that emerges from the market will be set by the needs and capabilities of early users and suppliers. A sound route for long-term development—a route that creates dynamic possibilities above static efficiencies—will not automatically emerge from the market. Because the externalities from private choices are so great, government policy can have enormous positive influences.

Yet policy makers are powerfully limited in their capacity to make real choices. Paul David explains this well.[22] First, there is the "Narrow Policy Windows Paradox." The "windows for effective public policy intervention at comparatively modest resource costs" tend—as we argued earlier—to be at the beginning of a technology development. There is only a brief moment, a narrow window, during which policy can influence technology development. The difficulty is that at the moment when policy influence is greatest, the problem is understood the least by policy makers. This is the "Blind Giants Quandary":

> . . . public agencies are at their most powerful in exercising influence upon the future trajectory of a network technology just when they know the least. The important information . . . concerns which characteristics of the particular technologies . . . users eventually will value most highly; and what possible differences exist between the potentialities which the available variants have of undergoing future technical enhancements as a result of cumulative, incremental innovation.[23]

We would add that the question of *what* user needs is also the question of *which* users will have access to the possibilities of the network. David contends that the task of policy must be to prevent the "windows of opportunity from slamming shut before the information needed for policy is available."[24]

American policy has decided to allow the market to create the new infrastructure and set the network standards. It will not, as a matter of national policy, attempt to shape the next generation media. Nor will it attempt to create market advantage for American firms or exploit the close link to the other information industries. The infrastructure that emerges in America will reflect the needs of our major businesses and government as delivered in the form of network products and services by the new AT&T, the divested Bell local operating companies, and the myriad of competitors that are emerging at the national and local levels. The infrastructure will undoubtedly be highly diverse, composed of both wholly private and public information networks that are interlinked but are accessible, for the most part, only to major users rather than to all Americans. The hand of policy will be limited, and as a consequence, important strategic issues will not be faced up-front. These include the loss of Bell Labs as a national R&D facility in electronics and related technologies, and the loss of opportunities to set standards in ways that could create advantage on world markets for domestic and foreign firms operating in the United States. The significance of the change in the role of Bell Laboratories cannot be overestimated. In the years of regulation, Bell Labs was virtually a public laboratory. AT&T's own service operations were a regulated monopoly, and they were restricted by regulation from competing in component and equipment markets. Consequently, the laboratory was free to be wide open to all. It would make certain it had access to international technology advances, but it would transfer its technology to all comers. Bell Labs acted as a technology pump for the economy, pulling technology in and watering the national technology garden.[25]

Other serious strategic issues, like the opening of our market to foreign competition without reciprocity, will be dealt with on an ad hoc basis by Congress—something that will alternately create and resolve international tensions. "Overall, market-led development of the information industries and infrastructure in the U.S. will create tremendously dynamic competitive market opportunities, but the apparent cost is the loss of strategic and reasoned policy guidance over the changes taking place."[26]

By contrast, the new telecommunications infrastructure emerging in Japan will combine competition in the market between Nippon Telephone and Telegraph (NTT), major Japanese companies both private and public, and foreign firms like IBM and AT&T, with continued policy guidance aimed at ensuring that the new infrastructure serves important public goals. Japanese policy seems to be consciously shaping the character and configuration of the network. This combination of market competition and policy guidance is certainly quite different from the completely market-led approach adopted in the United States. We suspect that Japan's efforts will be highly successful in creating a very efficient new communications infrastructure for the Japanese economy. Japan's way through the maze of changes also strategically retains the potential to use the procurement for that network as an instrument of development for Japanese industry. The American concern is that the Japanese market will continue to be closed in strategic ways and that Japanese policy will continue largely to favor established Japanese producers and help to prepare them for competition on world markets. U.S. firms should find increased opportunities to sell equipment and services in Japan as a result of the partial liberalization of the domestic market effected by the new laws. However, the Japanese market business of U.S. firms will continue to be subject to regulatory control by the Japanese government—in particular, the Ministry of Posts and Telecommunications (MPT). Indeed, because that continued regulatory control will be less formal than in the past, U.S. firms worry that they will find their opportunities systematically limited in ways less amenable to resolution through government-to-government negotiations. If Japanese policy appears to discriminate against American firms, it makes their domestic policy an international issue. We emphasize that an asymmetry in telecommunications trade—a substantially open American market and a substantially closed or difficult to access Japanese market—will not be politically stable.

The trade issue may fade or be resolved; but the dynamic possibilities represented by network configurations will be enduring features of each national economy. Those configurations will set constraints on how the new technologies can be exploited and by whom.

As in the case of production technology, the central point is that public choices will shape the terms of the transition. Government policies about how networks are organized will massively influence *which* possibilities for sustained, competitive economic growth are captured and which are missed. Those policies will result in differently configured telecommunications networks with distinct potentials for use and industrial development.

12

Choices America Faces:
Issues That Will
Shape the Transition

THE SHAPE of the industrial transition is an open question. It will depend on the choices America makes. We have focused here on new production technology, particularly programmable automation, and on telecommunications as elements of the shifts occurring in industry. We might, alternatively, have examined such matters as how robots and robotic vision systems affect the range of tasks that can be automated, or the possibilities of biotechnology altering chemical processing in another generation. Or along an entirely different line, we might have chosen to focus on the purely organizational changes that have begun to alter the image of the modern corporation as a tightly structured bureaucracy or on the emergence of flexible manufacturing in small firms in Italy and Japan. We have tried only to convince the reader that profound, enduring changes in the production process are occurring that have substantial implications for corporate strategy, work organization, competitiveness, and productivity —just take your pick from this or a longer list. What is not open, however, is the necessity of making the transition quickly and competitively.

Even if the United States rapidly begins implementing the new technologies, its problems and choices will not end. Many fear that the new automation will destroy more jobs than it creates, that in defending industry against new competition the United States will be undermining the manufacturing employment base of the economy. In autos and apparel, American production has dropped as American firms have lost market share to imports. The corporate efforts to defend these markets by lowering costs through domestic automation meant that direct employment on the production lines dropped even further.[1] BRIE studies demonstrate that the major effect of trade on employment is an acceleration of production innovation.[2] Only the firms—be they in so-called advanced or traditional sectors—that can effectively exploit the potentials of new technologies through product and production innovation will survive. In sectors such as telecommunications and semiconductors, even though output rose, employment did not keep pace and even fell.[3] Manufacturing innovation resulting from the character of new products stripped jobs off the production line. A central office switch was once an electromechanical product produced by 3,250 workers. Today it is a digital product manufactured by 120. While direct production employment has dropped, the costs of design and development have skyrocketed from $50 million to between $500 million and a billion dollars.[4] Design and development is principally sophisticated labor. The chain of support behind manufacturing has lengthened, and certainly many of the new workers are in firms categorized as being in the service industry.

The fears that automation will destroy employment have been heard before, of course, and were not fulfilled. Rather, increased productivity generated new demand and new employment while the arrangements for production were reorganized. Is there anything new that should alter a calculus based on past experience? Perhaps there is. In periods of slow growth, new jobs in expanding sectors and related activities are not generated as rapidly as old jobs are destroyed by production modernization. This, precisely, is the meaning of rising unemployment rates in Europe and of dropping manufacturing wages in the United States.[5] Is this slow growth a phenomenon of the business cycle or a new feature of the present stage of development? We do not wish to enter this debate because the answers—as important as they are—do not affect the case we are building. The changes in production must come. The traditional assembly line will be altered and employment stripped out. America could avoid these changes only by insulating itself from world markets and accepting a decline in the American economic position. Two political problems bound America's choices. First we must recognize that any long-term declines in wages and job availability will politically strain a society and pose macroeconomic problems. Second, we must ask who will pay for and benefit from the reorganizations required to sustain growth? A failure to resolve these problems equitably will reduce the nation's capacity to adjust to new markets and technologies. The politics of industrial adjustment are indeed central to the process of economic growth in each advanced country.

Here we confront a narrower question: What kind of production revolution will be created? We raised two questions at the start of this part of the book: Will firms automate at home or move production offshore in search of cheaper labor and less expensive components? Will the United States attempt to implement the technology to reinforce, or to undermine, the skills of its workers. In our minds the two issues are inextricably intertangled and of extraordinary importance.

American producers over the last years have moved their production offshore, not simply to be closer to their foreign markets, but to find inexpensive labor and components to reduce the cost of products they sell in the United States. Offshore production has been spawned both by the pressure of imports and by competition among American firms. It has been sustained by policy both in the United States and in the countries where export platforms have been located.[6] In the last years some American firms found another reason to move production abroad: they sought to escape some of the consequences of the high value of the U.S. dollar.

The move abroad is cumulative—that is, for each firm or group of firms, the move abroad builds on itself in two ways. First, an offshore production network has been developed that functions as a real alternative to a domestic net. When the first producers went abroad they had to supply many of the component parts and production services from an American base. Their suppliers often moved offshore with them, to be closer to the point of final production and to capture some of the same advantages of government aid and low-cost labor. Foreign component makers also began to supply American offshore producers. For example, the American semiconductor industry has found that when their clients move offshore they begin to buy components from offshore sources as well.[7] In some cases American firms have subcontracted their production abroad, transferring the product and production know-how. Once component sources are offshore, there is often a temptation to move product assembly offshore; as product assembly moves, additional moves offshore of component suppliers are again encouraged. Once the bulk of production is offshore, there comes a moment when it is seriously tempting to move product engineering abroad. This is not fanciful. We have heard such discussions in American firms. Offshoring has often speeded the emergence of a company's own competitors by transforming technology production. Let us be clear though; the move offshore gives a one-time labor cost advantage. Production innovation and investment in capital offshore is required to sustain that advantage.

Second, after years of moving abroad to find cheap labor to produce existing products at lower costs, American firms built up an expertise in the management of offshore production. Often investment in offshore production expertise is an alternative to building up expertise in implementing the most advanced production technologies or in designing or redesigning a product to facilitate automated production in the United States. Over time, the perception that foreign competition could be met by offshore production took form and force. Even a few years ago, when it was already evident that the Japanese had invested massively in domestic production, some in the semiconductor industry were still calling for more offshore locations as a viable response. Some major corporations have built formal models to set a framework for these choices, but the models (in our view) are often built on quite incorrect assumptions about exchange rates and on learning curves that serve simply to justify their biases.

We do not intend to exaggerate. There are many reasons for moving offshore. Sometimes it is necessary to locate production facilities close to foreign markets, and sometimes access to foreign technology requires research and production facilities abroad. There are often good cost-of-production reasons for being offshore. Many goods or pieces of production processes cannot be automated effectively and absorb enormous amounts of labor; those that can be cheaply and easily shipped are thus clear candidates for offshore production or assembly. The Japanese pattern has been different, but we also do not wish to glorify Japanese management. Initially, lower wage rates and an undervalued currency encouraged Japanese firms to move offshore. The Japanese did invest massively in domestic production innovation. Only with the radical increase in the value of the yen in 1986 have Japanese firms begun to consider whether the limits of domestic production innovation for standard goods have been reached.[8] Many are building on their domestic manufacturing strength.

However, as programmable automation emerges, the mix of activities that can be carried out in the United States will expand. We suggest simply that earlier moves offshore may blind firms to the possibilities—and now needs—to automate at home. We have considered in our discussion consumer electronics and semiconductor production choices. Let us take still another case, computer disk drives, where the earlier stories seem to be repeating themselves. Our reaction to this case runs to the old saw about not learning from our mistakes. American producers have made product innovations, but their manufacturing technology has not kept pace. The bias of American producers is for product—but not process—innovation.[9] Japanese competitors have emphasized both. Once again it appears that Japanese production advantages will allow them to push ahead of their American competitors.

> *Given the lack of advanced manufacturing processes and the low level of verticle integration of U.S. disk drive manufacturers, some industry observors wondered whether the U.S. firms could move down the steep learning curves associated with product costs in an industry like disk drives.* While the use of state of the art production technology applied in judicious product redesigns combined with aggressive purchasing could do much to improve product costs, *failure to use automated process technology and verticle integration might slow such improvements enough so that more aggressive competitors could outstrip U.S. drive manufacturers as volumes increased and products matured.* [our italics][10]

How did one American producer, Shugart Corporation, deal with this problem when making choices about where to manufacture? Shugart was not comfortable with a strategy of domestic production innovation, and consequently chose to put off to another day what it recognized as the need to build distinctive manufacturing competencies that would be needed for survival.

> . . . for Shugart's management, [domestic automation] did not appear to be a serious contender. This was due in part to their lack of familiarity with automation and its requirements, to their desire to limit capital investment, to their desire to maintain flexibility, and to their desire to maintain what had historically been very high return on assets. One of the firm's manufacturing engineers had argued eloquently that such automation would create barriers to entry for would-be competitors, it would enhance product consistency, and would give Shugart an early start in developing these distinctive competencies —which most agreed would eventually be required to stay in the business. However, the general consensus among Shugart engineers was that a product had to be "designed" for automation for it to be successful. *Besides, to most of Shugart's management, such an option just didn't feel comfortable.*[11]

So what did Shugart do? They established an offshore joint venture with MCI, a piece of the Matsushita group.

> Basically Shugart provided product designs (based on their close customer contact and their in-house design capabilities), MCI procured the materials (often from other Matsushita companies) and manufactured the product, and then Shugart distributed and serviced the drives to its worldwide customers (excluding Japan).[12]

In essence, Shugart transferred its core advantage in product innovation to one of its strongest potential competitors, allowing that competitor an enormous home market in which to gain mastery of the product.

Other American firms have turned to domestic automation. A crucial question then is what will it take for American firms to routinely turn to domestic production innovation as a means of holding market? What will it take in terms of management understanding and support of flexible production and process innovation? What will it take in the form of workplace relationships and work force skills to implement such strategies? American production must confront high wages and, compared to its competitors, high capital costs. What troubles us, though, is that traditional manufacturing strategies, aimed at using capital simply to replace and to control labor, have the double disadvantage of requiring expensive capital and stripping out of the production process what must in the end be a distinctive American advantage—a skilled and educated labor force.

What then should America do, in its firms and in government policies? That is the subject of the last part of this book.

PART III

Creating

Advantage

13

Toward an
American Consensus

WHAT, then, do we do? To establish priorities for America, policy makers must take as fundamental assumptions the conclusions we reached in Parts I and II. First, manufacturing matters. There is, as yet, no such thing as a post-industrial economy, no matter how the sociology of work may evolve. And its advent is not imminent. Erosion of American mastery and control of production will result in the erosion of American wealth and power. Second, American industry is not doing at all well in international competition; its capacity to remain competitive in the high-wage and high-value-added segments of industry is eroding. The problem is not simply one of exchange rates, though the high value of the dollar in recent years certainly exacerbated matters. Rather, the competitive problems lie in a long-term weakening of our capacities to make and sell products in world markets. Third, industry worldwide is undergoing a fundamental transition, a transition driven by shifting patterns of competition and evolving technology.

We must also recognize that three constraints on America's choices exist. First, the United States cannot compete in world markets by cutting wages. We did not do this in the past when wage differentials with our leading competitors—the advanced countries—were far greater than they are now. And to cut wages to Korean or Brazilian levels would represent a total, and catastrophic, change in our society. Second, a retreat to defensive trade protection will not serve as a sustained or long-term policy to support high wages and sustained productivity. The arguments against protection are quite clear. Protection triggers reciprocal responses by other nations and ultimately shrivels the volume of international trade so that everyone loses—but not, we should note, equally. It simply reduces the pressure on firms to make the product and production changes required to be competitive. It reduces the effectiveness of the fundamental, long-term process of wealth generation. Over time, as U.S. firms fall behind in innovation and in competitiveness, they will need more and more protection. Certainly, British efforts at constructing a system of Imperial Preference to insulate its industry in international markets from the emergence of Germany and other competitors did not succeed. Not only did the system not protect British industry, but it fooled British firms about the nature of the competition they really faced and resulted in catastrophic strategies and tactics. There may be circumstances in which the costs of adjustment or unfair tactics abroad make us turn to tactical protection, but as a long-term national strategy it will not work as a solution to our economic problems.

Internationally, it would mean America walking away from its role as leader of the international economic system. The lesser problems associated with such a move might be the collapse of the world debt structure. The biggest ones fall into categories of alliance instability. The policy problem of assuring our own competitiveness is not a matter of capturing gains from others, but of assuring our own ability to participate fully in the possibilities of the new economy that is emerging. Third, policies that are radically inequitable are unlikely to generate the broad political support required to sustain a national commitment to the priorities of competitiveness. The evidence is overwhelming that sustained growth requires a stable political solution to the question of how to allocate the costs and gains of development. When the gains are allocated to some and the costs to others, such arrangements are rarely stable. When controversy about who wins and who loses from industrial changes percolates, stable deals about how to promote competitiveness are rare. So the question is: How do we assure sustained growth with high-wage labor and without protection?

These assumptions and constraints make certain national objectives clear. America requires high-wage industry that is competitive in world markets. High-wage industry requires that American firms be well situated in high-value-added segments of production, for only high value added will permit us to sustain high wages. Unfortunately, there are no automatic or clear-cut answers to where high value added is to be found. Some rather complex components that go into assembly are commodity products with prices driven down close to cost by competition, while others are unique elements that command premium prices. Likewise, some final goods are premium goods with distinct qualities that permit the "economic rents" needed to support high wages, while others are not. And the lists change quickly. Only a sustained capacity for design and manufacturing innovation will permit American firms to sustain high-value-added industry, and that in turn depends upon mastery and control of production as well as innovation and design.

Policy should pursue the competitive evolution of the American economy. We must—for the first time perhaps—make policy with priority attention to the dynamics of international competition, and to manufacturing competition in world markets in particular. We must succeed in and adapt to changing world markets, for we can no longer ignore them or shape the rules of play in those global markets to suit our preferences. Let us elaborate upon the definition of national competitiveness introduced in Chapter 5:

> A nation's competitiveness is the degree to which it can, under free and fair market conditions, produce goods and services that meet the test of international markets while simultaneously expanding the real incomes of its citizens. International competitiveness at the national level is based on superior productivity performance and the economy's ability to shift output to high-productivity activities which in turn can generate high levels of real wages. Competitiveness is associated with rising living standards, expanding employment opportunities, and the ability of a nation to maintain its international obligations.

As we noted:

> it is not just a measure of the nation's ability to sell abroad and to maintain a trade equilibrium. The very poorest countries in the world are often able to do that quite well. Rather, it is the nation's ability to stay ahead technologically and commercially in those commodities and services likely to constitute a larger share of world consumption and value added in the future. Clearly, a nation's ability to compete internationally is reflected by its ability to maintain favorable terms of trade, which in turn governs the ease with which its citizens can maintain their international obligations while enjoying steadily rising real incomes.

We emphasized that:

> national competitiveness will . . . rest on competitive firms generating productivity levels needed to support high wages, especially in growth sectors. The

competitiveness of firms depends upon the quality and quantity of physical and human resources, the manner in which resources are managed, the supporting infrastructure of the economy, and the policies of the nation.[1]

National and corporate competitiveness are analytically distinct but practically intertwined.

Competitive adjustment of the firm or the nation must, in this transition, be built on the ability to generate and apply product and process innovation. As we explored in Part II, it is not just a matter of innovation, but of the ability to exploit innovation in the market. That depends mightily—for both company and nation—on the capacity to produce competitively. Competitive production capabilities will depend on the effective introduction and mastery of the new programmable production equipment in a strategy of dynamic flexibility that permits rapid adaptation to markets. Policy must target the processes of production and of technological evolution and diffusion. *First,* production is our competitive weakness, a weakness that makes our very real strengths vulnerable. If we do not get substantially better than we now are at production, we will lose the value of our advantage in product innovation and, before very long, the advantage itself. American firms will not be able to control what they can't produce. Technology diffuses quickly, and when sold as licenses captures few rents. The lessons of the last years make that very clear. Because technology spreads quickly, it leaves few advantages in the simple creation of scientific or technological knowledge or in the investment in simple machines. *Second,* we emphasize that a central characteristic of this transition is the profound effect that the new technologies will have on traditional industries. The United States cannot advance along narrow but isolated lines of technological development. The nodes, the intersections of high technology with traditional industries will prove critical in national development. The new technologies of this era are transformative in their effect. Thus, all depends on how this knowledge is used throughout the economy. Nor is the problem purely technical, for only a strategic and organizational imagination permits the possibilities the new technologies represent to be explored fully. Using technological innovation to create and hold market positions for entire industries requires a deep and broad effort. That, in the end, rests on the investment in people, in human capital, and not just narrowly in engineers or scientists—though certainly that— but broadly in the community as a whole. In a world where technology and capital are highly mobile, the quality of a nation's work force will be critical to its ability to apply and diffuse technology.

The stakes in the choices we face are high. There are a variety of possible economic futures open to America. Let us exaggerate and imagine a spectrum. At one end lies an internationally competitive U.S. economy in which highly productive, skilled workers apply their abilities to make use of the new technologies and flexibly produce a broad range of high-quality, valued goods and services. They thereby earn the high wages necessary to sustain both the standard of living to which some Americans have grown accustomed and most aspire, and the open society that has been so closely linked with a strong and open economy. At the other end of the spectrum lies a real danger of a competitively struggling economy in which a small minority of high-skilled research, development, and service jobs coexist with a majority of low-skilled, low-wage jobs and massive unemployment. Living standards—perhaps along with social equality and political democracy—would deteriorate rapidly as manufacturing and services, in order to compete, move offshore and automation strips the labor content from the remaining U.S. goods and services.

The Quixotic Pursuit of the Magical Cure: The Search for Solutions

There are no simple formulas to cure our national economic ills, no one magic thing to do that will right it all. America's policy makers must try to avoid the temptation to search out and believe in the instant solution. It is not primarily an intellectual-scientific problem amenable to a techno-logical solution: a vaccination, a nuke, a heart transplant. Even a cursory glance at the history of economic crises shows that remedies do not come fully constructed from the "Solution Store" nor (*pace* Keynes) are they strokes of inventive genius.[2] Political bargaining and policy experimenta-tion have often produced unexpected answers, answers that only took on names and orthodox respectability after their success. Keynesian theory was formally developed in England, but the notions were implemented on an ad hoc basis and without the benefits of labels and theories elsewhere. Sometimes those very solutions had been sitting on the cluttered shelves of the Solution Store, but they were not part of an understanding of a problem, a ranking of priorities, an organization of trade-offs. They were not yet part of a political debate and therefore far from being part of a political solution.

Solutions abound. There are lists and lists of them. First there are the "we musts": We must lower the cost of capital. We must make investment capital more patient. We must change our system of industrial relations that is grounded in mistrust, scorn, and inflexibility. We must debureaucratize the corporation. We must make an effort to sell abroad. We must learn foreign languages. We must reduce theft—or at least push it out of the plant and into the store. We must educate our youth, and perhaps our not-so-young, for productive survival in a competitive and changing world. All of these ideas and many, many others are eminently sensible.

There is also an abundance of "how to" solutions: First, of course, cut the deficit. Then, in no particular order, and with no endorsement at all: shift taxes from producers to consumers; force open Japanese capital markets so that world prices and terms prevail there; cut government spending on social programs and undeserving causes and use the resources to underwrite the competitive economy either through tax cuts or through direct spending; ditto for defense spending; again, for farm programs; increase government health spending, but finance it out of consumer incomes (not payrolls), thus removing the burden of health and pensions from the competitive sector; provide protection at the border to a particular industry; go whole hog and protect them all; the list could be extended almost indefinitely—the shelves of the Solution Store are piled high, and the classification schemes confused.

Politics and Priorities: The Framework for Debate

At its core the challenge is political not technical. Deciding what our goals are must precede a debate about how to implement them. Successfully adjusting to the emergence of new competition, to the changes in world markets, and to the appearance of transformative technologies is as central a national concern as defense or security policy. If we fail to do that, all our other objectives become secondary because we won't have the resources to achieve them or the social and political will to pursue them. Nonetheless, a competitive and efficient economy is ultimately a means not a goal in itself. There are other essential national objectives. Not least among them, for instance, is the need to assure a just and decent community not just a rich society. The investment and reorganization required to adjust to world markets must—at least in the short run—clash with other social objectives. Indeed, industrial development can aggravate social divisions. It always involves gains and costs, but these are never evenly or equitably spread. The question of course is who reaps the gains and who pays the costs of an emphasis on competitive development and of the particular strategies chosen to pursue that emphasis. A politically stable settlement allocating these costs and gains must be achieved. Otherwise the endless conflicts about such matters as whose consumption is reduced to assure savings and which protections against market changes are removed to assure a flexible economy will stalemate American development.

How do we go about accomplishing this central political task of reorienting our priorities? There are three mechanisms by which advanced countries have set priorities and established stable political settlements on which to base growth in the years since World War II.[3] First, in many of the smaller European countries as well as in Germany there have been direct negotiations among crucial social and economic groups, between labor and business. Indeed, in the years between World Wars I and II in some countries quite explicit bargains were reached.[4] In Sweden the deal was clearly enough specified that it could be expressed as a formal economic model.[5] These social bargains meant that the stronger groups did not use the full force of their power against their rivals, but rather tended to compensate those damaged by industrial growth. In these countries rapid growth and labor power have been perfectly compatible. It is a style of governance that has come to be called "corporatism." But America does not have a social structure with highly centralized interest groups that would permit a bargain built on a corporatist style of negotiation.

Second, in Japan and France, where the state executive imposed a pattern of policy that both forced growth and amounted to a settlement of how the price of rapid growth would be paid.[6] Labor's power was fragmented, and it had no role in direct policy making in either country. In Japan a mixture of company unions, lifetime employment, and dual labor markets integrated labor in production while blocking the organization of a radical national movement. In France a politically and ideologically divided labor movement had little influence in the firm or plant and none in politics. Through the fast-growth years, policy in both countries rested on conservative coalitions. In both countries the process of development and industrial modernization inevitably displaced the very groups that were the natural constituencies of the conservatives. Managing modernization, indeed creating and preserving market processes, was thus a very delicate political game. The Japanese conservatives, but not the French we might add, managed the political consequences of the social transformation generated by industrial growth without losing power although the French conservatives did far better at holding power than they ever imagined or even permitted themselves to remember. The United States has neither the bureaucratic structure nor the political system to even begin thinking about a strategy of state-led development.

Finally, in the United States there has been a pattern of market-led growth in which there has been no purposive direction of growth and no explicit social bargain. Individual groups have won aid or protection, but not as part of or the price for a larger strategy. We have sought to protect corporate autonomy not exploit government leverage.[7]

Of course, in the last forty years we haven't needed to have an economic goal. We were confident that the unmanaged market was moving in the proper direction, because the outcomes favored us. We have been dominant. Nonetheless, we now must reorient our priorities and objectives if we want to retain our economic position. We must find a mechanism for confronting and making difficult choices. We must be able to debate analytically evident but politically charged truisms. For instance, we must confront the facts that raising national savings means reducing someone's consumption and that national investment today means savings from current consumption or borrowing abroad. If current consumption is to be reduced, does that mean that we must cut welfare or eliminate the deductibility of interest on consumer spending and housing? In the American system a reorientation will not mean just one set of decisions, however complex, at the national level, but an abundance of choices about schools and taxes throughout the complex federal system. A multitude of competing social objectives must be acknowledged and incorporated. The sheer diversity of decisions and choices to be made across the continent in state legislatures and local governments almost requires and demands a broad national agreement that we must make the adjustment to a changing world economy that our national hopes and goals require. We must build an American consensus.

The first step toward an American consensus is a framework for political debate that does not assign responsibility for America's problems on one group or require that certain groups adjust their lives so that others can carry on undisturbed. We must each abandon many of our sacred myths and think fresh about the problems we face. The framework of the debate must be constructed before the solutions can be recognized and selected. The framework—the way we define and order our understanding of the society in which we operate, the nature of our problems and their relative importance, and the scope of our options—is initially what matters most. Indeed not only does the framework—the optic through which we view the world—determine what choices and possibilities we see, but it often dictates our priorities as well. The framework and not the specific solutions is the concern of this book. Indeed, pursuing the quick fix or the magical solution is a means of avoiding the tough choices that reorienting U.S. priorities involves.

14

Policy and Competitiveness in a Changing World Economy

THE FRAMEWORK for debate must permit America to reorient its priorities and use government policy to help reestablish the competitive evolution of the economy. The difficulty is to make the policy discussion a concrete consideration of how best to use the multitude of policies America does have and will make. Far too often the debate is not about what policy to adopt, but about whether there should be any policy at all. In the United States there is a strong current of opinion, backed by a powerful and rich intellectual tradition and a long national experience, that holds that government focus on industrial competitiveness will only serve to make things worse. American political debate about the role of government in the economy is caught up in an unfunny fun house where ideological mirrors reflect distortions of intricate, but unproven theories. Three strands of argument in particular entangle the debate.

Interest Group Standoff

First, some would have it that government and the clutch of special interest groups that steers government simply clog the machinery of the economy and prevent growth. An important image in American politics and a theme in our political discourse is that government cannot effectively act in the public or general interest and can only be an impediment to economic development. Politics, we are told, is dominated by narrowly drawn interest groups incapable of acting in any but their own particular and selfish interests. The government apparatus is a weak one, permeated by these organized groups and unable to articulate its own purposes and directions. The American government may be strong internationally in competition with other nation-states, but it is weak internally. Some formulations highlight iron triangles that link interest groups, congressional committees, and executive agencies. Policy is made, in these conceptions, fundamentally through an addition of special favors, through pork-barrel politics. This view has found formal exposition in recent years.[1] We are told that groups cannot act politically from common purpose and concern with public interest. The gains to a community that might be realized by members of a group acting together cannot be easily achieved if each person acts rationally. If the individuals that compose the group are rational, each will tend to act as a free rider and permit others to act on his behalf. Of course, if everyone is rational, then creating collective action is very difficult. The implication is that interest groups form only when there are concrete side payments that equate value added with the costs of participation. The very logic by which groups are formed means that they will use government selfishly and will tend to redistribute wealth through politics rather than create the conditions through which greater wealth is generated.[2] In a milder version of the same vision it is argued that the parties that aggregate interests have weakened; consequently there is a fragmented series of interest groups all trying to feed like pigs at the trough of government.[3] In both formulations, the result is that an accumulation of interest groups will generate a steadily growing number of private deals which distribute income rather than generate wealth. Interest groups are seen as the fat cells in a kind of economic arteriosclerosis. An accumulation of groups is held responsible for inflation and slow growth, stagflation, and sundry other economic ills. Indeed, in a peculiar kind of correlation, the destruction of interest groups facilitated economic development in Japan, France, and Germany; while the survival of interest groups through stable politics in Britain meant an inevitable economic slowing down.[4] Consequently, the most important link between government and politics is a negative one. There is a policy consequence to this analysis. The best thing to do about interest groups is to limit them or their access to government, while the best thing to do about government is to keep it away from the market.

The theory behind these arguments is limited and, when applied to modern economic development, flawed and weak.[5] But most importantly, the record does not support the case that the advanced economies have been fouled in the undergrowth of interest groups and an excess of democracy.[6] In each fast-growth country a coalition for rapid growth and development was established. When, as in the case of postwar France, new purposes for government had to be established, a transformation of the groups active in politics—not a limitation of their numbers—was critical.[7] From a historical perspective, each change in the character of world markets and economy provoked tensions within the several national polities. Growth resumed when new bargains and solutions were worked out.[8] America's political problems do not stem from the slow buildup of interest groups that submerge the market. Rather, they have their source in America's unwillingness or inability to define its new political choices in the radically changed world economy and build political coalitions in support of innovative solutions on which growth can once again be built.

Markets and Strategies

The second notion that complicates American policy debate is, stated in its simplest form, that government cannot outguess the market. This completely misposes the problem. There are those who would simply try to force government out of the economy and leave our fate to their faith that, over time, the market will produce the best outcome. They rarely recognize that government, through the rules and institutional structures of the markets can and—as we argued in the case of Japan—does structure the dynamics of competition. Often those effects are powerful and positive. It is increasingly obvious that there is more than one form of market capitalism, and America's policy makers must recognize that differences in the role of government mean that there are several different market dynamics. Even a belief in the market cannot avoid the question of what markets we want to set up and what kind of market infrastructure we want to build in an era of rapid market and technological change. It is not a matter of markets or politics, but of the precise ways that governments relate to business and structure markets.

Coming to terms with the role of government in an era of transition demands an understanding of how policy can shape a nation's position in international trade. Precisely because economic theory is concerned with static equilibrium, not with the dynamics of development, it is hard to find within traditional theory a basis on which a systematic and positive policy for competitiveness or development can be built. There are whole categories of exceptions to any conclusion that government can only distort market processes, but as each is an exception, it must be justified separately. The misleading consequences of the static character of such a conclusion is evident from an international and developmental perspective. Indeed, the powerful role of government in domestic economic development can best be seen from an international perspective. Governments can —and do—create enduring advantage for national firms in international trade. By enduring advantage we mean, again, a defensible competitive position that can be sustained after subsidy or policy measures to create advantage are withdrawn. The advantage need not, therefore, be arbitrary or temporary. Nor are the advantages necessarily limited to a few isolated sectors; indeed, they can influence the dynamics of an entire economy. Government policy can recast the position of the domestic economy as a whole in international markets.

This touches on a core notion that has shaped American policy debate, the forbidding doctrine of Comparative Advantage, remembered by the millions who once took Economics 101 in rather the same way Latin declensions are remembered by their parents. Revealed Comparative Advantage, to give it its full name, is the economic doctrine that addresses foreign trade. It tells a nation what its economy will specialize in: the British (because they wrote the text), in manufacturing textiles; the Iberians (because they believed it and lost), in port wine. A nation should, and will, find itself specializing in those activities in which it is the most efficient (or least inefficient) compared to all the others. Having a comparative advantage in something, say machinery or, better yet, complex manufacturing, does not mean that you are world class good at it or even better at it than the other guy. It means that you are just less worse at it than at other things. Your wage level tells you how good you are.

The American policy debate on trade is based on the prevalent view of comparative advantage in American economics. Our policy choices are framed by the notion that comparative advantage is revealed, not created. A nation finds its comparative advantage by looking backward in the trade statistics. It does not choose it by looking forward in its policy councils.

Policy should not try to create comparative advantage. We are constantly told that nations that subsidize exports are only deluding themselves and, at the same time, subsidizing their consumers by lowering the price of the goods they import. Pull away the subsidy, and things will rubberband back to "normal." Enduring comparative advantage can not be created by policy.

It is of course true that, in a strict definitional sense, comparative advantage cannot be created. But saying that is a little like saying, as economists do, that foreign trade will always balance out. Prices simply need time and freedom to adjust. That is true, but nugatory. If, for example, the price of the dollar were permitted to adjust to the point where one dollar equaled one yen, we could sell the entire economics building at the University of Chicago, brick by brick, to the Japanese to use as disco space. The trick is not to balance trade; it is to balance trade at a high wage level. Similarly, a country always has a comparative advantage in something— that is the way the thing is defined. The interesting question is, in what? Can we keep it in activities that pay a high wage? Government policy, we argue, can to a significant degree move the list of its industries upward (or downward) in the hierarchy of value added. It can reshuffle its national list itself by influencing which industries are able to apply the power of the new transformative technologies to their products and processes.

What is comparative advantage? It is *not* the same thing as competitive advantage for a firm. Competitive advantage means that a firm can successfully sell its products in a given market. In economics jargon, this is called "absolute advantage." Firms have competitive or absolute advantage, nations have comparative advantage. What, then, *is* comparative advantage? The classic explanation is simple, but consistently misunderstood.

> . . . countries export goods which they produce most efficiently and at lowest cost and import goods that they produce least efficiently and at highest cost. A nation then exports in sectors in which it has a comparative advantage and imports in those in which it has a comparative disadvantage. A nation, of course, can have an absolute advantage in international competition in all sectors, but it will still—by definition—have a comparative advantage only in some sectors.[9]

Does all this get us anywhere? It lays the groundwork for analysis. The question is how interesting is the analysis? The answer is, not very.

The standard textbook example of trade uses a two-sector/two-nation economy, usually Britain, which has a comparative advantage in textiles, and Portugal, which has a comparative advantage in port wine.

According to the classic analysis, both countries are better off if each one specializes in the product in which it has a comparative advantage and the two countries trade with each other.

What the example fails to note is that Britain, with its advantage in textiles, becomes a richer nation than Portugal, with its advantage in port wine. If your comparative advantage is in bananas, a cheap, readily available commodity, then national GNP and per capita income will be less than if your comparative advantage is in numerically-controlled machine tool production. Many of the most successful of the newly developing countries understood clearly what American textbooks have not acknowledged; consequently, they have aggressively pursued policies aimed at altering the structure of their economies and hence their comparative advantage. Japan, for example, has consciously sought to shift the structure of its economy from one in which its comparative advantage was in labor-intensive goods to one in which it was in capital-intensive goods, and now to one in which its advantage is in knowledge-intensive goods and goods that require manufacturing expertise. If, by contrast, a nation's position in the high-value-added activities of an era erodes, its relative wealth will erode as well. Britain is the counterpoint example to Japan. Thus, it matters a great deal what a nation's comparative advantage is. This is another way of saying that the composition of a nation's trade matters.

How, finally, can we understand the link between the competitive dynamics of industry which we observe in the business pages of the daily newspaper, and the comparative advantage of nations, which we observe by analyzing their trade statistics? Is there a link between comparative advantage and competitive advantage? Recognizing the link will begin to illuminate how governments can influence comparative advantage through policy. Tyson and Zysman have pointed out:

> Whether comparative advantage is real or policy-induced at any moment in time, the competitive dynamics of industry form the link between static and dynamic comparative advantage. Over time, shifts in competitive advantage for particular firms in particular industries can accumulate into a change in national comparative advantage. The crucial point is that comparative advantage rests on the accumulation of investments, and that a long-run strategy can slowly alter a country's comparative advantage by altering its capital stock. Generous endowments of specific raw materials may give firms in one country a competitive advantage over international competitors. Thus in paper products, a firm with domestic access to ample timber resources will presumably have lower timber costs (a real Ricardian absolute advantage). In electronics assembly, cheap labor may give developing countries a competitive advantage in the labor-intensive phases of production (a real Heckscher-Ohlin absolute advantage). Port facilities give Japan cheap access to imported

raw materials required for steel production; in automobiles, an elaborate national policy to promote the components sector provides a substantial competitive advantage to all companies.

The main point, again, is that accumulated investment, whether in physical infrastructure or in the infrastructure of related markets and firms, is crucial to determining both competitive advantage and comparative advantage over time. In essence, a nation creates its own comparative advantage by the efforts of industries and government to establish competitive advantage in the market. Where the eroding competitive positions of individual firms unravel a web of infrastructure, the outcome can be a long-term loss in competitive advantage which amounts to a shift in national comparative advantage. This is especially true in industries composed of a few large firms. Although there may be no comparative disadvantage underlying the initial competitive difficulties of a particular firm, these difficulties can have a cumulative effect that leads to a national disadvantage. The costs of recapturing a lost market share will go up if the infrastructure, in the form of suppliers and distribution networks, is undermined. The collapse of suppliers may affect the industry's collective ability to sustain its technological position. As this discussion suggests, in advanced industrial economies, comparative advantage—a concept much in vogue and often loosely used—is to be understood as the cumulative effect of both company capacities and government policy choices, not simply as the effect of given endowments in capital, labor and resources.[10]

Policy can help to upgrade a nation's position in international competition in a substantial and enduring way. Like much in economic reality, but little in economic theory, the relationship is not symmetrical. Policy, all by itself, can hold back an economy that has most other things going for it: over the decades Argentina has been a recurrent reminder. But policy, however enlightened and astute can, by itself, only contribute to the upgrading process. It can't do the whole job. But the contribution can be very important.

The one thing policy is least able to do is to have *no* impact on a nation's competitive position. And that, of course, is what conventional American economics sternly prescribes for it. That policy cannot simply go away, or be "held harmless" in its impacts on the economy, is true not only for America, but for any complex, modern society. Like it or not, government affects the economy—both as a direct economic actor (taxing, spending, and often, doing) and as a set of all-pervasive and ever-changing rules. That truth is compounded by the fact that economic reality today consists of several large and complex economies that are all heavily policy-impacted. One nation's policies affect another nation's position. Were it achievable, policy neutrality in all nations might well be the best rule for the System as a Whole (though not necessarily for any one nation in that

system). In the absence of such universality, it loses any claim for being
the best rule for any particular nation.

A Hierarchy of Policies and the Fear of Intervention

Creating advantage requires a systematic and sustained effort. The quick
fix won't work. There is, though, a fear in the United States that acknowl-
edging a powerful role for government in industrial development, let alone
embracing a bold policy initiative, would lead to government entangle-
ment in and direction of the daily affairs of American corporations or,
worse, in the details of the affairs of the corner grocery. However, recognition that an active and positive government always plays a role in economic development should not lead to the conclusion that selective intervention—government mucking around with specifics of corporate strategy
—is the only role possible. Understanding that this third element of America's instinctive distaste for government action to promote development is,
at the least, exaggerated is essential for an intelligent policy debate.

There is a clear hierarchy of possible policies, which run from the most
general to the most specific. (1) At the top are the aggregate policies
addressed at objectives that will affect all sectors—macroeconomic stability or balance of payments equilibrium are examples. In principle these
policies affect all groups in the economy equally, but in practice they
powerfully influence specific sectors in very different ways. (2) Then there
are the market-perfecting policies aimed at improving the economic infrastructure and the quality of inputs available to all firms in the economy.
These include a collection of policies intended to improve the output of
the market process by making the markets themselves work better. Policies
to improve the working of telecommunications, transportation, or financial
systems as well as policies to raise the educational quality of the work force
or to encourage longer-term lending will affect the choices open to all
firms. (3) At the bottom there are the policies aimed at dealing with the
problems of specific sectors. Despite America's ideological distaste for
industrial policy, the United States has an abundance of programs that do,
in fact, have specific and intended consequences for a whole range of
industries. They were not made, however, with attention to problems of
international competitiveness.

This hierarchy corresponds quite neatly with a ranking of policies
based on their political acceptability—the more general the policy ap-

proach, the greater the political acceptability. The least general policies—
and the least politically acceptable—are sectoral specific: subsidizing, protecting, favoring, or fostering specific sectors, industries, or firms.

The interconnection between the three types of policies in the hierarchy matters. We can all agree that the deficit should be reduced. That is
a macro or aggregate policy. Reducing the deficit demands concrete choices
about whose taxes to raise or whose programs to cut. Many of the mechanisms for implementing aggregate policies involve decisions that affect
how markets work and the quality of the economic infrastructure. Similarly, problems in specific sectors often have their origins in the rules and
resources in the economy at large. For example, the American semiconductor industry is composed of merchant firms that are smaller than their
highly integrated and diversified Japanese rivals. Alliances between the
companies to support research and production development, even while
competing on product, may permit a competitive response. Whether those
alliances are possible depends on the antitrust rules about how the market
game should be played. Identifying the problems that firms face will help
suggest how the market system can be improved by altering the rules and
raising the quality of inputs and infrastructure. The fear that policy action
to promote competitive development would mean an extensive and interventionist industrial policy is unwarranted.

15

Toward a Policy Agenda for Competitiveness

T HE current economic transition—the transformation of industrial society—sets an agenda of change and policy choice. Competitive adjustment, we have argued, will be built on the ability to generate and apply product and process innovation. Competitive advantage will rest not just on product innovation, but on sustained manufacturing expertise. Those economies that diffuse and apply technologies widely will find advantage because they will both create markets for new and advanced technologies and transform traditional industries in the process. But there is nothing inevitable about the outcome. However, the policies we adopt will be an important element in determining the choice we make about the outcome we create.

Creating Economic Resources

How in an era of transition can government help create advantage? It can do so principally by substantially upgrading the quality of what goes into production, the factors of production—raw materials, capital, labor—and the networks and rules that affect how those factors are combined—the economic infrastructure. Government must act primarily at the second level of the policy hierarchy (see Chapter 14). Even traditional theory suggests this. Comparative advantage rests on the relative factor proportions required in the production of different types of goods—that is, a nation will tend to specialize in those sectors that require factors of production that it has in abundance.

Classical trade theory does not worry about *how* a nation got its particular pattern of comparative advantage, just what it is. National factor endowments are not, however, simply given by nature; they are, to an extent that matters, created over time by policy. Moreover, policy powerfully affects the real price and quality of these inputs, and does so all the more when the crucial endowments involve technology, know-how, and skills. Let us look at the effect of policy on, respectively, land (raw materials), capital, and labor (which includes technological know-how)—the basic inputs to the economy.

RAW MATERIALS

The power of policy to create advantage by creating national factor endowments and affecting their quality and price is evident even in the case of raw materials. Geology is a natural given; economics isn't. Policy can play a role—a big role—in transforming geological factors into factors of production. In economics the question is not what raw materials a country can locate beneath its soil, but at what price they can be delivered to the point of use. And delivered price can be massively influenced by policy. One country may have abundant coal or iron or copper in the ground, but since the coal is deeply buried in isolated areas, the cost of getting it to the surface and shipped to the point of use may be very high. A second country may have no iron, coal, or copper, but may have decided to invest massively in port facilities and ships; it may be able to buy the raw materials at prices lower than that of its naturally endowed competitor. Japan, for example, has been blessed by a relatively solid absence of natural resources: no iron, no oil, no copper, though to their regret, the Japanese do have some coal. Japan consciously set out to turn its lack of raw materials to an advantage. It located steel mills on the coast, invested in modern port and off-loading facilities, and innovated in shipping design and production, while at the same time obtaining access to and control of raw materials around the world. The delivered price to Japanese producers of such raw materials as coal, iron ore, and copper has often been at prices lower than that paid by its competitors who have such resources in the ground. Indeed, Britain and France, as well as other naturally endowed nations, have been compelled by domestic political pressures to maintain high-cost domestic production of coal and other raw materials; their resource endowments have become comparative disadvantages.

Infrastructure development was the key policy choice involved in transforming a geological disadvantage in raw materials into an economic advantage. The provision of infrastructure can be considered a market-perfecting policy; infrastructure improvements make markets work better by eliminating "frictions," in this case—as with ancient Roman and modern American roads and harbors—the frictions of physical distance.

CAPITAL

If policy, along with lots of effort, can decisively influence even the most "natural" of production factors—raw materials—it can play a bigger role in the other factors—such as capital—which are clearly not a matter of natural endowment. The level of savings, the allocation of access to that pool of savings, and the price of that money to different kinds of users are not simply matters of "natural" market forces. They are strongly affected, sometimes even set, by domestic and international policy decisions.

Sometimes the decisive character of policy is overlooked and people start to believe that capital costs or savings rates lie in our national character, so let us construct some illustrative examples of policies that have enormous impact. Let us make the market for savings competitive by eliminating traditional ceilings on interest paid to small savers; open the market to all borrowers, worldwide; allow interest payments on housing and consumer goods to be deducted from income for tax purposes; and create a social security system whose benefits are not based on actual past savings but on entitlements funded from current taxes. If we follow these policies, the cost of funds will rise. This is clearly the American case. Now let us choose a different set of policies. Let us fund pensions entirely from the earnings of past savings; administer the flow of funds to limit and to discourage consumer credit, which will not be granted tax advantages; keep a lid on interest paid to small savers; and moreover, limit foreign access to the pool of domestic savings thus generated. This is clearly the Japanese case (at least up through the mid-eighties). Other things being equal, as the economists say, savings will be higher in Japan, the pool of savings more readily available to national industrial investment, and crucially, the costs of capital will be lower in Japan than in the United States.

Our choice on capital costs—keeping America's higher than that of our most powerful competitor—has substantial consequences. Since Japanese capital costs are lower than ours, Japanese firms will have an advantage in capital-intensive businesses and an incentive to convert competition into a game of capital-intensive manufacturing, something they have done, with disproportionate benefit to themselves in industry after industry, most recently in semiconductors. In this way the nature of competition is itself shaped by policy, ours and that of other governments. A big difference, however, is that, for the most part, our policies are being set with little concern for competitiveness while those of our most successful competitors are being strategically determined.

Not only do the differences between American policies for capital and those of other countries matter, but it is no longer possible to just have a domestic policy for savings and investment. We must make the policy with attention to international markets and do so strategically, with an eye to foreign government policies. International markets and the strategic logic of policy now make even seemingly simple and direct solutions into complex conundrums. It may prove more difficult than expected to gain or close a cost-of-capital disadvantage. Take the deficit. Can it be assumed that slashing it would lower the competitive disadvantage of U.S. firms in capital costs? The answer must be: only maybe. First, a reduction in U.S. government borrowings should relieve demand pressure on capital markets. Interest rates should then decline. But there is no reason to assume that foreign governments would not take advantage of that reduction to lower their interest rates and thereby negate any catching up on the costs of capital. Also, and more important, if world capital markets were indeed open—and the U.S. market is, for both borrowers and lenders—there is no reason to assume that U.S. savings, even if lent at lower prices, would be channeled into onshore U.S. productive investments; they could go, as they have in the past, to finance French nuclear power plants, or Korean semiconductor factories, or nonproductive spending in Latin America, or to finance American spending on housing and on imported goods. This is not to say, "Don't slash the deficit." It will have a big and positive impact on U.S. industry. But that impact might well come less through lowering the relative costs of capital to U.S. industry than through lowering the exchange rate of the dollar. The point is that the impacts are strategically determined; the effects of our move will depend upon the responses of policy makers in other nations.

If international capital markets were truly open, it wouldn't necessarily matter where the savings took place. American, Swedish, and Dutch firms could draw on Japanese savings at those same low rates of interest Japanese firms enjoy. However, in the Japanese case, policy has prevented this. Foreigners who might have wanted to draw on the Japanese national pool of savings have, until now, had only limited access. That capital cost differentials have been an important element in international competition in recent years is largely the result of a Japanese policy choice. The policies were originally established to generate capital in postwar Japan, when investment funds were short. They have simply never been dismantled. In an international economist's dream world, perhaps the whole question for America and for others could be mooted by eliminating the possibility of substantial international capital cost differentials. In recent years there has been much movement in opening capital markets—though many of the capital markets in the advanced countries, especially Japan, the biggest after the United States, are far from open. In a world of open capital markets—that is, in a single world capital market—in which there were no successful national policies to favor certain sectors in the pricing and allocation of capital, competitive advantage in capital-intensive production—long a U.S. strength and now a weakness—would be hard for anyone to achieve. Capital cost differentials—and policies designed to foster them—would cease to be a strategic concern of government and would drop out of the international competitiveness equation. It would be a solution to the policy problem in that it would simply eliminate it. In fact, international capital markets are already open enough, large enough, and efficient enough that the advanced countries will not be able to build capital barriers to entry against new producers.

If the prices and availabilities of raw materials, as well as the costs and availabilities of capital become smaller and smaller factors in differentiating production possibilities and costs across nations, the burden of competitiveness will fall on much softer factors of production: the ability to generate and use the most advanced technologies, the intelligence and dutifulness of the work force, and the relative ability of organizations to combine smart and flexible technology with smart and flexible people. The level of skill—perhaps education or productive smarts are better words—and the flexibility, robustness, and astuteness with which that intelligence is organized and mobilized will become the critical differentiating factor. This leads us to technology and education.

TECHNOLOGY

Technological development and diffusion, we have suggested, is where advanced countries may be able to gain an edge and establish themselves during the transition. Importantly, this is an area in which it is widely accepted that markets often fail, and because of that it is an area where government policy can make a major difference to competitiveness.

The root of market failure is to be found in the fact that the social gains from technological investment and use often exceed even the enormous private gains. Since the socially optimal amount of effort will not occur spontaneously through markets, government support is considered appropriate to capture these externalities. There are an abundance of historic policies in America and in countries around the world aimed at making the markets for technologies work more effectively, or at least more effectively for them. In Japan the government adopted strategies in advanced electronics and manufacturing to encourage technological development in Japanese firms by funding what we call "generic" technology, thereby lowering the risk to firms entering new technological arenas. It has adopted ambitious policies to diffuse NC machine tools and robots among small producers who would otherwise be reluctant and slow to adopt these new apparatuses. In the United States the famed agricultural extension service and the land grant colleges were organized to develop and diffuse agricultural technology and upgrade skills in the agricultural sector. They were, as these things go, extraordinarily successful policies. In all these cases governments have acted, in the language of economics, to correct market failures. The improved use of labor and capital embedded in new technology gives advantages to firms that accumulate national comparative advantage in the high-value-added sectors.

For the development and, critically, the diffusion of today's production technologies, America currently has created two major disadvantages for itself. First, the American investment in civilian technologies now lags behind that of its partners. Civilian spin-offs from military R&D could, of course, offset some of that disadvantage. But studies at BRIE and elsewhere suggest that these commercial advantages are now much more restricted than they were in the 1950s and early 1960s.[1] While it is difficult to judge the effect of military development and procurement on civilian industry, on balance the impact is, in our view, to distort the capacity of firms to adjust to competitive international markets. To promote civilian R&D, government can do a number of things. It can subsidize, directly or through taxes, firms that undertake or increase levels of R&D. The R&D tax shelters and tax credits are instances of such policies. Government can also support the basic scientific research and the education required to transform basic science into products. Policy can promote more applied research. Here, often, there is a concern that government will either support the wrong firms or the wrong technologies. There are ways of avoiding that problem.

In critical areas such as semiconductors or new materials, support for generic technological development is a means of addressing international competitive problems. In current American policy there is a category called "basic science," which is heavily funded in the United States. Pour money into the science machine, the theory goes, and out will come product and economic growth. Of course the Japanese did fine without pouring much in at that point. They borrowed the results of that basic research from elsewhere, usually the U.S., at no or very low cost. There is a second category called "product development." In between basic science and product development is a third category known as "applied science"—the application of basic principles to something useful. In fact, policy makers need to examine these categories more carefully. At any moment a range of products will depend on resolving particular scientific problems or building up enough knowledge about particular materials or processes. Those problems are not basic science, but they precede product development. In the sweep of applied technologies and science, certain problems can be identified that are likely to have substantial economic consequences if solved. Here is where the Japanese have put their money.[2] It is the generic quality of these technologies, which are essential to many products but not specific to any, that permits joint research corporations among competing firms such as Microelectronics and Computer Technology Corporation to be established. In passing we should note that Bell Laboratories once played this role with extraordinary distinction. It was a national treasure and resource, a center of research that solved many generic problems and pumped the results into the national and, indeed, the international industrial community. The AT&T divestiture, the breakup of the Bell System, has changed the nature of Bell Laboratories' role in the economy. Generic research is a suitable and underdeveloped target of competitiveness policy.

Second, there is the task of diffusing the use of emerging technologies. In the nineteenth century American policy took the lead in this area when we established the Agricultural Extension Service both to do research for farmers, none of whom could individually conduct that research, and to diffuse this advanced agricultural know-how. That policy had a strong and positive impact on raising the competitiveness of American high-income agriculture. In the twentieth century the Japanese have created a virtual manufacturing and machine-tool extension service.[3] It does for a broad range of industry what the Agricultural Extension Service did for American farmers, introducing them to new ideas and equipment and providing technical expertise to help them choose and use that equipment productively. Japanese policy has gone even further. It has organized programs to help small and medium-sized firms lease and purchase the advanced equipment vital for increasing their competitiveness and, therefore, the competitiveness of other Japanese firms linked to them. These policies have helped Japan diffuse NC machine tools and robots among smaller producers, who would ordinarily be slow to adopt new techniques, much faster and more broadly than in the United States. A Manufacturing Extension Service, patterned after the Agricultural Extension Service, would be a good device for bringing new technologies into smaller U.S. firms. It would help U.S. competitiveness across a range of industries, not just those that make the technologies. With a similar objective of diffusing technology, but at a much higher technical level, the National Science Foundation is purchasing a number of supercomputers for major U.S. universities to train the next generation of computer scientists on the newest, albeit very expensive, machines rather than on outdated technologies. Technological diffusion is critical because the current industrial transition is being driven by the application of emerging transformative technologies to traditional sectors. When microelectronics, new materials, and biotechnology touch established products, those established products, as well as the processes to make them, are altered. Moreover, the new technologies interconnect, creating an economywide wave of advance.

There are now extensive international markets in technology. Just as international capital markets have made investment funds more widely available, technology, which diffuses ever more rapidly, is more quickly available to more potential producers. Consequently, the way technology is employed will prove decisive. That will turn, in our view, on the character of the U.S. work force. Technology will be a complement not an alternative to a skilled work force.

EDUCATION AND SMARTS

In the present transition, the nature of work-force skills and the level of those skills will change. However, the distant and disembodied force of technological development driven by competitive pressures will not unilaterally determine the kinds and number of skills that a competitive U.S. economy will require. Skill requirements—the market's demands for labor —will be significantly shaped by skill availabilities, and not only in the static and conventional sense of markets always clearing at some price. Work at BRIE suggests the hypothesis that the availability (or scarcity) of skills shapes competitive strategies as well as the development of particular technologies.[4] This has always been the case:

We can see it as far back in the American past as in the origins of mass production of muskets, an organizational and technological response to perceived shortages of craft skills. Former Labor Secretary Ray Marshall has observed a similar phenomena in the period after World War II. He argues that the GI Bill played a key role in creating a supply of well educated workers that shaped a demand for their skills. A similar adjustment to skill availability also occurred during the 1960s when highly trained solid state electronics engineers—the result of government grants to graduate engineering education during the 1950s—began to enter the labor force in significant numbers. Educated labor is an economic resource that is strongly shaped by policy. In this transition it may prove decisive. We should admit that our close work with the Carnegie Forum on Education and the Economy during the last year simply confirmed our own biases. Nonetheless it does appear that "organized smarts" will massively determine a nation's competitive success in the current transition. An educated, skilled labor force broadens rather than forecloses choice in the competitive development and application of technologies. In the end it permits firms to get new technology into place more cheaply.

Similarly our research and the work of others suggests that across the industrial spectrum, competitive mastery of the new technologies rests on successful employment of workers' skills. In continuous processing plants, for example, microprocessor based instrumentation generates a large integrated data base. To maximize the power of the technology, workers have to be able to monitor, analyze, and intervene in the continual flow of electronic data; they have to "both theoretically apprehend the data and convert their understanding into articulate processes in order to communicate it to others." Similarly metal workers using computer-controlled machine tools need to rely on a reservoir of craft skills to prevent disastrous breakdowns and bottlenecks in the production process. In white collar industries the introduction of office automation technologies makes it possible for clerical workers to assume functions formerly reserved for professionals, but only if they are sufficiently skilled to use the new technology and sufficiently educated to understand the new functions. Even the speed of change itself places new demands on the work force, requiring that it adapt continually to new products and new processes.[5]

Labor as a factor of production is not just people, but people with particular skills, attitudes, and habits. Production can be organized differently with literate workers than it can in an illiterate community, to take just one element of the labor package. The skill base of a nation and how it is employed is likely to be the decisive factor in determining national competitiveness—the country's ranking in the international hierarchy of wealth and power. America has a rather substantial range for choice in this matter. The pool of skills is a product of education policy. In the nineteenth century America benefited from a uniquely egalitarian system of public education that produced an unusually broadly skilled work force. At one time America could be confident that, in competition with Europe, its egalitarian, literate, and homogeneous community of skilled workers represented a distinctive asset. We cannot have such confidence now. We have lost that advantage. American literacy rates are low: functional illiteracy of U.S. seventeen-year-olds is estimated to be somewhere between 8 and 20 percent.[6] Some estimates are radically higher. Less than one percent of the Japanese population[7] is functionally illiterate. On the basis of internationally administered achievement tests, American high school seniors do very poorly in international achievement comparisons—worse than the students of any other developed nation.[8] The number of engineers per capita in Japan is roughly double that of the United States.[9] Unless we avert this, the United States will find itself with one of the lowest skilled work forces among the advanced countries, and this will directly and powerfully shape our pattern of advantage, converting it to a pattern of disadvantage in industries that can employ high-wage labor.

Unless we have the skills to employ the new production possibilities, no amount of investment capital will make us competitive with countries that have invested in human as well as in physical capital. Economic development and productivity in Japan and the newly industrializing countries rests firmly on their development of a skilled work force. The unexpected and impressive success of Korea in advanced electronics is an excellent illustration of creating advantage through factor policies, especially skills policy. That nation entered electronics with none of the three necessary elements: it had no supply of skilled electronics engineers or technicians, little capital, and no homegrown technology. It sent its promising young people off to MIT and Berkeley, borrowed the money, licensed the technology, and built, over the years, an emerging and probably self-regenerating comparative advantage in electronics. An explicit policy about skills and an all-out effort to develop them was an indispensable element in Korea's success in electronics. It is not just that their labor was cheap, but that it was disciplined and—for the production tasks needed—educated and skilled. Now, as our competitors, both the newly industrializing countries and the advanced economies of Europe and Japan, move into higher and higher value-added production, the educational levels of their work forces and the investment in education at all levels of their societies are increasing more than proportionally. The United States will not again be the economy with the most skilled work force. The question is whether we will find ourselves at a substantial disadvantage.

Equally important, the skill pool of the population shapes how tech-

nology is used. Firms in different countries use different production technologies; cars are made differently in Britain, Japan, and the United
States.[10] The origins of those differences do not lie, as we saw, simply in
the cost of different factors of production. Rather they reflect different
approaches to the problems of manufacturing—different solutions to be
found under different social conditions and in which labor and capital costs
are merely one element. Indeed, there are many instances in which factories in different countries use identical machines in radically different ways
and achieve distinctly different results in terms of productivity.

Certainly, until five years ago the debate over how robots should be
used was on different tracks in the United States and Japan, with the
Japanese emphasizing production flexibility and the Americans emphasizing labor replacement.[11] There are clues emerging, not systematic evidence
but clues, that the consequences of the new competition and technology
for the labor force depends on how it is used. How the technology is used
depends on the problems it is called on to solve. If there is a shortage of
skilled labor, then the technologies will evolve in ways that require less
skilled labor. Where skilled labor is abundant, technology can emerge to
reinforce the abilities of the work force.

In the formulation we have chosen—seeing the economy through
factors of production—skills appear as the most important element of
policy affecting labor. Yet, if the optic is shifted slightly, it is the organization of labor relations and the character of labor-management conflict that
will shape the technological strategies of firms. Where skilled labor is
absent but technological development is easy to attain, technology will be
used to substitute for the missing labor. However, where skilled labor is
abundant but powerful and perceived by management as an obstacle to
corporate operations, the technology will be used to displace the work
force and eliminate the obstacle—the power a skilled work force can exert
over operations in plant and shop floor. The technology will be used to
eliminate perceived obstacles to management strategies and autonomy.
Consequently, labor relations are a vital counterpart to work-force skills.
This is not a technical matter of the best way to arrange "bargaining" and
negotiations. Rather, it is a matter of resolving the conflicts between labor
and management in a manner that assures flexibility and encourages participation and cooperation. In one form or another this involves security
of employment. The politics of labor is the vital counterpart to the politics
of education.

America has substantial choice here. We could try a strategy of stripping skills out of jobs. We can try to replace skilled labor—on the shop
floor and in the office—with technology and offshore that which we can't

replace or think we can't yet replace. As argued in Part II of this book, how the technology is to be developed and how it will be used is not determined. It is a question of choice or, more accurately, a question that will be resolved by a long series of iterative choices, each one being influenced by the previous one.

Shaping and using technologies to displace skilled labor runs deep and serious national risks. At any single moment it may be possible for a firm to pursue this tactic, but it will start us down a dangerous technological path, one that in the long run will make national competitiveness in world markets difficult. There are three dangers or risks. First, we suspect that technologies that displace skilled workers are more rigid and less flexible than those that complement and require skills. Such production systems are inherently more capital-intensive. They generally require far higher levels of capital investment and technological complexity to achieve comparable results. In part, as a consequence of the greater investment of capital and the elimination of skills, entire production systems must be reformed from the top down in larger discreet steps. They are more difficult to reform from within. This simply reinforces a weakness of American firms—their inability to adapt rapidly to changing technologies. Second, worker replacement technologies are harder to develop and more expensive to implement. Take, for instance, artificial intelligence control systems for production. If they are used to supplement worker skills, they can be much simpler than if they must embody vast levels of expertise and knowledge required to replace the workers. Look at the Bay Area Rapid Transit system (BART) in San Francisco. The technological dream was to replace drivers with an automated control system. To do so required enormous development costs and heavy capital investment. Yet, that system has never worked. In sum, simpler technologies that rest on worker skills will be implemented sooner and be more widely diffused, we hypothesize, because they are easier to develop and cheaper. But, we must not exaggerate. Fully automated factories will emerge and do provide remarkable efficiencies. Yet the question, we suspect, is how one closes on the design of such "lights out" operations. If the automated factory implements production systems initially developed progressively with skilled labor and less automated technologies, they are likely to move into operation smoothly and effectively. When the design is conceived whole cloth by engineers and cast into concrete and machines, serious difficulties may be expected. In other words, skilled labor may be a decisive element in the experimentation required to develop new production systems. Third, and centrally, can we as a nation—as opposed to an individual firm or even the sum of individual firms—really adopt fundamental strategies based on stripping labor skills from jobs and, therefore, accepting a relative decline in overall educational levels?

To pose the question as a national choice raises some unpleasant fundamentals about the different strategies that can be used to contend with our competitiveness problem. For the nation, the low-skill choice leads to dead ends. Competition on wage rates is one dead end. We cannot, we are learning, keep capital costs substantially lower in America than abroad, so that American unskilled labor could command much higher wages than foreign unskilled labor because it could be given much more powerful tools with which to work. It is also a fantasy to hope that an elite group of American engineers can keep production technology in this country so far ahead of technology in other advanced countries and developing nations that we can retain decisive production or product advantage. The realities of the past few years should by now have shattered that illusion.

That America will lose if it takes the low-skill route does not mean that America will close down or that all Americans will lose. It does, however, mean that most of us will lose a lot, and that this country will be transformed in ways that many of us find terribly unattractive. We would become more like a Latin American society. We could have a small minority of high-skilled research, development, production, and service jobs coexisting with a majority of low-skilled, low-wage jobs, and massive underemployment and unemployment. For the vast majority of Americans, living standards would deteriorate rapidly—probably along with social equality and political democracy—as, in order to compete, manufacturing and services move offshore and automation strips the remaining labor content from the remaining U.S. goods and services. It is not an attractive scenario.

THE NEW INFRASTRUCTURE: TELECOMMUNICATIONS
AND ORGANIZED SMARTS

Infrastructure, as we have just seen, remains vital, even in its most traditional forms: ports, rails, and roads. But the critical form of infrastructure is now telecommunications. Chapter 11 made this argument and showed how the development of new telecommunications-based technologies and their adaptation in a vast range of commercial settings are radically altering production strategies and recasting the competitive equation.

It also showed how different nations are responding differently to the possibilities of the new telecommunications. Japan, in particular, is making an enormous effort, investing way ahead of market, to provide the most sophisticated possibilities to the broadest possible range of users—that is, to both small and large businesses (and even households). The United States, on the other hand, has devised policies that focus on providing, at very rapid speed, new and sophisticated technologies primarily to big users. It is, in the final analysis, a policy that conceives of telecommunications as an investment service purchased through the market by firms. And the United States has cleared away the obstacles to letting the market fit the technology to those clients who occupy the biggest places in the launch markets—the big users. The Japanese strategy is differently conceived. It sees telecom primarily as an infrastructure, and the Japanese government is setting the pace and the form of that infrastructural investment in order to orient and improve the working of the market. The improvements they have in mind are clear: get the benefits of the new technology to small-and middle-sized firms as well as big ones so that it will help them to compete in the ever more difficult international competitive environment. That strategy aims at helping not only small Japanese firms but also, because many of them are subcontractors to big firms, at increasing the competitiveness of those large firms. At the same time, by investing ahead of market demand, Japanese infrastructural policy structures and launches what Japanese policy makers consider the most important high-tech sector for the future—enhanced telecommunications—in a way designed to enhance mightily the competitive advantage of Japanese firms.

Infrastructural policy cannot be divorced from competitiveness policy. But telecom, however enhanced, is more than a physical and software network that, once laid in, will quickly give a nation's producers a launch-market lead down the learning curve and, when applied broadly, will offer vital production advantages to that nation's producers. Ultimately, productive use of that infrastructure depends upon the "quality" of the person on the other end of the line. That takes us back to the new economics of educated and organized "smarts," which treats national endowments of trained intelligence as productive infrastructure for the entire economy as well as just assets (actual or potential) for a particular firm.

Put more formally, as the division of labor becomes more and more complex—and that, after all, is what the colossal growth of producer services represents—the productivity of any worker, or any firm, depends on that of workers in other firms. The workers in other firms provide not simply a priced and purchasable input that can be warehoused and used as needed. Instead, they are integrated into the production "on-line" as it were. The telecom revolution is all about enhancing this interactive approach to complex production. The productivity of a doctor, for example, is substantially a function of the ability of the patient to describe symptoms accurately and quickly and to understand complex instructions the first time through, as well as a function of the productivity of lab technicians, medical-imaging centers, and insurance claims processors, to name but a few. They are all external to the doctor's organization. In still more formal terms, when a firm's production function is written out in mathematical form, the factors that determine output are listed, rather like the ingredients in a cooking recipe: so much capital, so much raw materials, so much labor, and so on. But there is a whole set of factors that are not generally included in the written equation; they remain implicit. One such factor is public order: revolutions that will disrupt production are not listed; power outages that will short-circuit the works are also not factored in. The implicit part is growing bigger, or at least it is changing its composition. As the division of labor extends itself, the production function of any firm—be it a manufacturer or a service firm—is becoming increasingly dependent upon the production function of other firms. If this is not true, we have no explanation for the growth of services to producers that we examined in the first part of this book. It becomes harder and harder to shield or isolate the productivity of your firm from that of other firms—clients as well as providers—and from the organizations upon which your own productivity depends; for example, by buying up all the good people, because your good people have to interact with their less good people. Accountants, lawyers, travel agents, financial advisers, and consultants of all sorts confront similar "interdependent" production functions. So do software writers, venture capitalists, and air traffic controllers. Production more and more resembles an on-line network.

Should Government Intervene in Specific Sectors?

Sectors are a fact of life. However lowly the place they occupy in economic theory, sectors are where industrial change is experienced and where political pressure for government to act concentrates. As long as there is industrial change, there will be sectoral pressures for government to act; given those pressures, sometimes, perhaps often, government will act, and the target of its actions, explicitly or otherwise, will be the sector. The realistic question is not whether we will or will not have policies at the sectoral level; we have many of them. The issue is whether America will or will not make its policies with attention to the purpose of encouraging positive adaptation to international competition and whether we will or will not respond to the sectoral policies other nations adopt to create advantage for their firms in international markets.

Sectoral policy is pervasive; and it's not just about competitiveness. Government intervenes on a selective basis all the time. It does so on the sly and with a bad conscience. More importantly, it does so with no strategic aim. Our agricultural policy protects particular groups and forms of productions; our tax policies steered investment into real estate, oil, and farming; our pension policies encourage short-term investment; massive government credit guarantees distort financial markets in specific but scattered directions; and, of course, our defense policies both aid and impede competitiveness in major hunks of the economy. The list of protected industries could be made very long: coastal shipping, trucking, textiles, tobacco, oil, steel, offshore pipes, aeronautics, and many, many others each get their special, sectoral treatment. We do not develop strategic aims in part because we do not want to, in part because we have never had to, in part because we are quite unprepared intellectually, institutionally, and politically to take on the task, and in part because we assume that domestic interventions simply serve to advantage some groups rather than others and that they advance the particular rather than the general interest. Americans do not believe that attention to sectoral problems can translate into general increases in national welfare or affect our international comparative advantage.

Even a modicum of political realism also tells us that there is absolutely no sense paralyzing ourselves in an irresolvable discussion of whether or not to have sectoral policies. The United States already has them, hundreds of them, especially for existing industries that succeed in getting themselves made into objects of positive policy. And we will have many more, soon. What policy makers must do is change them, reorient them in a competitive direction. The fact remains, that despite popular belief, our domestic interventions, for better or worse, do shape our comparative advantage. And so do those of other nations.

The new debate about selective intervention as a policy issue in this country emerges in response to foreign government policies to promote their industries by "targeting," as the policy has come to be popularly labeled. Industrial policy and planning have few firm roots in purely domestic U.S. politics or in American intellectual life. Rather, American industrialists who consider themselves to be in "targeted" sectors focus attention on foreign selective policies when they contend that their foreign competitors are given an "unfair" advantage in international competition through subsidized research and financing often along with protected home markets. Their complaints are frequently answered in very simplistic, static terms. Those static analyses generally conclude that the foreign government is wasting its money and subsidizing us and that we should take their subsidized goods, enjoy them, and send the foreign government a note of thanks. According to these analyses, the subsidies and promotional efforts—the targeting—will not, over the long term, affect national comparative advantage; the government will not succeed in reaching its goal.

In assessing foreign government sector-specific policies and deciding on U.S. response, there are two issues to consider. First, can promotional policies aimed at specific sectors permanently alter the competitive balance in those industries? The answer is a clear yes. In microelectronics and civilian aircraft, American firms had a dominant world position, built in no small measure on the base of military programs and procurement in the 1950s. Japanese electronics and European aircraft programs have created real and enduring rivals. Particularly in the electronics industry, Japanese policies helped firms overcome real barriers to entry into world markets. It assisted them in catching up technologically and in launching production in a closed market. The same story can be told about optical fiber technologies. The structure of the worldwide industry was, as a consequence, permanently altered. Policies can act in a variety of ways to alter market structures. If market position rests on a service network, then subsidized sales that allow the service network to be built up will permit a market position to endure after subsidies are ended. If market position depends on technological development and a country protects its market while investing in a particular product development, then its targeting efforts can help create enduring competitive positions. New trade theories have at last begun to provide a theoretical foundation for what was already known by most policy makers in the countries that have been making the best economic progress, but denied by those who looked at competition through a traditional economic lens. In imperfect competition—and most important international industries involve imperfect competition—strategic trade policy can work. When governments provide subsidies or protection, or both, they increase the resources available to firms competing in oligopolies. Those increased resources can alter firm strategies, allowing them to pursue different market, pricing, production, and product tactics. Of course, whether a particular firm can use those resources to build an improved and defensible market position is always an open question. We have argued elsewhere that policies that seek to affect the structure of an industry by promoting specific market outcomes without regard to the logic of competition or the dynamics of the companies in that industry will ultimately undermine the firms such policies purport to help.[12] There is nothing automatic about market success, no matter who is playing the game. But there should be no question that governments, through their policies, both intended and not, do shape market outcomes in international competition, and they do it very often.

Second, if a government helps firms in an industry create advantage in a specific sector, can the outcome in that specific sector affect, in any important way, the national comparative advantage? For the country promoting its industry the question is whether, even if it succeeds in helping firms to establish competitive position in world markets, it has not really wasted its money by diverting resources from those sectors where firms without subsidy could establish themselves in world markets. For the United States the question is whether it should accept the subsidy as a gift or fear it as a Trojan horse.

The answer to both questions depends on how one thinks the economy works and what the nature of the interconnections between sectors are. If resources move smoothly between uses without generating unemployment or economic dislocations, then perhaps the United States might want to accept the subsidy gift. If there are other opportunities for the workers and the communities in which they live and if the time of adjustment is brief, then the United States still doesn't have a national problem. (Of course, we might ask why we should allow those in the targeted industry to bear economic dislocations imposed on them by foreign government choice not market logic, but that is a separate issue.) The static, one-time costs of adjustment that might be paid to adjust the economy to imports based on foreign subsidy are an important policy problem, but they are not the central issue in this discussion.

Our central concern here is with the longer-term development of the economy and with the structure of the nation's comparative advantage. Let us put the question differently, then. Can foreign targeting of one or several sectors affect the structure of American comparative advantage? Conversely, could support of particular sectors assist America's way through the industrial transition and keep us at the top? Sustained investments, both public and private, are the link between competitive advantage in particular sectors and changing national patterns of comparative advantage.

If sectors are all equal so that we can be indifferent as to what we produce or if they are so thoroughly disconnected that what happens in one sector is of no consequence to the others, then the United States can be indifferent to the displacement forced by industrial development policies abroad. We may then wish to value those foreign subsidies as a gift.

However, the larger the consequences of development in one sector on the evolution of others, the more we should hesitate and inspect the gift to make sure that accepting it doesn't entail taking real risks. In Parts I and II of this book we examined these linkages between sectors from different vantages. When the Japanese supported the development of the steel industry in the 1950s, MITI argued that investment in this capital-intensive industry in a period of capital shortage made sense because of the possibilities it would open to the rest of the economy. Universally in Japan, and for some analysts in the United States, the semiconductor industry has the same critical or economically strategic character. The real economywide consequences of the rise or decline of a single industry depend on the linkages between sectors, the spillovers of technology, and the character of international markets. The linkages of particular importance are those between different high-technology sectors—links that sustain technological dynamism—and those between high-technology centers and traditional sectors where products and production processes are being transformed. We have already emphasized that sectors and activities in an economy are linked together. Some of those linkages are very strong—that is, if one activity disappears, the other will as well: production equipment repairmen without factories full of equipment are sorry souls. Other linkages are very weak: an appliance repair firm is indifferent to the national origin of the washers it services. But glass manufacturers who sell to General Motors or disk drive producers who sell to computer companies are likely to lose their clients if foreign cars or foreign computers capture the American market. British glass manufacturers are not likely to find markets in France or Germany to compensate for the loss of British-produced cars, and American auto or computer parts manufacturers are unlikely to find markets in Japan.

However, it is the interconnections not just in the sale of products that tie sectors together, but also in the flow of technologies.[13] Why can't the United States simply buy semiconductors and embed cheap semiconductors into expensive computers? The value added would come from architecture, software design, and applications. The Danes did something like this in the nineteenth century when they imported cheap American grain and fed it to pigs and cows rather than trying to defend the domestic production of grain. The character of sectoral interconnections—the nature of a sector's linkages to other pieces of the economy—and the process of technological "spillover" are crucial. The spillovers flow forward from products such as semiconductors. Certainly semiconductor products can be purchased in the market by all producers. However, those from computer makers through television producers who themselves use microchips to innovate require knowledge of products in development months and even years before they are available in the market. The merchant semiconductor producers—those who make the product to sell to others rather than for their own use—require an intimate relationship with clients to design and develop next-generation products. Will U.S. producers of computers be able to stay ahead of Hitachi if they depend on Hitachi for semiconductors? Will U.S. semiconductor makers be able to stay ahead of—or keep up with—Fujitsu if they have to depend upon Fujitsu for new production equipment? Can GM ever surpass Toyota in productivity if it relies on Japanese production equipment and control systems for its productivity gains? If the technology in question is quite mature—that is, if it changes little—the urgency of the question is much reduced. If the technology is changing rapidly, the question becomes vital. The interplay between users and technology producers is the critical element. Final product companies that have distinctive needs induce innovation from component and equipment companies. We have examined the consumer electronics industry, where Japanese firms which dominate the sector have been large users of a low-speed but low-heat technology known as CMOS. Their experience with this technology gave them an advantage in turning this consumer electronics technology into a base for dense high-speed computer chips.

The spillovers—the know-how and the technological sparks—pass through two sets of channels: *markets* and *communities.* A microchip may be purchased in the *market* and the engineering then reversed to discover how the chip works, but that takes time. Dependence on foreign sources for a technological innovation could affect the entire range of user industries, but only if the transfer time for that technology through the market were too slow to permit users of one nation to implement that technology fast enough to remain competitive in their own product designs. The debate has become intense because many Japanese firms are highly integrated, producing production equipment, components, and final systems. Indeed, we know of instances where materials in the production process for semiconductors have—with reason—been withheld from the market by integrated Japanese firms. Thus the question of whether markets will pass along technologies from one nation to another is not an abstract one; rather, it turns on the organization and dynamics of specific markets in specific countries.

Equally, knowledge passes through *communities,* the learning and diffusion of technology occurring through conversations and from job switches. Certainly, scientific communities are highly international, and business dealings and transnational alliances diffuse new technology internationally. Indeed, while actively suing Japanese semiconductor producers for dumping, American producers are busily insisting that technology-sharing arrangements would be honored. Yet business and technological communities remain more densely national than international. This is especially true in some countries. If new experimentation, both technological and in business strategies, takes place in the telecommunications and semiconductor industries, it is essential that those ideas spread throughout the American economy. Of course, this is not an abstract problem. The reality is that our major competitor is Japan. The Japanese community is organized around business groups from which there is very little outward movement of personnel. Microchip innovation within a group will be used to advance final products produced within that group, and the producers of final products within that group serve, at least in part, as a captive market. The Japanese community itself is quite closed, certainly when compared with the United States and Western Europe, and spillovers of technological innovation within Japan will almost certainly move more rapidly inside Japan than out from it. Those innovations will most likely move as final products through market channels. The economy, as we have argued, is not a set of disconnected pieces, but an interwoven fabric.

The fate of specific sectors, carrying both the technological code of the future and the market demand to implement it, can affect the pace and character of economic transitions. At particular times particular sectors have been the keystones of whole structures of technological and economic advance. The claim that some sectors are critical can quickly degenerate into a claim that all are, and that strategic policies become programs of generalized subsidy and protection. Nonetheless, at particular historical moments, some sectors are quite clearly crucial. In the middle part of this century, automobiles became both a symbol of mass production and a source of innovation in production technologies. That production knowledge unquestionably spilled over into related sectors that could use similar strategies and technologies. Similarly, in Japan, autos and consumer electronics served to generate machine tool and production technology industries and helped to create a manufacturing advantage in the Japanese economy as a whole. Knowledge spreads and diffuses.

The policy problem is to know which sectors are critical, so let us not run ahead of ourselves to a series of sector-specific policies. Just because we might accept that some sectors are economically strategic, even if we admit that their emergence could alter the comparative advantage of a nation by driving a broad wave of development, how do we know which sectors they are? In the years after World War II those countries that adopted systematic sectoral policies were relatively backward. They were less developed than their rivals and, consequently, could look at the industrial structure of their more advanced competitors. They had maps of the future. Still, the question was how to read the maps. There were a number of evident criteria, including those used by MITI:

1. Was it a growth sector?
2. Were there substantial potential export markets?
3. Were there long-term declining costs either from scale or learning curve economies so that, if volume of production grew, costs would fall?
4. Were there substantial income and price elasticities so that, as Japanese incomes rose and prices fell, demand would steadily grow?

In the present period additional criteria might have to be added.

5. Does a sector have the potential to influence the product characteristics and production processes of other industries?
6. Is it a transformative sector? Will a mastery and lead in this particular technology open big new possibilities in other sectors of the economy?
7. Will there be substantial negative consequences elsewhere in the economy of not being state-of-the-art and competitive in this particular technology and being, therefore, dependent upon foreign providers and the next round of foreign developments and applications?

Much depends on the channels through which the technology and know-how flow and the link between component development and final product design. Many in Japan believe that there are strategic sectors that historically allow one country to be dominant during a particular period of history. The notion is that semiconductors are at the beginning of a decisive industrial chain.

Strategic transformative sectors are those emerging industries whose products alter goods and production processes throughout the economy, as we argued in Chapter 6. They transform the rest of the economy. The technologies spill over into other sectors and often do so through channels that are tied to national communities. The emerging character of the industries which are the source of these technologies gives competition in them a strategic character in which decisions by one firm can alter the very character of the market and the choices open to other firms. In such emerging or shifting sectors—industries with strategic competition—government policies can shape the very character of international markets. Moreover, establishing position in these industries can indeed give a firm or a nation a dominant position in a stream of product and process innovation.

Perhaps, then, America can act in specific sectors in ways that can affect the nation's industrial development and comparative advantage, and, perhaps, it can identify those sectors which are strategically located in the economy. That does not mean that the solution to those sectoral problems ought to be sectoral policy. There are many risks in sector-specific policies. First, it is not always evident what should be done. Let us say we should support the development of the semiconductor industry. There would be limited agreement as to which firms and which strategies should be supported. The uncertainty is inherent because the industry is in the process of unfolding. The lines of development, as we argued earlier in this part, are yet to be established. Second, if we open wide the Pandora's box of sectoral-specific policy, we may not support the development of key sectors or competitive firms, but rather may lavish resources on those sectors which have the greatest political clout, usually those with the biggest battalions and the longest political experience.

We should be relieved therefore that the conclusion that particular industries matter disproportionately to the national economy ought not to suggest that we should automatically run after these sectors with buckets of money trying to pick the specific firms to back or that we should suddenly waive all taxes on all firms that produce electronics gear. Identifying the problems and potentials of particular sectors does not mean that the policy solution should be specific to the industry. Sector-specific policies are certainly not the only answers to the problems of sectors, nor are they necessarily the best. They are the most difficult to sell politically and the hardest to implement well. Once understood in terms of the strategic questions we have just reviewed, they can be answered, more often than not, through the factor level and market perfecting policies we discussed previously.

In many ways America is in a particularly fortunate position insofar as making policy to improve competitiveness is concerned. We have done so little that there is a huge layer of easy things we can do before we get to the hard ones. And those easy ones have by far the biggest impact. Most countries have already geared their basic economic policies toward international competition. We haven't. That gives us a kind of "advantage of backwardness" position in policy making. It is a little like energy conservation a few years back. The United States had done so little in that direction compared to Europe or Japan that, while other countries were at a stage where they had to take very difficult measures, we could do easier things —things they had done years before—and get huge returns. The same is true in competitiveness policy. Only let's hope that in competitiveness policy we take better advantage of our privileged position. Because we have done so little in the past to shape policy to the goal of competitiveness, we are, among all our competitors, uniquely privileged.

16

Trade Policy in an Evolving World Economy[1]

I N THE YEARS after the Second World War the United States helped structure the international trade and monetary system with the objective of increasing economic efficiency through unrestricted and nondiscriminatory trade. We were the preeminent economic power with the bulk of world exports and a currency which itself became a reserve and transaction instrument for international finance. Consequently, the United States could, for example, permit other countries to devalue or undervalue their currencies against the dollar because, despite those devaluations which increased the competitive position of foreign products, we still ran substantial current account surpluses. The United States invited Europe and Japan to join it in an open trading game in which the American market was the single largest prize because we were confident of our ability to compete. Not surprisingly, the rules reflected our preferences and served the interests of both American security policy and the multinational corporations that were already establishing themselves around the world. America had a substantial competitive surplus that was invested in maintaining and advancing the open trade system.

Our dominance rested in part on a monopoly created by the war, and our relative position diminished as the war-torn economies of our trade partners were rebuilt. As traced in Chapter 5, the slow rate of American productivity growth continues to compromise our competitive capacities and our strength in the international economy. While the erosion has been slow, the consequences have often appeared quite suddenly. For example, in 1971 we were obliged to break the link between the dollar and gold and devalue our currency to restore our ability to sell in world markets. When in the 1980s we had to finance our colossal deficit by borrowing from foreigners, America discovered that its domestic macroeconomic policies were constrained by interest rate policies abroad. The United States could not, in 1986, lower its own interest rates without cooperation from Japan for fear that large spreads between Japanese, German, and American interest rates would perturb the flow of foreign capital on which U.S. macroeconomic policy now depends. Domestic policy must now be made with an eye to international constraints; conversely, international economic policy must be made with attention to the requirements of domestic competitiveness. Indeed, U.S. policy must increasingly be made in negotiation with our allies.

Certainly the United States remains the single most powerful international economic force, but for once it must horde it resources. Because trade rules, and sometimes outcomes, must be negotiated with an ever wider range of ever stronger trade partners, the United States must establish its own priorities and concentrate on them. What are the issues and stakes?

THE LIBERAL ECONOMIC ORDER

The rules and arrangements that govern most international trade were set forth after World War II in the General Agreement on Tariffs and Trade and came to be referred to as the GATT trade system.[2] That system evolved through seven multilateral trade negotiations that succeeded in substantially reducing tariffs and quotas as barriers. The GATT was constructed around four premises. First, trade arrangements that are built on multilateral negotiations among all nations are preferable to bilateral or other partial arrangements. Second, trade will be conducted by private actors in markets in which prices are set by a free interplay of supply and demand. Third, government intervention is a distortion of the market aimed centrally at delaying domestic adjustment to international price signals. Fourth, free trade will generate the expansion of all economies, if only each will bear the strains of internal expansion and adjustment. The GATT emphasis on private actors in international trade was reinforced in the 1960s by the dramatic growth of the multinational corporations and the rapid expansion of the Eurocurrency markets which produced an international financial system of similar scope to the one inside the United States, but outside the control of any governmental authority. Compared to these new and powerful private forces, government interventions were treated as relatively negligible, rather rearguard exceptions to a transforming liberal order.

The enduring ability of governments to shape economic outcomes could be ignored while negotiations were focused on tariff restrictions to trade and as long as the United States was able to ignore or downplay the effect of foreign government choices on its trade. In the Tokyo Round of discussions (1973–1979), trade negotiators reached the bottom of tariff restrictions and confronted so-called nontariff barriers. They did so roughly at the same time that the United States confronted both its declining trade position and the pressure of state policies abroad. Suddenly "nontariff restrictions" were on the agenda. National differences that might be considered trade barriers cannot be negotiated away in the same manner as tariffs and quotas. Eliminating *external* barriers and putting *internal* pieces of the domestic economy up on the negotiating block are in fact very different things.

WHAT ROLE FOR GOVERNMENT? THE REAL QUESTION OF NONTARIFF BARRIERS

Let us identify nontariff barriers for what they are: specific arrangements of policy, of business organization, or of social life that give advantage to domestic national producers in an era of international competition. Sometimes the obstacles to trade created by these arrangements are the unintended results of domestic objectives, but the protections created may still be dear to national firms. Sometimes those nontariff obstacles are indeed the intended outcome of governments that no longer feel they can resort to outright restrictions to guarantee the interests of their national companies. Technical differences in product safety, government procurement, telecommunications regulation, and financial markets, for example, are often at issue and create intense controversy.

Nontariff barriers are difficult to negotiate both because reconciling different national approaches will create advantage for some producers and force others to adjust and because the changes often require the agreement of domestic policy bodies concerned exclusively with domestic issues. Many of the details can, of course, be negotiated. If the issues were all technical, perhaps a complex web of concessions could be created. At the core, however, the conflicts are political, not technical; they are struggles about what the proper role for government is in managing and developing the productive economy.

Brush aside the fuss and furor of the trade conflicts, and there are centrally different conceptions about the proper role of government in the domestic economy. Most European economies give much greater emphasis to social protection and organize the rules of the domestic market to assure that. Many also accept that industrial promotion and the direct support of private interests is a legitimate function of government, not one to be closeted. The Japanese and Korean experiences have emphasized the vital role government policy can play in industrial development. The United States cannot simply declare alternative approaches to economic development illegal. To impose our opinion about the proper organization of international economic life, we might temporarily limit access to the American market, but for the most part this isn't a remedy for the real U.S. problem of a slow pace of productivity growth. Protection, if used indiscriminately, becomes a habit and drug. Moreover, it is a threat that cannot be used repeatedly. Once closed, a market cannot be reclosed. Consequently, the threat loses credibility. Even when restrictions are imposed, the mechanisms of government support can be changed, sustaining its purposes while hiding or clouding its techniques. Similarly, foreign firms can often pursue strategies of entry into the United States by using different tactics. Some in the United States may not approve of the varied forms of market capitalism and the tactics of America's trade competitors. They label certain practices of foreign governments as "unfair," and they may well be correct. Certainly the United States can and must block many specific practices it finds unacceptable. But as a general matter, the United States can't enforce such judgments about the domestic strategies of other nations.

STATE STRATEGIES IN INTERNATIONAL TRADE

The premises of the GATT system only awkwardly fit many of the new realities of international trade. Indeed, as Michael Aho and Jonathan Aronson contend, if policy makers had understood the manner in which the Japanese economy worked in the postwar years, they would never have settled on the rules for the GATT.[3] The assumption—half fact and half fiction—that governments are negotiating about the rules of trade, leaving the market to settle the outcomes, is increasingly less tenable. Governments are increasingly negotiating directly about trade outcomes. Moreover, the rules concerning domestic economy and the appropriate use of national government power in the world economy have themselves become the subjects of negotiation.

In the last few years governments have reappeared in international trade negotiations in three forms. First, there is government as the manager of surpluses. The management of surplus capacity involves negotiations among companies and governments to reduce supply to a level consistent with existing demand. Surplus capacity may result from a sharp drop in demand. In that case, the negotiations are among established producers about who will bear the pain of the downturn. However, surplus capacity may also result from the entry of new producers, often from developing countries, into established markets. In this case, the negotiations are among governments about how to handle a reshuffling of the division of labor among nations. Second, there is the state as trader. States may directly negotiate the terms of sales and influence the terms of supposedly private bargains. State trading, barter, buyback, offset and mixed trade arrangements are not new, but their volume is increasing.[4]

Finally, there is government as advantage creator. Governments may follow purposive strategies to create advantage for specific sectors as a means of advancing the development of their economy as a whole. Before we consider the dynamics of developmental states, we must ask, "Do we care whether foreigners promote the development of their domestic industries by subsidizing industries that will later export goods to the United States?" We have already discussed this issue, but we must be clear about our analysis. Is the subsidy a gift or a Trojan horse? Suppose that a foreign government subsidizes the production of autos and machine tools. If those autos or machine tools are then sold in the United States below the price of American produced goods, American firms will be required to reduce production or close down, and consequently labor and communities will be forced to "adjust." Is this a serious problem for the United States? Does it harm American welfare? Should America do something about it? Milton Friedman has argued that the United States should consider such subsidies as gifts from foreign governments—transfers from their consumers, who pay for the subsidies with taxes, to U.S. consumers, who benefit in lower prices. The unused resources of the firms who lose sales will be shifted to other uses, and the national welfare will improve.[5] Such subsidies serve to create advantages. The notion embedded in American trade law is that such advantage is temporary and will end as soon as the subsidy is withdrawn. The analogy again is to a stretched rubber band that reverts to its original form. In our view, those gifts may in the end represent Trojan horses. But in a range of industries, such subsidized sales have served to create long production volumes that helped to reduce long-term production costs and establish sales beachheads in the United States. The subsidies bought volume production and market share; under the right conditions these can be self-accumulating advantages. Enduring, not arbitrary, advantage can be created by concerted effort and policy. The analogy is not to a rubber band, but to something more fundamental and Darwinian—survival and prosperity in a changing environment.

Competing in a World of Developmental States

In the United States the notion of using government policy to create advantage—that is, using policy strategically to help industry establish enduring competitive position in world markets, to shape the national production structure and the pattern of comparative advantage to assist the evolution of wages and production—is new and controversial. As a policy, if not as a formal theory, these objectives are pursued by many governments, most notably and most successfully Japan.

The central purpose of the "developmental state"[6] is the upgrading of the nation's position in the international economic hierarchy. Critical sectors—those that by their links to other industries can affect the entire economy—are thus seen as a form of industrial infrastructure. Such critical industries are treated as the equivalent of railroads and harbors in an earlier era and consequently are seen, even in a capitalist economy, as an appropriate concern of government. The state pursues the competitive development of specific economic sectors in the short run with the long-term purpose of assuring the industrial base required for the expansion of the entire economy. Japan is the most successful developmental state and, because it is our most serious competitor, the most closely examined example. There, systematic government policies have sought to move the economy from labor-intensive goods, such as textiles, to consumer durables, such as televisions and automobiles, and then into the advanced technology sectors of computers and, soon, aircraft. The Japanese have demonstrated clearly that under some circumstances developmental policies can work, and that when they work their impact is powerful. They have shown other nations the path and the stakes.

In promoting internationally competitive industries in telecommunications, aerospace, nuclear energy, petrochemical and offshore engineering, avionics, and transportation equipment, the French have also understood the power of this approach. They have demonstrated to such interested nations as Brazil that success is not tied to inimitable particularities such as Japanese management traditions, the dutifulness of Asian labor, or a natural (or imposed) political consensus. Rather, with careful planning success is open even to nations with communist workers, cultivated managers, and a political and social heterogeneity perhaps best characterized by de Gaulle's complaint, "How can you govern a nation with three hundred different kinds of cheese?"

The governments of the newly industrializing countries (NICs) are attempting to repeat the trick, starting again at the beginning of the cycle with labor-intensive production or in sectors with stable and easily available technologies. Such late developers have a series of advantages, including the ability to apply the best available technology, which in established industries is not difficult to obtain or to use. The notion that comparative advantage can be created and not, as static trade theory suggests, just revealed lies behind the concerted government strategies to create international industrial advantage that are the core of developmental policy. The developmental state, then, pursues clearly defined goals of industrial expansion rather than attempting simply to umpire the economic rules while leaving the economic outcomes to be settled in market competition. In doing so it acts as a player in the market through specific financial and administrative arrangements.

The argument about which economic theory should guide government policy has been absent from U.S. trade theory literature. Traditional trade theory does not deal well with questions that do not fit its static orientation and its assumptions of perfect competition. It certainly does not confront the role government can play in creating comparative advantage. The theory behind the developmental state, however, took concrete form in Japan a generation ago. The theory became the underpinning of policy. There was a fight over policy between the Bank of Japan, which followed traditional principles and advocated support for labor intensive textiles, and the Ministry of International Trade and Industry (MITI), which wished to restructure industry and promote steel. MITI won the fight. Japanese policies for industry since have followed the logic of theorists less attended to in American economics—List and Schumpeter. Is it simply by chance that they wrote in and about an economy, Germany, that was a latecomer to the industrial world and that followed a developmental strategy of its own? Proponents of developmental approaches argued, in effect, that government policies can gradually turn a temporary competitive disadvantage into enduring comparative advantage because government policy affects the gradual accumulation of physical and human capacity that underlies production technologies. National comparative advantage is, in part, a product of national policies over time.

That implication has been absorbed by many governments that are attempting to create enduring advantages and to alter their national place in the world economic hierarchy. In competition among the advanced countries, these government strategies create intense trade controversy in sectors such as electronics, telecommunications, and aircraft. The U.S.–Japanese high-technology trade negotiations—currently underway—are sparked by just these issues. The developmental strategies of the NICs pose problems in other sectors. Although many American industrialists would like to forbid such state strategies, it would be difficult at best to enforce a judgment that Japanese or Korean, French or Brazilian practice is simply illegal. Those who pursue developmental strategies do not accept "free" market outcomes as inevitable or automatically legitimate.

Since we cannot here review a long series of country and sector stories, let us at least briefly consider some fundamentals of the Japanese case. The Japanese experience, we noted earlier, must be understood in three steps: (1) the effect of policy on market dynamics, (2) the influence of market dynamics on corporate strategy, and (3) the influence of corporate strategies on shop-floor organization. In Part II we examined steps 2 and 3, here we will look at step 1.

The Japanese government exerted influence on the economy during its boom years of the 1950s and 1960s in two important ways. First, it was a gatekeeper, controlling the links between the domestic and international economy. It was, in T. J. Pempel's terms, an "official doorman determining what and under what conditions capital, technology and manufacturing products enter and leave Japan."[7] The discretion to decide what to let in and, at the extreme, out of Japan permitted the doorman to break up the packages of technology, capital, and control that the multinational corporations represent. In almost all cases, neither money nor technology could in itself allow outsiders to buy or bull their way into a permanent position in the Japanese market. This closed market then gave Japanese firms a stable base of demand which permitted rapid expansion of production and innovation in manufacturing.

Second, government agencies—most notoriously MITI—sought to orient the development of the domestic economy. Although government bureaucrats did not dictate to an administered market, they have consciously contributed to the development of particular sectors. MITI is not so much a strict director as a player with its own goals and its own means of interfering in the market to reach them. Government industrial strategy assumes that the market pressures of competition can serve as an instrument of policy. It is not simply that the government makes use of competitive forces that arise naturally in the market, but rather that it often induces the very competition it directs. This intense, but controlled, domestic competition substituted for the pressures of the international market to force development. The competition is real, but the government and private sector work together to avoid "disruptive" or "evasive" competition. We do not need to select between cartoon images of Japan, Inc., or a land of unfettered competition. It is the particular interaction of state and market in Japan that is interesting.

Seen from the perspective of the firm, government policy helped provide cash for investment, tax breaks to sustain liquidity, research and development support, and aid to promote exports. These public policies—the web of policies rather than any individual elements of it—changed the options of companies. Without the protected markets, the initial investment could not in many cases have been justified by private companies. Without external debt finance, the funds to expand production rapidly would not have been available to the firms. Within a protected market, the easy availability of capital and imported technology was bound to attract entrants to favored sectors.

However, MITI viewed the stampede for entry, which it had encouraged, and the resulting battle for market share, which limited profits, as excessive competition that had to be controlled. The intensive domestic competition was controlled by a variety of mechanisms, including expansion plans agreed to jointly by government and industry, debt financing of rapid expansion that made the bankruptcy of major firms a threat to the entire economy and hence unthinkable, and the oft-cited recession cartels. The dual facts of purposive government influence on economic outcomes and real market competition are reconciled by seeing the system as one of controlled or limited competition.

The very success of Japanese industrial development—combined with intensifying pressure from Japan's trading partners—has begun to loosen the network of relations that characterized the developmental state and on which the strategy of creating advantage in world markets rested. Many formal restrictions on entry to the Japanese market have been lifted. Serious trade problems still remain, however. As long as Japan had to borrow generic technologies on which to build its growth and had undeveloped potential markets that could be seized by domestic or foreign producers, formal closure of markets was essential to a system of orchestrated development. Now less formal obstacles to entry may matter as crucially to competition in advanced technology as formal restrictions did a generation earlier.

Japan's imports of manufactured goods remain dramatically below those of the other advanced countries and have not increased as a portion of the national economy since the early 1970s. Japan's unique trade characteristic is a tendency, relative to its trade partners, not to import manufactures in sectors in which it exports.[8] The system of administrative guidance that affects government programs of finance and procurement, the Byzantine distribution system, and the habits of private coordination amid competition all evolved slowly. Indeed, the Japanese state still exercises a leadership role and exerts substantial influence in high-technology industries, on the one hand, and in declining or mature industries faced with oversupply, on the other.

There is a crucial interplay between these two sets of interventionist policies that is likely to continue to spark problems in international markets and to create enduring tensions between Japan and its trading partners. Promotional policies in which the risks of domestic oversupply are at least in part insured against or underwritten, depending on how one chooses to characterize the particulars of Japanese policies, encourage bursts of investment for domestic demand that translate directly into export drives. Now that Japanese producers tie domestic investment decisions directly to world market strategies, the relationship between strategies in the Japanese market and their impact on the American market is immediate. There is a pattern of aggressive promotion of advancing sectors and of determined insulation and cushioning of mature sectors. This amounts to confining open international competition in the domestic market to sectors in which major Japanese firms are dominant worldwide or at least able to withstand foreign entry into home market and to sectors from which Japanese firms are absent. It implies sustaining closure in those sectors that are under pressure from abroad.[9]

The Japanese system may slowly open and become fully integrated with its advanced-country trade partners. But other would-be Japans stand in line. The challenge of the developmental state, the challenge of nations deeply committed to promoting their own industrial development, will not pass from the contemporary scene.

THE CONSEQUENCES FOR AMERICAN TRADE POLICY

The success of state policy in many of the developmental economies shows clearly that government policy can effectively promote industrial development and a repositioning of a nation's economy in world markets. It is not a matter of markets or governments, but of how governments shape the behavior of markets. Policy can set the dynamics of market competition by establishing the rules of the game and the resources available to play it. In the Japanese case, market dynamics gave a very particular logic to corporate strategy, which in turn generated production innovation. Japan is our largest and most recent competitor, but not our only one. America's competitive problem is not limited to developmental states.

It is the erosion of American competitiveness, not just the success of developmental strategies, that challenges our nation's place in the international economic hierarchy and the positions of Americans in the international division of labor. The success of other nations and America's difficulties at home put pressure on us to navigate the industrial transition faster and better. They force us to find ways to apply new technologies to production to create opportunities for high-skilled, high-wage, high-productivity employment—our only long-term developmental path. The strategies adopted by other nations also change the impacts of the policy measures we would adopt absent such approaches abroad.

We have a choice between protection and positive policies to promote adjustment and competitiveness. Firms, workers, and communities naturally see market protection as one mechanism to survive in the face of intense and successful foreign competition. By itself, normal industrial dislocation in a period of rapid change in production technologies and new forms and patterns of international competition would generate political dislocation and demands for protection. The suddenness and extent of our exposure to such competition vastly heightens those pressures.

The present wave of protectionist pressures should not surprise us. Nor should its increasing amplitude as things refuse to get better. What is perhaps more surprising, and more frustrating, is the limited and inadequate range of our responses. Since World War II, the general thrust of American policy has been aimed at creating a world that favors open trade —the free flow of goods and finance—with labor being a notable exception. Importantly, alongside international agreements to free the flow of goods were policies to support the multinationalization of American business. More precisely, American rules were structured to favor direct foreign investment. Two forms of support were crucial: first, the tax laws tended to encourage overseas investment rather than domestic adjustment; and second, the trade laws were arranged to allow American firms to invest overseas, producing part of their product at these offshore locations, and to be taxed on only the value added abroad when the goods reentered the American market. A third element of support for direct foreign investment was provided by U.S. aid programs that helped the developing countries establish themselves as export platforms. As a matter of policy the United States encouraged the corporate search for cheap wage locations that, we believe, has slowed the adaptation of production processes.

In a series of cases we examined a few years ago,[10] it was clear that policies for specific manufacturing sectors ran a different course from general policies. The exceptions are more numerous than one would have expected from the rhetoric. The United States has had one basic response to industries that have been weakened by foreign competition. It has consisted fundamentally of one form of protection or another. For the most part those policies involved "voluntary" restrictions on trade negotiated on a bilateral basis between the United States and exporting countries. Those policies have not stemmed the trade pressures. Rather, in a quite predictable manner, they have encouraged firms in each sector to do three things. First, to avoid restrictions on specific categories of goods, foreign producers have modified their products. Restrictions on leather shoes generate synthetic, rubber-soled shoes. Restrictions on cottons encourage new blends. Restrictions on the number of passenger cars encourage small truck imports. Second, restricted in the total number of products they could ship to the United States, foreign firms have moved their mix of production to the more expensive, higher-value-added end. Cheap T-shirts have given way to designer jeans in the same way that inexpensive Japanese cars have been replaced by more expensive models. Third, production at new locations has sprung up. Either existing producers have changed location or new producers have entered the market. In sum, the policies have generated new products and new producers as well as pressing competition into higher-value-added parts of the market.

Positive policies to promote adjustment or to rebuild competitiveness have not been part of our political tool kit. Chrysler stands out as a remarkable exception that required mobilizing half the government. (Lockheed, of course, was not a response to trade pressures.) There is a debate about how effective the protection dosages were, and indeed how serious the doctors were. Many believe the dosages were intentionally diluted by officials who were committed to free trade and considered it their duty to make those compromises necessary to contain protectionist forces in order to resist real protectionism.[11] What matters now is the change in scale, the vast increase in the number, diversity, and size of industries seeking some form of substantial trade relief. Rather than individual cases that can be treated in isolation, we may be watching the outlines of a protectionist coalition take form. If trade pressures continue, and we believe they will even if the dollar returns to a more moderate level, there will be enduring competitive problems.

Many fear that the individual compromises with open trade will accumulate to change the principles of American trade. As long as the principle is open trade, each act of closure requires justification. If the principle changes, then the trickle of protectionist acts could become an undirected flood. There are in the United States, three lines of political defense for free trade: a broad ideological commitment to the idea that open trade is in the national interest became entrenched in the years after World War II; a set of institutions were created and staffed to implement that ideal; and a strong political coalition supported the institutions and the ideology. As the American trade position has shifted, neither the institutional commitments to open trade nor the broadly based ideological bias in that direction have truly changed.

A real change in trade policy would require a shift in the political or coalitional basis of trade policy. The coalition for open trade has continued, but it has been severely weakened. The position of American industry in international markets has deteriorated, and American agriculture and large American financial institutions are more dependent than ever on open markets. The international position of American agriculture is deteriorating rapidly. Only a radical shift in the interests and position of finance or agriculture would fundamentally alter the political bases of our trade policy. Such a shift is now possible; it is a possibility of enormous consequence. A complete collapse in this free trade coalition is not very likely, but substantial increases in the number of exceptions and restrictions on access to American markets are. The continuation of overwhelming dominance of the free trade coalition should no longer be counted on.

Defensive protectionist policies will neither stop the import pressure nor help American firms adapt and adjust. They won't suffice.

A Strategic Trade Policy

American trade policy must give priority to the goal of promoting the competitive development of American industry in world markets. A strategic trade policy is a complement to a domestic policy that promotes adjustment and development in response to shifting world markets. If we do not choose our own priorities they will be chosen for us by other countries that can select their purposes and will consequently set our negotiating agendas. In that case, our policy agenda would be set fundamentally by priorities abroad and lobbying within.

There is adequate legal basis to pursue the purposes we as a nation may choose.[12] The precise legal framework is not essential; nor is a precise policy agenda, since the flow of events will dictate the issues. Let us sketch by example what a strategic trade policy means. Given our focus, three emphases are evident. First, manufacturing matters critically to American domestic development and to our international trade position. Services are a complement to manufacturing that can both create markets for industrial products and can be sold on the basis of manufacturing advantage. They ought not represent a hope and emphasis on their own. Second, the development of manufacturing skills based on the introduction of programmable automation and skilled labor will be decisive in international competition. Production at home was the basis on which Japanese innovation was built. Production in the United States or in other advanced nations when market conditions require will be the basis of an American response. To the extent that policy has built incentives for American firms to locate abroad, it has pushed them in the wrong direction. Third, foreign domestic and trade policies that affect the evolution of America's rapidly evolving high-technology industries should be a central concern. It is in emerging industries where sales volume is growing rapidly, technologies are unfolding, and production costs dropping that development strategies are most effective. It is in these evolving sectors, with the technologies that will transform the rest of the economy, that enduring advantage in world markets—advantage that is difficult to reverse—can be established through temporary foreign promotional policies that can be removed later. It is here we must put the weight of our efforts to alter foreign practices and unacceptable business strategies.

Of course, we must avoid the idiocies that result when we make domestic policy as if our internal choices had no consequences in international markets. Glaring at us is the example of the deregulation that ended AT&T's monopoly. In so doing we opened the American market to foreign competition without asking for any reciprocity. We gave up quids without asking for quibus. Bell Laboratories was transformed from a development lab and technology pump for the nation into the private lab of the reorganized AT&T. In one stroke we created a competitive disadvantage for our firms in international markets. We permitted foreign markets to function as developmental preserves while offering the American market as the prize in the competitive competition. We made these choices in one of the industries that will define national competitive advantage in the future. We made these decisions purely on the basis of domestic concerns. We can't afford many such choices. Fifth, we must link domestic policy to international policy in a more positive way. If we are going to be dependent on foreign savings to finance our deficit, then fully open international financial markets are indispensable. If high interest rates are a competitive problem, then each pool of savings to which American companies are denied access is an essential issue. Japan, with its enormous trade surplus, is presently a huge pool of savings. Full deregulation and international liberalization of the Japanese financial markets are, in fact, crucial. Finally, we can no longer so readily use pieces of economic policy as gifts to our allies to cement strategic deals. Consistently subordinating economic goals to alliance objectives was only possible when we had a dominant position. A competitive commercial weakness will now begin to become a strategic weakness by weakening the pace of technological and production evolution. Production of defense goods will cost more for less adequate equipment, which will be based on technologies that may no longer be at the cutting edge.

COOPERATION IN MANAGING CHANGING INTERNATIONAL ROLES

Changes in the relative power of nations, be it economic or military, are always hideously difficult to manage. Roles that have been established have to change. We are in such a period now with the diminished position of the United States and the growing economic power of Japan. Europe matters vitally, but its position and role are not shifting sharply. The European issue is what stance Europe will take toward the converging roles of the United States and Japan.

The United States is compelled to attend increasingly to its short-term domestic needs in making international economic policy. Because of the sheer scale of the American economy, domestic decisions have massive international consequences. Managing those consequences, both economic and political, will require cooperation. Put baldly, for the United States to act narrowly in its short-term interests, some might say selfishly, without disrupting international economic relations demands conscious toleration from its trade partners who are also its trade rivals. This is not to say that the United States was magnanimous in earlier years, but rather that the interests it pursued corresponded with the international system as we had constructed it. Now we can shake the system but not shape it to our design.

Conversely, Japan's increased international economic strength, represented by its trade surplus and overall creditor position, which is not yet fully acknowledged or understood in Japanese politics, requires that it increasingly act from its long-term interest in the stability of the international economic order and, if need be, purchase through concessions the continued participation of its partners in an open system.

In essence, an American strategic trade policy will require a shift in the dynamic of competition and cooperation in the international economy. America's allies have a real stake in such a strategy. Unless America can define its priorities and pursue a set of limited objectives, a less controlled and more generalized departure from open trade and international cooperation is a real likelihood. The question is not whether the American position and role will change, but what the terms of that change will be and whether it can be managed without extensive turmoil.

17

Conclusion:
The Myth of the
Post-Industrial Economy

S OMETIMES new notions capture our fancy, resonate to some element of our experience, and color the way we see the world. The concept of a post-industrial society is just such a notion. It resonates to our experience of big changes, shapes our perceptions of their tone and texture, and organizes our understanding of their direction. But the notion obscures the precise location of those changes and their meaning.

Things have changed of course. Production work has changed. People go home cleaner; more of them leave offices than assembly lines. Service activities have proliferated. The structure of enterprises is different; the giant bureaucracies of finance and corporate conglomeration dominate the skylines of our cities, even while economic rejuvenation depends on a myriad of more entrepreneurial firms. The sociology of work and the organization of society have changed along with the technologies of product and production.

But the relationship of those changes in technology and society to changes in the fundamentals of economics and politics is less clear. Despite predictions, political power has not passed to a new class of technical experts who dominate access to scientific knowledge. There has not been even the faintest trace of it happening at the national level, nor has it happened at the corporate level. While formal knowledge matters enormously—more than ever—the expert and his knowledge are, for the most part, embedded in the corporate bureaucracy. IBM, despite its efforts, may not be able to control the lives of its scientist employees the way employers in some factory towns did a century ago, but the economic value of the knowledge they embody is captured quite as successfully by the corporation, and a salary is paid to the employee. Indeed, the fruits of their knowledge are captured in silicon and sold by the corporation as a commodity quite as successfully as more humble mechanical knowledge was sold a hundred years ago. However strange and wondrous their products, the entrepreneurs of Silicon Valley have much in common with the entrepreneurs of Manchester in 1840. And for the vast majority of service workers, continuity is as strong and depressing a reality as change. The majority of employees in McDonald's are little different—in any positive ways—from employees in the thousands of small luncheonettes of an earlier era. For the vast majority of hospital workers and schoolteachers the promise of new scientific knowledge contrasts in ways that are difficult to resolve with the realities of their daily work experience.

The growth of service employment, even of white-collar employment, has not put an end to labor struggles and class conflicts of earlier industrial periods. Whatever its merits as a principle for organizing our understanding of sociological change, we have yet to arrive at post-industrial politics. Nor is there post-industrial economics. The division of labor has become infinitely more elaborate, the production process far more indirect, involving more and more specialized inputs of services as well as goods and materials located physically as well as organizationally far from the traditional scene of production, the proverbial shop floor. But the key generator of wealth for the expanded and differentiated division of labor remains mastery and control of production. Niche economies can specialize in one part of this division of tasks. New York City, or Washington, D.C., or Monaco, or the Bahamas, or Switzerland can specialize in services or a particular subset of services and prosper. But an economy as vast as that of the United States cannot be fit into any niche. Our labor force may well be located in services. Yet as we have seen, the jobs of many, and the income levels of almost all, depend upon American mastery and control of production.

The transition we are experiencing is not out of industry into service, but from one kind of industrial society to another. The choices we make as a nation, the policies and priorities we choose, will determine whether the transition marks the end of a half century of American power and industrial leadership.

The argument of this book is straightforward. It can be summed up as follows:

1. There is no such a thing as a post-industrial economy. Manufacturing matters. The wealth and power of the United States depends upon maintaining mastery and control of production.

2. Changes in the extent and forms of international competition coupled with the mass application of microelectronics-based technologies are revolutionizing production. The United States is not doing very well in this new international competition. The most important competitive weaknesses of U.S. firms are in the production process. These weaknesses endanger the strengths of those firms.

3. A flight offshore for cheap labor will not provide a winning long-term strategy; after a few rounds of product and process innovation it will just compound the problem. A strategy of trying to hold onto the high-value-added activities while subcontracting production to foreign producers who have a manufacturing edge defines the fast track to disaster. Over time American firms will not be able to control what they cannot produce. The only viable strategy for American firms is to combine advanced technology with high-skilled labor and innovative management to create high-wage, high-productivity, flexible production capabilities.

(4) Policy sets the terms of the new competition. Policy can help to upgrade a nation's position in international competition in a substantial and enduring way. Or it can handicap national producers and accelerate a downward spiral of weakening production capability, offshoring, further weakening, more offshoring, and a flight into pure distribution and defense contracting. The one thing policy is least able to do is to have no impact on a nation's competitive position. And that, of course, is what is conventionally prescribed for American policy making. That policy cannot simply go away or be "held harmless" in its economic impacts is true not only for America, but for any complex, modern society. That truth is compounded by the fact that the international economy consists today of several large and complex national economies that are all heavily policy-impacted. One nation's policies affect another nation's competitive position. Were it achievable, policy neutrality in all nations might well be the best rule for The System as a Whole (though not necessarily for any particular nation in that system). In the absence of such universality, it loses any claim for being the best rule for any particular nation. America has, to date, formulated economic policy with no attention to competitiveness. If we are going to be able to choose our own future and not just submit to it, the focus of our policy-making attention will have to change. Competitiveness will have to become a primary concern. Concretely, the United States will have to develop policies to promote investment in technological development

and diffusion, in a skilled work force, and in the offices and factories that embed and house the technology and workers.

(5) We suggest that there is a better way to talk about development —about what matters and what does not matter to sustaining the prosperity and international leadership of the U.S. economy in world competition —than that provided by the paradigms, perspectives, and arguments of conventional economics. It is not that the standard arguments are technically flawed; they have been not so much disproven by keen debate as betrayed by changing reality. We suggest an alternative approach which, though less conventional, is, in the final analysis, far more prudent. It leads not to simple answers and pat policies, but to real choices. Rather than just letting a future happen to us—a future that is coming on fast and that we may not at all like—we can—not completely, but to an extent that matters —shape our future.

Our conclusion is upbeat in substance, strategic in perspective, though guarded in prognosis. The outcome of America's passage through the industrial transition need not be exclusively the affair of impersonal and imperturbable technological and economic forces. There is room for choice and action. That is the good news. It is good because at present we are not doing terribly well. The competitiveness of U.S. producers has been showing signs of serious weakness for quite a few years, even discounting the crippling effects of the overvalued dollar.

The bad news is contained in that same sentence: there is room—and need—for choice. Just because we have a choice about our future does not mean that we will take advantage of that opportunity, use it well, and even enjoy the freedom and responsibility choice provides. We have a political system which we cherish that is artfully constructed to avoid clear choices. And we cling to an economic ideology based on a notion of choice that minimizes the opportunity and desirability of making important, strategic ones.

There is a spectrum of possible economic futures open to America. At one end lies an internationally competitive U.S. economy in which highly productive, educated workers use new technologies flexibly to produce a broad range of high-value-added goods and services. They thereby earn the high wages necessary to sustain both the standard of living to which many Americans have grown accustomed and most aspire, and the open society that has been so closely linked with a strong and open economy. At the other end of the spectrum lies the real danger of a competitively weakened economy in which a small minority of high-skilled jobs coexists with a majority of low-skilled, low-wage jobs and massive unemployment. Living standards—perhaps along with social equality and political democracy—would deteriorate rapidly as, in order to compete, manufacturing and services move more and more value added offshore and automation strips the labor content from the remaining U.S. goods and services.

The transition sets the agenda of change, but there is nothing inevitable about the outcome.

The position we argue is simple. If we are wrong, the policies we propose will amount to accelerating the pace of industrial change by investing in people, plant, and technology at the expense of consumption. The medicine may prove unnecessary, but in the end America may be wealthier, more confident, and less troubled. If we are right, then there is reason for urgent concern and a need for immediate action. We propose the course of least national risk and, indeed, the course of least national regret.

NOTES

NOTE: The acronym BRIE, which appears frequently in the notes, stands for Berkeley Round-table on the International Economy, University of California, Berkeley, California.

Chapter 1

1. U.S. Department of Commerce, Bureau of Economic Analysis, *Survey of Current Business,* June 1981, pp. [S-11]–[S-12].

2. Office of the U.S. Trade Representative, *Annual Report of the President of the United States on the Trade Agreements Program, 1984–85,* p. 43.

3. New York Stock Exchange, *U.S. International Competitiveness: Perception and Reality* (New York: N.Y. Stock Exchange, August 1984), p. 32.

4. *Forbes,* 11 April 1983, pp. 146, 149. For a more academically respectable voice carrying the same message to a broad public, see Gary S. Becker, professor of economics and sociology at the University of Chicago, who writes: ". . . Strong modern economies do not seem to require a dominant manufacturing sector" (*Business Week,* 27 January 1986, p. 12).

5. See Daniel Bell, *The Coming of Post-Industrial Society: A Venture in Social Forecasting* (New York: Basic Books, 1973); Colin Clark, *The Conditions of Economic Progress and Security* (London: Macmillan, 1940); Allan Fisher, *The Clash of Progress and Security* (London: Macmillan, 1935); Allan Fisher, "A Note on Tertiary Production," *Economic Journal* 62 (December 1952); Allan Fisher, "Tertiary Production: A Postscript," *Economic Journal* 64 (September 1954).

6. See Daniel Bell, *Post-Industrial Society.* For a review of these basic developmental theories, see Simon Kuznets, "Quantitative Aspects of the Economic Growth of Nations, II: Industrial Distribution of National Product and Labor Force," *Economic Development and Cultural Change* (July 1957, supplement); Simon Kuznets, "Quantitative Aspects of the Economic Growth of Nations, III: Industrial Distribution of Income and Labor Force," *Economic Development and Cultural Change* (July 1958); M. Lengelle, "Growth of the Commerce and Services Sector in Western Europe," in OECD, Manpower and Social Affairs Directorate, *Manpower Problems in the Service Sector: Supplement to the Report* (Paris: OECD, 1966).

7. In addition to the president's report, see also *Los Angeles Times,* 2 September 1984, section IV, p. 1; Ronald K. Shelp, *Beyond Industrialization: Ascendancy of the Global Service Economy* (New York: Praeger, 1981). For a survey of opinions, both pro and con on this issue, see the *National Journal* 30, 27 July 1985, pp. 1725–36.

8. See the U.S. Department of Commerce, Bureau of the Census, *Historical Statistics of the United States,* series w 1–11, p. 599.

Chapter 2

1. Daniel Bell, *The Coming of Post-Industrial Society: A Venture in Social Forecasting* (New York: Basic Books, 1973), p. 124; While Bell uses a 4 percent figure for agricultural employment, it has since moved to 3 percent. See the Council of Economic Advisers, *Economic Report of the President,* February 1984, table B-29, pp. 254–55.

2. New York Stock Exchange, *U.S. International Competitiveness: Perception and Reality* (New York: N.Y. Stock Exchange, August 1984), entitles section 2 (pp. 27–39) of its upbeat report on the shift out of manufacturing and up into services "Creative Destruction." The origins of the term and the concept of "creative destruction" are to be found in Joseph Schumpeter, *Capitalism, Socialism, and Democracy* (New York: Harper & Row, 1962), pp. 81–87.

3. Council of Economic Advisers, *Economic Report of the President,* February 1985, tables B-93 and B-94, pp. 339–40. Note that while table B-94 shows the secular decline in agricultural labor intensity, the increase in capital intensity is less dramatic, especially since 1976. Of greater importance would seem to be the growth of technology and skills over the same time span (pp. 339–40).

4. Council of Economic Advisers, *Economic Report,* 1984, table B-29, p. 255.

5. Robert Z. Lawrence, *Can America Compete?* (Washington, D.C.: Brookings Institution, 1984), pp. 98–99.

6. USDA, Economic Research Service, *Economic Indicators of the Farm Sector: Farm Sector Review 1983,* Report #ECIFS3-2 (August 1984); William Edmondson and Gerald Schluter, "Food and Fiber System Employment in the South" (Washington, D.C.: Economic Research Service, USDA).

7. The Farm Bureau, the Grange, and state level farm lobbies all use this 7:1 agricultural employment and income multiplier. While politically powerful, the figure has no empirical basis. In the late 1930s Carl Wilkins, an Iowa farmer and lobbyist for federal farm aid, noted that over the preceding twenty years cash farm receipts had been equal to one-seventh of national income. He inferred from this that $1 of farm income generated $7 of national income. This piece of spurious thinking is now incorporated into Farm Bureau estimates. See also the work by John Davis and Raymond Goldberg of the Harvard Business School, *A Concept of Agribusiness* (Boston: Division of Research, Graduate School of Business Administration, Harvard University, 1957). These two authors utilized input-output analysis to measure the economic activity required to deliver food, clothing, shoes, and tobacco to domestic consumers and to support agricultural exports. As the following pages will show, employing pure input-output analysis to measure the extent of employment in *any* sector, especially the services sector, is fraught with methodological problems.

8. USDA, *Economic Indicators.*

9. See the *New York Times,* 2 February 1985, editorial page, for a policy-related example of the "3% who heroically produce for all of us and for all the world."

10. Council of Economic Advisers, *Economic Report,* 1984, table B-37, p. 263.

11. Office of the U.S. Trade Representative, *Annual Report of the President of the United States on the Trade Agreements Program,* 1983, p. 25.

12. Congressional Budget Office, *The Industrial Policy Debate,* December 1983, p. 13.

13. Ibid., p. 12. The figures of 47 percent and 53 percent reflect the ratios of goods and services to GNP, where GNP excludes structures.

14. Trucking and warehousing have an indirect employment multiplier of .49 for each $1 million of apparel sales. Sales are valued at the site of production (producer's value) and exclude transportation and handling charges. Furthermore, the multiplier only includes employment required through the manufacturer and thus excludes trucking and warehousing employment and its induced employment that is related to wholesaling and retailing. In 1977 dollars, the 1984 producer's value of apparel production was approximately $40.6 billion and generated about 19,000 jobs linked to warehousing and trucking. See the Department of Labor, Bureau of Labor Statistics, Office of Economic Growth and Employment Projections, *Input-Output Sectoring Plan,* 7 October 1985. The I/O table is based on the aggregation of the Bureau of Economic Analysis, 1977 I/O table and the 1984 Bureau of Labor Statistics' estimates of the producer value of outputs.

15. See Jay Stowsky, "Beating Our Plowshares into Double-Edged Swords: the Impact of Pentagon Policies on the Commercialization of Advanced Technologies," *BRIE Working Paper* 17, BRIE, University of California, Berkeley.

Chapter 3

1. Council of Economic Advisers, *Economic Report of the President,* February 1984, p. 43.

2. Ibid., Table B-99, p. 332.

3. See for instance the New York Stock Exchange's *U.S. International Competitiveness: Perception and Reality* (New York: N.Y. Stock Exchange, August 1984), pp. 30–32; comments by the Office of the U.S. Trade Representative, *Annual Report of the President of the United States on the Trade Agreements Program,* 1983, pp. 25–26, 99–101; see also Ronald K. Shelp, *Beyond Industrialization: Ascendancy of the Global Service Economy* (New York: Praeger, 1981), p. 2.

4. Council of Economic Advisers, *Economic Report,* 1984, pp. 42–45.

5. Office of the U.S. Trade Representative, *Annual Report of the President of the United States on the Trade Agreements Program,* 1984–85, p. 2.

6. Ibid., p. 5.

7. U.S. Department of Commerce, International Trade Administration, *United States Trade: Performance in 1984 and Outlook* (June 1985), p. 33.

8. Ibid., table 1, p. 81. In 1983 the surplus was higher, $5.6 billion (but the merchandise deficit was also better: $69 billion); in 1982 the surplus was $9 billion. It peaked at $9.5 billion in 1981 and wound back down to $2.5 billion in 1977.

9. See Jonathan David Aronson and Peter F. Cowhey, "Trade in Services: A Case for Open Markets" (Paper prepared for the American Enterprise Institute for Public Policy Research, *Public Policy Week,* Washington, D.C., 1984).

10. Economic Consulting Services, *The International Operations of U.S. Service Industries: Current Data Collections and Analysis,* June 1981.

11. On telephone destinations see Mitchell L. Moss, "Telecommunications and the Future of Cities," *Land Development Studies* 3 (1986), pp. 001–012.

12. See Congress of the United States, Office of Technology Assessment, *Trade in Services: A Special Report,* September 1986.

13. U.S. Department of Commerce, *U.S. Trade: 1984,* p. 38.

14. Ibid., p. 39.

15. Ibid.

16. Ibid., pp. 12–14, 34–40.

17. "The Shrinking World of U.S. Engineering Contractors," *Business Week,* 24 September 1984, p. 84.

18. See Stephen S. Cohen and John Zysman, "The Mercantilist Challenge to the Liberal International Trade Order" (Paper prepared for the Joint Economic Committee, Congress of the United States, November 1982), pp. 46 ff; Francisco Colman Sercovich, "Development Discussion Paper No. 96" (Unpublished article for the Harvard Institute for International Development, Cambridge, MA).

19. For an enlightening discussion of the development of this phenomenon in Southeast Asia, see Allen J. Scott, "The Semiconductor Industry in South-East Asia: Organization, Location and the International Division of Labor" (UCLA, 1985), pp. 4, 23–35; forthcoming in *Regional Studies,* 1987. Of special note is figure 4, detailing the growing clusters of semiconductor service and manufacturing linkages in Manila.

20. *Institutional Investor,* June 1984, pp. 269–80.

21. *San Francisco Chronicle,* 20 July 1984, p. 37.

22. *Wall Street Journal,* 19 June 1984, p. 34. On the shrinking relative position of U.S. banks, see C. Stewart Goddin and Steven J. Weiss, *U.S. Banks' Loss of Global Standing* (Washington, D.C.: Staff Paper, Comptroller of the Currency, 1980–83), p. 2; and see also Philip A. Wellons, *Passing the Buck: Business, Governments, and Third World Debt* (Boston: Harvard Business School Press, forthcoming).

23. See Stephen S. Cohen and John Zysman, "Countertrade, Offsets, Barter, and Buybacks," *California Management Review* (University of California, Berkeley, Winter 1986); Stephen S. Cohen and John Zysman, "Is the World Bartering Itself Out of One Crisis Into Another?," *Los Angeles Times,* 23 March 1986, section IV, p. 3.

24. Cited in *Business Marketing* (January 1984); *Forbes,* 12 March 1984. p. 41.

25. *Forbes,* 12 March 1984, p. 42.

26. *Business Week,* 19 July 1982; *Countertrade,* 19 March 1984.

27. See Gary Banks, in *World Economy* 6 (June 1983). Mr. Banks prepared the GATT briefing book on countertrade policy. See also *International Management* (August 1984), p. 25.

28. *Finance and Development* (published by IMF, January 1984).

29. David Yoffie, "Profiting from Countertrade," *Harvard Business Review* (May/June 1984), p. 8.

30. See *Business Marketing* (January 1984).

31. For an excellent discussion of the *amakudari* (interlocking public-private directorate)

networks in Japanese industrial structure, see Chalmers Johnson, *MITI and the Japanese Miracle* (Stanford: Stanford University Press, 1982), pp. 280–87. See also Andrew Shonfield, *Modern Capitalism* (London: Oxford University Press, 1965), pp. 251–53, for a discussion of interlocking directorates in Germany, as well as the excellent discussion by Wellons, *Passing the Buck.*

32. Michael Borrus et al., "Telecommunications Development in Comparative Perspective: The New Telecommunications in Europe, Japan, and the U.S.," *BRIE Working Paper* 14 (1985), p. 12.

33. See Patrick Cogez, "Telecommunications in West Germany," *Supplement to BRIE Working Paper* 14 (1985), pp. 45–72. See also Karl-Heinz Neumann, "Economic Policy Towards Telecommunications, Information, and the Media in West Germany," in Marcellus Snow, ed., *Marketplace for Telecommunications* (New York: Longman, 1986); Marcellus Snow, "Telecommunications Deregulation in the Federal Republic of Germany," *Columbia Journal of World Business* 18, no. 1 (1983), pp. 53–61.

34. This view was urged by the Services Policy Committee in the *Chairmen's Report on a New Round of Multilateral Trade Negotiations* (submitted to the U.S. Trade Representative, May 1985). See also Jonathan David Aronson and Peter F. Cowhey, *Trade in Telecommunication Services: Prospects for Negotiation* (Cambridge, MA: Ballinger, forthcoming); Geza Feketekuty and J. D. Aronson, "Restrictions on Trade in Communication and Information Services," *The Information Society* 2, no. 3–4 (1984).

35. In belated recognition of this oversight, Senate Bill 2094, the so-called Danforth Bill, was introduced in 1982 and received favorable treatment by the Senate Finance Committee in June of that year. The bill proposes to "achieve the same degree of access to foreign markets for competitive U.S. exports, services, and investment that we [the U.S.] accord to other countries." See the *Congressional Record* Jan. 1982, 2nd sess., 128 (11), p. 5. See also the fuller treatment of the bill in William Cline, ed., *Trade Policy in the 1980's* (Washington, D.C.: Institute for International Economics, 1983), pp. 123, 153 ff.

36. See Joan Edelman Spero, "Trade in Services: Removing Barriers," *Political Science* (Winter 1983), pp. 17–24; see also Office of the U.S. Trade Representative, *Report on Trade Agreements, 1984–85*, pp. 99–100.

37. Many foreign governments consider the current U.S. effort to cast trade in services in a GATT format to be a new tactic, after the failure of the direct approach, to push deregulation on them. It is an interpretation that presages resistence—at a minimum long, slow negotiations. For a summary of the U.S. policy position, see William E. Brock, USTR, "A Simple Plan for Negotiating on the Trade in Services," *World Economy* 5 (November 1982).

Chapter 4

1. The literature on service growth as a sign of development has been cited in the notes to Chapter 1. For arguments that the growth of the service sector represents economic stagnation, see Barry Bluestone and Bennett Harrison, *The Deindustrialization of America: Plant Closings, Community Abandonment, and the Dismantling of Basic Industry* (New York: Basic Books, 1982); Bob Kuttner, "The Declining Middle," *The Atlantic Monthly* (July 1983); Emma Rothschild, "Reagan and the Real America," *The New York Review,* 5 February 1981.

2. Jorge Luis Borges, "The Analytical Language of John Wilkins," *Other Inquisitions* (Austin: University of Texas Press, 1964), p. 103.

3. *National Journal,* 27 July 1985, p. 1724.

4. *Forbes,* 11 April 1983, p. 146. For other sources on the conceptualization and operationalization of services categories, see H. C. Browning and J. Singlemann, *The Emergence of a Service Society* (Springfield, VA, National Technical Information Service, 1978); Colin Clark, *The Conditions of Economic Progress* (London: Macmillan, 1940); Allan Fisher, *The Clash of Progress and Security* (London: Macmillan, 1935); Allan Fisher, "A Note on Tertiary Production," *Economic Journal* 62 (December 1952); Allan Fisher, "Tertiary Production: A Postscript," *Economic Journal* 64 (September 1954); Victor Fuchs, *The Service Economy* (New York: National Bureau of Economic Research, 1968); Jonathan Gershuny and Ian Miles, *The New Service Economy: The Transformation of Employment in Industrial Societies* (New York: Praeger, 1983).

5. SESAME *Travaux et recherches de prospective* (Paris: La Documentation Française, 1974).

6. Bell's tendency to define services by residual classification is aptly pointed out by Jonathan Gershuny in his book *After Industrial Society?: The Emerging Self-Service Economy* (Atlantic Highlands, NJ: Humanities Press, 1978), p. 56.

7. Colin Clark, *Condition of Economic Progress.*

8. Ronald K. Shelp, *Beyond Industrialization: Ascendancy of the Global Service Economy* (New York: Praeger, 1981), pp. 10–11.

9. George J. Stigler, *Trends in Employment in the Service Industries* (Princeton: Princeton University Press, 1956), p. 47.

10. Office of the U.S. Trade Representative, *Annual Report of the President of the United States on the Trade Agreements Program,* pp. 7, 24.

11. Congressional Budget Office, *The Industrial Policy Debate,* pp. 11, 13.

12. Office of the U.S. Trade Representative, *Report on Trade Agreements,* p. 24.

13. Congressional Budget Office, *Industrial Policy,* p. 14.

14. U.S. Department of Labor, Bureau of Labor Statistics, *Employment and Earnings,* August 1984, Table B-1, p. 43.

15. Council of Economic Advisers, *Economic Report of the President,* February 1984, Table B-37, p. 263.

16. Council of Economic Advisers, *Economic Report of the President,* February 1985, p. 263.

17. Council of Economic Advisers, *Economic Report,* 1984, Table B-37, p. 263; Department of Labor, *Employment and Earnings,* August 1984, Table B-1, p. 43.

18. U.S. Department of Labor, Bureau of Labor Statistics, *Employment and Earnings,* 1975, 1980.

19. Ibid.

20. Ibid.

21. Ibid.

22. Ted K. Bradshaw, "California as a Post-Industrial Society" (Institute of Governmental Studies, University of California, Berkeley, 1973), p. 13.

23. Office of the U.S. Trade Representative, *Report on Trade Agreements,* p. 26.

24. Shelp, *Beyond Industrialization,* p. 21.

25. Bradshaw, "California Post-Industrial Society"; Shelp, *Beyond Industrialization,* p. 13. For French services/industry employment figures see Institut National de la Statistique et des Etudes Economiques (INSEE), *Annuaire statistique de la France,* 1985, Tableau C.01-4, pp. 101–104.

26. On France see Maurice Parodi, *L'Economie et la société française depuis 1945* (Paris, 1981), pp. 80, 369.

27. For data on the period between 1950 and 1970, see INSEE, *Tableaux de l'économie française,* 1980, p. 83; for data on the period between 1974 and 1979, see Parodi, *L'Economie française,* p. 48.

28. Commissariat Général du Plan, *Rapport sur les emplois dans les services,* 8e plan, p. 33.

29. Shelp, *Beyond Industrialization,* p. 23.

Chapter 5

1. Computed from Alan Altschuler et al, *The Future of the Automobile* (Cambridge, MA: MIT Press, 1984), table 2.3, p. 19.

2. See François Hetman, *Les Secrets des giants americains* (Paris: Seuil, 1969).

3. J.J. Servan-Schreiber, *The American Challenge* (New York: Atheneum, 1968).

4. Altschuler, *Future of Automobile,* p. 19.

5. See Lester C. Thurow, *The Zero-Sum Society: Distribution and the Possibilities for Economic Change* (New York: Basic Books, 1980), pp. 3–5.

6. "The Hollow Corporation," *Business Week,* 3 March 1986, p. 59.

7. Office of the U.S. Trade Representative, *Annual Report of the President of the United States on the Trade Agreements Program,* 1985, table 5, p. 20.

8. Robert Z. Lawrence, *Can America Compete?* (New York: Praeger, 1981), p. 5.

9. Ray Marshall and Norman J. Glickman, "Choices for American Industry" (Paper prepared for the Industrial Union Department of the AFL-CIO, Austin, Spring 1986), p. 4.

10. The preceding definition of competitiveness is taken from vol. 3 of *Global Competition: The New Reality*, the Report of the President's Commission on Industrial Competitiveness, by Stephen S. Cohen, David Tecce, Laura D'Andrea Tyson, and John Zysman, (Washington, D.C.: GPO, 1985) from which the following pages draw heavily.

11. Among the problems associated with measuring changes in world market shares, the most salient is over the choice of volume (units of goods and services) or value (currency value of the goods and services) as a measure of market share. Any devaluation of a currency will, ceteris paribus, result in medium-term gains in the number of *units* of domestically produced goods a nation exports during a given period. In the short run, however, the *value* and revenue which those goods bring to the nation are lessened by the weakened position of the devalued currency.

12. Thurow, *Zero-Sum Society*.

13. Robert Z. Lawrence argues, we believe wrongly, that national economies *can* realize long-term growth by the instrument of competitive devaluations—so long as the positive effect of relative currency price differentials offsets the slower growth rate of the nation's productivity. See Lawrence, *Can America Compete?*, pp. 4, 43–44, 95. While this may be true in a static sense—while competitive devaluations may bring increased exports in the short run —we argue that the *dynamic* and deleterious effects of productivity stagnation far outweigh any immediate benefits of competitive devaluation.

14. The methodological problems associated with the calculation of world export shares and comparative national productivity levels are discussed by Irving B. Kravis and Robert E. Lipsey of the National Bureau of Economic Research (NBER) in "Productivity and Trade Shares" (Washington, D.C.: NBER Conference on Research and Recent and Prospective U.S. Trade Policy, March 1984), and in greater detail in Robert E. Lipsey and Irving B. Kravis, "The Competitive Position of U.S. Manufacturing Firms," in Banca Nazionale del Lavoro, *Quarterly Review* 153 (June 1985), pp. 127–54. The Robert Lipsey–Irving Kravis finding is that American multinationals increased their share of world trade between 1966–77, while America's share declined. Their later work shows that though the increases in share stopped around 1977, American MNCs have held onto their relative position up to 1983 when the data stops.

First, the central question is not the accuracy of the data but rather their meaning. What is significant is that American-based MNCs are increasing their share of world trade? Is it, as Lipsey-Kravis present it, a positive indicator of American managerial and technical performance (with an implicit critique of the United States as a production location)? Or does it mean that they are sourcing on a world basis and hence generating massive increases in international transactions for the same (or even shrinking) volumes of output? Is the sourcing from their own plants that use their own technologies and their own people or are joint ventures with partners who have (or will soon have) superior production technologies becoming more commonplace? Is the sourcing from high-wage countries or from cheap labor platforms? Does it mean that restrictions on domestic content in country after country have propelled those firms into a complex production strategy of producing a share of value added in a maximum number of locations and then engaging in massive international shipments? There are many possible meanings.

The Lipsey-Kravis discussion suggests that they attribute the strong showing of the U.S. MNCs to their technological, production, and organizational advantage. But a look at some of the major sectors that dominate the statistics (excluding oil) creates more than some doubt about that conclusion.

The revealed American MNC advantage in the Lipsey-Kravis study is in transportation and machinery. Transportation means automobiles and aircraft. These are delightful sectors to analyze because the number of firms selling the final products are so small we can talk about the companies, their strategies, and not just aggregated trade numbers. In 1977 the United States dominated world auto production and held a strong position in markets throughout the world. Certainly the competitive position of our major automobile multinationals— General Motors, Ford, Chrysler, and American Motors—has deteriorated radically since. Thus, any trade numbers used to suggest a continuing strong position should be carefully examined. In the last ten years American firms were responding with a world car strategy to local content regulations in many markets. This meant exchanging components across national borders. Such a strategy will, of course, produce enormous "export" numbers. In a competitive context where the share of the American market held by the American firms drops and their shares of third markets also declines, a rising share of world trade should not be taken as a prima facie indicator of competitive strength. American firms still dominate aircraft competition. But Boeing is not an MNC in the Lipsey-Kravis sense; its stellar performance does not support their argument, indeed it provides a powerful counterexample. In railway equipment, American producers have lost market share badly; and American truck producers and the very multinational American producers of agricultural equipment (Harvester, Deere, Ford) have also experienced serious erosion.

Machinery is a more ambiguous category in this particular data set. Yet, certainly, in a wide range of machinery sectors American producers have lost position in the last years. Machine tools, NCs, robots, fork lifts, construction equipment, and production equipment in general would be a good instance. A steady position for American MNCs in machinery, in the face of a decline in the position of some major equipment industries, must mean an expansion in the market share and export position of others. This will in all likelihood be in sectors such as computers and computer components. Yet here American firms are facing substantial and growing competition, particularly from the Japanese. Take semiconductors. World market share has declined. Our exports of semiconductor equipment is endangered by a basic shift in technological position. Similarly, in the last two years with the deregulation of the American telecommunications market, we have begun running a major trade deficit in these sectors. In sum, a much closer look at much more refined data than is available would be needed to conclude that only the American production location and not the production, technology, and management of American MNCs is at issue. A somewhat casual examination of the data, all that is really possible because of its level of aggregation, suggests that the position of American multinationals in general is following more basic national trends. There is a lag, and these are our strongest national firms, but the difficulties we see in the national data can be seen here.

The second question is whether the extent of multinational exports reflects sourcing decisions that will emerge as decisive competitive weaknesses. There are reasons to think so. In some cases firms have moved production abroad to be closer to markets, either because governments have compelled them to or because market requirements force it. In other cases, American firms have moved abroad to source components or conduct assembly in cheap labor locations. They have done so, in sectors such as color televisions, as an alternative to developing their mastery of production. The result in televisions and semiconductors has been that a lack of manufacturing expertise, resulting from procurement decisions in the 1960s and 1970s, has emerged as a decisive competitive disadvantage. Some firms are waking up to this. IBM, for instance, has decided that only competitive production—which means a capacity to manufacture competitively in the advanced countries—will allow them to continue to capture returns from innovations.

15. Council of Economic Advisers, *Economic Report of the President,* 1986, p. 301.

16. See Elizabeth Kremp and Jacques Mistral, "Commerce extérieur americain: d'où vient, où va le deficit?," *Economie prospective internationale* 22 (Paris: Centre d'Etudes Prospectives et d'Informations Internationales) (CEPII), 1985, pp. 5–41.

17. It is worth noting that the elasticity of imports into Japan is very low—that is, as the price of American or European goods rises and falls, the change in volumes purchased is very small. This can be an indication of the competitiveness of Japanese industry, the impermeability of many of its markets, or both. See Clyde H. Farnsworth, "Trade Gap with Japan is Expected to Grow," *New York Times,* 9 December 1985 A1–107, col. 1.

18. The view that the U.S. trade problem is one of an overvalued exchange rate is critiqued by Cohen et al., *Industrial Competitiveness,* pp. 29–32. Our *structural* competitive problem was in fact compounded by currency overvaluation in ways not easily reversible.

19. For information on the rising (trade-weighted) value of the dollar, see the Council of Economic Advisers, *Economic Report of the President,* February 1985, pp. 351. For information on the declining price of imported goods over the same period, see U.S. Dept. of Commerce, *United States Trade: Performance in 1984 and Outlook,* June 1985, p. 108. NOTE: This table shows import *prices* as the same or even rising, and *volumes* increasing at an even faster rate.

20. Farnsworth, "Trade Gap with Japan."

21. Lawrence, *Can America Compete?,* pp. 74–75, writes: "In summary, the effect of trade has not been to shrink the U.S. manufacturing sector, and the United States has not lost its comparative advantage as a whole. The United States has been developing a growing comparative advantage in high-technology and resource-intensive products, while its comparative advantage in labor-intensive and capital-intensive products manufactured with standardized technologies has been eroding."

22. See "National Strategies: Key to International Competition," in Bruce R. Scott and

George Lodge, eds., *U.S. Competitiveness in the World Economy* (Boston: Harvard Business School Press, 1985), p. 32.

23. Ibid.

24. See Stephen S. Cohen, "Informed Bewilderment: French Economic Strategy and the Crisis," in Stephen S. Cohen and Peter A. Gourevitch, *France in the Troubled World Economy* (London: Butterworth Scientific, 1982), p. 30.

25. See *Textile Exports of Japan* (Tokyo: Institute of Textile Trade Research and Statistics, 1983).

Chapter 6

1. The U.S. doctrine of trade interdependence, reflected in steady pressure for tariff reductions and open trade, has been expressed in the multilateral tariff reduction rounds of the General Agreement on Trade and Tariffs (GATT), negotiations held each decade since World War II. As pointed out by Stephen Krasner, this doctrine was well suited to a postwar world in which the United States, by dint of its commercial strength, could afford to lead the world economy more toward a multilateral, freer, and "friendly" competitive trading network. Indeed, no other nation could seriously challenge U.S. industrial dominance, and free trade promised to increase demand for exports to rebuild the economies of Europe and Japan. See Stephen Krasner, "U.S. Commercial and Monetary Policy: Unravelling the Paradox of External Strength and Internal Weakness," in Peter J. Katzenstein, ed., *Between Power and Plenty: Foreign Economic Policies of Advanced Industrial States* (Madison, WI: University of Wisconsin Press, 1978).

2. See Etienne Davignon, Umberto Colombo, A.P. Speiser, and John Zysman, *Reviews of Innovation Policies: France,* Examiner's Report (Book I) on the Innovation Policies of France, prepared for the OECD Directorate for Science, Technology and Industry, Paris, January 1986.

3. Frank Press, "Technological Competition and the Western Alliance," in Carlo de Benedetti et al., *A High Technology Gap? Europe, Japan, and the United States* (Washington, D.C.: Council on Foreign Relations, forthcoming).

4. Davignon et al., *Reviews of Innovation Policies.*

5. Carlo de Benedetti, "The New Role of Europe in a Global World," in Carlo de Benedetti et al., *A High Technology Gap?*

6. Press, "Technological Competition."

7. Michael J. Piore and Charles F. Sabel, *The Second Industrial Divide: Possibilities for Prosperity* (New York: Basic Books, 1984).

8. Thierry Gaudin, "What Is an Innovation Policy?" in Frances Pinter, ed., *Innovation Policy in Six Countries* (London: North Holland, 1985), p. 26.

9. Ibid.

10. Centre d'Etudes Prospectives et d'Informations Internationales (CEPII), "Economie mondiale: la montée des tensions" (Paris: CEPII, 1983), p. vi.

11. See John Zysman, *Governments, Markets, and Growth: Financial Systems and the Politics of Industrial Change* (Ithaca, NY: Cornell University Press, 1983), chap. 1, for a discussion of this issue.

12. Two examples of this position are: Mancur Olson, *The Rise and Decline of Nations: Economic Growth, Stagflation, and Social Rigidities* (New Haven, CT: Yale University Press, 1982); and Michel Crozier, Samuel P. Huntington, and Jogi Watanuki, *The Crisis of Democracy: Report on the Governability of Democracies to the Trilateral Commission* (New York: New York University Press, 1975).

13. There are a wide range of authors who have written a great deal on the erosion of the postwar economic dynamism. A necessary, but by no means exhaustive, list of authors must include Robert Boyer, Jacques Mistral, Benjamin Coriat, and Pascal Petit. See, for instance, Robert Boyer, "New Technologies and Employment in the Eighties: From Science and Technology to Macroeconomic Modelling" (Paper presented to the International Institute of Management/Labor, Market Policy Conference, West Berlin, 1–3 October, 1985); Robert Boyer and Jacques Mistral, "The Present Crisis: From an Historical Interpretation to a Prospective Outlook," *Annales* 3/4 (Paris: Armand Colin, 1983); Robert Boyer, "Wage Formation

in Historical Perspective: The French Experience," *Cambridge Journal of Economics* 3 (1979); Robert Boyer, "Wage Labor, Capital Accumulation, and the Crisis: 1968–1982," *The Tocqueville Review* 5 (Spring/Summer 1983); Robert Boyer, "From Growth to Crisis: The Changing Linkages Between Industrial and Macroeconomic Policies" (Draft for the Brookings Conference on Industry in France: "Implications for the United States," Washington, D.C., 27–28 September 1984).

14. See in particular the works of Robert Boyer cited in note 13.

15. Gaudin, "What Is an Innovation Policy?"

Chapter 7

1. Joseph A. Schumpeter, *Capitalism, Socialism, and Democracy* (New York: Harper & Row, 1942).

2. Richard Nelson provides several examples of industries in which the introduction of new technologies of production has been accompanied by a shift in the dominant firm(s). For example, the commercial airline industry of propeller-driven aircraft was dominated by McDonnell Douglas, but with the introduction of jet technology, gave way to Boeing. See Richard R. Nelson, "Policies in Support of High Technology Industries" (Unpublished mimeo, Yale University, October 1983). See also Richard R. Nelson, *High-Technology Policies: A Five-Nation Comparison* (Washington, D.C.: American Enterprise Institute for Public Policy Research, 1984).

3. Burton H. Klein, *Dynamic Economics* (Cambridge, MA: Harvard University Press, 1977); and Burton H. Klein, "Dynamic Competition and Productivity Advances," in Ralph Landau and Nathan Rosenberg, eds., *The Positive-Sum Strategy: Harnessing Technology for Economic Growth* (Washington, D.C.: National Academy Press, 1986).

4. The structure of a system is determined by the list of factors that influence its operation and by the way in which those factors interact. A parameter measures the effect of any particular independent factor (or variable) on the state of the system (the dependent variable). Thus, in economics, a simple consumption function can be specified as: $C = a + bY$ where C is consumption (the dependent variable), Y is disposable income (an independent variable) and a and b are parameters reflecting the slope and intercept of this (linear) system. In a transition, both the structure of a system and its parameters can change. New factors (variables) can enter the game, and the importance of old factors changes. The system will be unpredictable until parameters stabilize and the new structure of the system is known.

5. Klein, *Dynamic Economics.*

6. As pointed out by Pranab Bardhan, at the University of California, Berkeley, even if there are no learning curve effects and no economies of scale in production, a new producer will still face major costs of entry into a market to establish consumer recognition (perhaps through advertising), set up a sales and distribution network, and perhaps a service network in a new territory. These fixed costs of entry serve as a major barrier to entry for a new producer vis-à-vis the established firm.

7. Michael Borrus, "The Politics of Competitive Erosion in the U.S. Steel Industry," in John Zysman and Laura Tyson, eds., *American Industry and International Competition: Government Policies and Corporate Strategies* (Ithaca, NY: Cornell University Press, 1983), p. 142. See also Sharon Oster, "The Diffusion of Innovation Among Steel Firms: The Basic Oxygen Furnace," *Bell Journal of Economics and Management Science* 113 (Spring 1982). Oster examined the diffusion of the basic oxygen furnace (BOF) in the United States. She found that three variables explained the pattern of diffusion in this country: (i) the size of the unit planned (cost advantage of BOF is greater for smaller units); (ii) the local price of pig iron (the BOF uses a higher ratio of pig iron to scrap iron than the open hearth furnace); and (iii) whether the unit planned is a replacement or an expansion unit (for a replacement unit the savings in variable costs must be large enough to pay for the cost of building the new furnace, whereas with an expansion furnace the total costs of both alternatives are compared—thus the level of growth of demand will influence the rate of diffusion of the innovation). Oster's research suggests that U.S. firms, faced with a stagnant domestic market and limited export potential, had little incentive to invest in the BOF. On the other hand, Japanese producers probably faced a

growing (and protected) domestic steel market, thus leading them to invest earlier in the BOF. We must also, however, acknowledge the importance of wages in the past and current trade problems of the U.S. steel industry.

8. David Teece, "Capturing Value from Technological Innovation," *Working Paper* (Berkeley: Center for Research in Management, March 1986).

9. William J. Abernathy, *The Productivity Dilemma: Roadblock to Innovation in the Automobile Industry* (Baltimore: Johns Hopkins University Press, 1978).

10. Charles F. Sabel, *Work and Politics: The Division of Labor in Industry* (New York: Cambridge University Press, 1982.), p. 32. Sabel's work implies but does not directly develop this position.

11. Richard Nelson points out that "It is important to recognize the essential uncertainties which surround the question—where should R&D resources be allocated—in an industry where technology is advancing rapidly. There generally are a wide number of ways in which the existing technology can be improved, and at least several different paths toward achieving any of these improvements. Ex ante it is uncertain which of the objectives is most worthwhile pursuing, and which of the approaches will prove most successful. Before the fact, aviation experts disagreed on the relative promise of the turboprop and turbojet engines; those that believed in the long-run promise of commercial aircraft designed around turbojet engines were of different minds about where to go forward with a commercial vehicle. Whether and when computers should be transistorized was a topic on which computer designers disagreed; later the extent and timing of adoption of integrated circuit technology in computers was a subject which divided the industry. . . . The uncertainty that characterizes technological advance in high technology industries warns against premature unhedged commitments to particular expensive projects, at least when it is possible to keep options open. The divergences of opinion suggest that a degree of pluralism of competition among those who place their bets on different ideas, is an important, if wasteful, aspect of technological advance." See Nelson, *High-Technology Politics*, pp. 10–13.

12. Harvey Sapolsky, *The Polaris System Development: Bureaucratic and Programmatic Success in Government* (Cambridge, MA: Harvard University Press, 1972).

13. It is this which Charles Sabel's imaginative and important work, *Work and Politics*, shows: technological development is a product of choice. He argues that case when talking about this transition: "by the end of the 1980s it is likely that comparable stories, different in substance but with equally uncertain ends, will be told for each of the advanced industrial countries. The reindustrialization debate in the United States, the wave of neo-liberalism in Great Britain and nationalization in France, and the discussion of democratization and social ownership of large firms in Sweden are surely just the first signs of an epochal redefinition of markets, technologies, and industrial hierarchies. The outcomes willl depend on the daring and imagination of trade unions, industrialists, and politicians, and on the ideas of different social classes about how they want to work and live. But as soon as a new system, however shaky, is in place, the scientific thinkers on the Right will tell you everything everywhere, down to the last detail, was determined by the pursuit of efficiency. Scientific thinkers on the Left will say that each group's inevitable pursuit of its interest, determined by its place in the division of labor, is the real explanation. Both will agree that ideas of dignity and honor, the political programs they inform, and the conflicts to which they give rise were only foam on the wave of history. If you have been persuaded by the book you have just read, you will not believe them." See Sabel, *Work and Politics*, p. 23.

14. Ira C. Magaziner and Thomas M. Hout, "Japanese Industrial Policy," *Policy Papers in International Affairs* 15 (University of California, Berkeley, Institute of International Studies, 1980), pp. 5–34.

15. Andrew Sayer, "New Developments in Manufacturing and Their Spatial Implications," *Working Paper* 49 (University of Sussex, Urban and Regional Studies, 1985).

16. Nathan Rosenberg, *Technology and Culture* (Chicago: University of Chicago Press, 1979), pp. 25–50. See also Nathan Rosenberg, "Technological Change in the Machine Tool Industry," *Journal of Economic History* (December 1963).

17. Nathan Rosenberg, *Inside the Black Box: Technology and Economics* (New York: Cambridge University Press, 1982).

18. Peter S. J. Dunnett, *The Decline of the British Motor Industry* (London: Croom Helm, 1980).

19. This term came into usage with the analyses brought into office by the French socialists. See, in particular, the works of Christian Sauttre, of the Centre d'Etudes Prospectives et d'Informations Internationales (CEPII), Paris.

20. CMOS (complete metal oxide semiconductor) is a logic family made by combining N-channel and P-channel MOS transistors.

21. Rosenberg, *Inside the Black Box*, pp. 74–76.

22. David Teece, "Technology Transfers by Multinational Firms: The Resource Cost of International Technology Transfer," *American Economic Journal* (June 1977); William H. Davidow, *Marketing High Technology: An Insider's View* (London: Collier, MacMillan, 1986).

23. Of course, the arguments of Schumpter already cited are the best known presentations of the position. However the argument appears in a variety of other forms. See Rosenberg, *Inside the Black Box;* and Alfred D. Chandler, *The Visible Hand: The Managerial Revolution in American Business* (Cambridge, MA: Harvard University Press, 1977). Chandler demonstrates the necessary link between the development of the transportation and telecommunication industries, and the development of markets and hierarchically managed firms. See also the excellent article by James R. Kurth, "Political Consequences of the Product Cycle Industrial History and Political Outcomes," *International Organization* 33 (Winter 1979), pp. 1–34.

24. Other good sources on long-term business cycles include Joseph Schumpeter, *Business Cycles: A Theoretical, Historical, and Statistical Analysis of the Capitalist Process* (New York: McGraw-Hill, 1939); Christopher Freeman et al., *Unemployment and Technical Innovation: A Study of Long Waves and Economic Development* (London: Frances Pinter, 1982); Gerhard Mensch, *Stalemate in Technology: Innovations Overcome the Depression* (Cambridge, MA: Ballinger, 1979).

25. See for instance Hiroya Ueno, "The Conception and Evaluation of Japanese Industrial Policy," in Kasuo Sato, ed., *Industry and Business in Japan* (White Plains, NY: Sharpe, 1980), p. 382; Miyohei Sinohara, *Industrial Growth, Trade and Dynamic Patterns in the Japanese Economy* (Tokyo: University of Tokyo Press, 1982), p. 88.

26. Some representative works that express this view include: Yasusuke Murakami, "Toward a Sociocultural Explanation of Japan's Economic Performance," in Kozo Yamamura, ed., *Policy and Trade Issues of the Japanese Economy: American and Japanese Perspectives* (Seattle: University of Washington Press, 1982), pp. 3–46; and Yasusuke Murakami and Kozo Yamamura, "A Technical Note on Japanese Firm Behavior and Economic Policy," in ibid., pp. 113–21; Kozo Yamamura, review article in *The Journal of Japanese Studies* 9 (Winter 1983), pp. 202–217, and his "Success That Soured: Administrative Guidance and Cartels in Japan," in Yamamura, ed., *Policy and Trade Issues of the Japanese Economy,* pp. 77–112. The rather ambiguous views of Gary Saxonhouse might also be included under this rubric as well as under the "more market, less policy" school; see Gary Saxonhouse, "Evolving Comparative Advantage and Japan's Imports of Manufactures," *The Journal of Japanese Studies* 5.

Chapter 8

1. Commission of the European Communities, *European Economy* 22 (Brussels: EEC, Directorate General for Economic and Financial Affairs, November 1984), pp. 201–234.

2. International Monetary Fund (IMF), *International Financial Statistics* (Washington, D.C.: IMF, October 1985).

3. The trade figures give us a tentative vindication of this point: Trade = Exports + Imports (cif). In the United States the 1984 figures were: Trade = $559.07 billion, and GNP = $3,662.8 billion; the Trade/GNP ratio was therefore 15.3 percent. In Japan the 1984 figures were: trade = $363 billion, GNP = $1,464 billion, and the Trade/GNP ratio was 25 percent.

4. IMF, *International Financial Statistics,* pp. 486–87.

5. Council of Economic Advisers, *The Annual Report of the Council of Economic Advisers* (January 1985), p. 346.

6. For an interesting story see the case study of Benetton undertaken by Fiorenza Belussi: "The Diffusion of Innovation in Traditional Sectors: The Case of Benetton," *BRIE Working Paper* 19 (1986).

7. U.S. Department of Commerce, *United States Trade: Performance in 1984 and Outlook* (June 1985), p. 109.

8. Numbers used to calculate this figure were drawn from ibid.

9. Susan Strange, "Protectionism and World Politics," *International Organization* 39 (Spring 1985).

10. Ibid, p. 248.

11. Department of Commerce, *U.S. Trade: 1984*, pp. 25–27. 1984 U.S. imports from Europe = \$60 billion = 17.6 percent of U.S. imports. 1984 U.S. exports to Europe = \$47 billion = 21.6 percent of total U.S. exports. 1984 U.S. imports from Asia (Japan + East Asian NICs) = \$99.4 billion = 29.1 percent of U.S. imports. 1984 U.S. exports to Asia = \$41.6 billion = 19.1 percent of total U.S. exports.

12. See Strange, "Protectionism and World Politics," p. 251.

13. Sam Jameson, "Japan a Hard Sell, Even for Asians," *Los Angeles Times,* 6 December 1985, part IV, p. 3.

14. John Zysman, *Governments, Markets, and Growth: Financial Systems and the Politics of Industrial Change* (Ithaca, NY: Cornell University Press, 1983), p. 32. See also Richard N. Cooper, *The Economics of Interdependence: Economic Policy in the Atlantic Community* (New York: McGraw-Hill, 1968).

15. John Zysman and Laura Tyson, eds., *American Industry in International Competition: Government Policies and Corporate Strategies* (Ithaca, NY: Cornell University Press, 1983), p. 27. The Hecksher-Ohlin theory assumes a standard production technology to which all countries have access, and given factor endowments in each country. Under these assumptions, the theory posits that free trade will lead to increasing specialization among trading partners, as factor prices and hence production costs of traded goods converge. The theory treats the determinants of factor endowments as exogenous and overlooks the important fact that technologies are not the same among nations producing the same goods. As a consequence, certain critically important policy issues are placed beyond the reach of theoretical analysis. One such issue is the impact of government policies on the process of both physical and human capital accumulation over time.

16. David Teece, "Toward an Economic Theory of the Multiproduct Firm," *Journal of Economic Behavior and Organization* 3 (1982), pp. 39–63.

17. Steven S. Cohen, David Teece, Laura D. Tyson, and John Zysman, *Competitiveness,* vol. III, *Global Competition: The New Reality,* Report of the President's Commission on Industrial Competitiveness (Washington, D.C.: GPO, 1985), pp. 5–7.

18. Zysman and Tyson, eds., *American Industry,* pp. 28–32.

19. Zysman, *Government, Markets, and Growth.*

20. Michael Borrus, James Millstein, and John Zysman, "U.S.-Japanese Competition in the Semiconductor Industry: A Study in International Trade and Technological Development," *Policy Papers in International Affairs* 17 (Berkeley: University of California, Institute of International Studies, 1982), p. 123.

21. See James Millstein's chapter on the declining market position of U.S. television producers in Zysman and Tyson, eds., *American Industry,* pp. 106–141.

22. Private conversation.

23. Private conversation.

24. Private conversation.

25. On the development of the semiconductor industries, see Borrus, Millstein, and Zysman, "U.S.-Japanese Competition in the Semiconductor Industry;" Michael Borrus, with James Millstein and John Zysman, "Responses to the Japanese Challenge in High Technology: Innovation, Maturity, and U.S.-Japanese Competition in Microelectronics," *BRIE Working Paper* 6 (1983); Michael Borrus, "Reversing Attrition: A Strategic Response to the Erosion of U.S. Leadership in Microelectronics," *BRIE Working Paper* 13 (1985); Leslie Brueckner, with Michael Borrus, "Assessing the Commercial Impact of the VHSIC (Very High Speed Integrated Circuit) Program," *BRIE Working Paper* 5 (1984); Jay Stowsky, "Beating our Plowshares into Double-Edged Swords: The Impact of Pentagon Policies on the Commercialization of Advanced Technologies," *BRIE Working Paper* 17 (1986).

26. Hambrecht and Quist, Investment Bankers, "Institutional Research Department Report" (San Francisco, CA, 21 January 1982).

27. T. J. Pempel, "Japanese Foreign Economic Policy: The Domestic Economy, and the Problem of Pluralistic Stagnation," in Peter J. Katzenstein, ed., *Between Power and Plenty: Foreign Economic Policies of Advanced Industrial States* (Madison, WI: University of Wisconsin Press, 1978).

28. See Carol Parsons and Jay Stowsky, "Semiconductor Industry," Jay Stowsky, "Telecommunication Equipment Industry," Robert Scott, "Motor Vehicles," and Carol Parsons, "Apparel Industry," in Laura Tyson et al., *The Effects of International Trade on Employment* (Berkeley: University of California, BRIE, 1985); Laura Tyson and John Zysman, "American Industry in International Competition," in Zysman and Tyson eds., *American Industry.*

29. General Motors Annual Report (Detroit, 1985).

30. Ray Vernon, "International Investment and International Trade in the Product Cycle," *Quarterly Journal of Economics* (May 1966).

31. David Teece, "Technology Transfers by Multinational Firms; The Resource Cost of International Technology Transfer," *American Economic Journal* (June 1977); and William H. Davidow, *Marketing High Technology: An Insider's View* (London: Collier, MacMillan, 1986).

32. Davidow, *Marketing High Technology*.

33. Teece, "Technology Transfers by Multinational Firms."

34. Ibid.

Chapter 9

1. International Energy Agency, *World Energy Outlook* (Paris: Organization for Economic Cooperation and Development, 1982), p. 95.

2. Ibid.

3. On the recent development of the automobile industry, see Alan Altschuler et al., *The Future of the Automobile: The Report of MIT's International Automobile Program* (Cambridge, MA: MIT Press, 1984). See also Robert E. Cole and Taizo Yakushuji, *The American and Japanese Auto Industries in Transition: Report of the Joint U.S.-Japan Automotive Study* (Ann Arbor: Center for Japanese Studies, University of Michigan, 1984).

4. Burton H. Klein, *Dynamic Economics* (Cambridge, MA: Harvard University Press, 1977); and Burton H. Klein, "Dynamic Competition and Productivity Advances," in Ralph Landau and Nathan Rosenberg, eds., *The Positive-Sum Strategy: Harnessing Technology for Economic Growth* (Washington, D.C.: National Academy Press, 1986).

5. Robert Scott, "Motor Vehicles," in William Dickens et al., *The Employment Effects of International Trade* (Berkeley: University of California, BRIE, 1985). We have also discussed these issues at length with union officials.

6. Private conversation.

7. Burton H. Klein, "Dynamic Competition and Productivity Advances," in Landau and Rosenberg, eds., *Positive-Sum Strategy*, p. 85.

8. Ibid., 78.

9. See, for example, Richard R. Nelson and Sidney G. Winter, *An Evolutionary Theory of Economic Change* (Cambridge, MA: Belknap Press, Harvard University, 1982).

10. Robert Boyer and P. Petit, "Forecasting the Impact of Technical Change on Employment: Methodological Reflections and Proposals for Research" (Brussels: Commission of the European Communities); and Diettrich and Morley, eds., "Relations Between Technology, Capital, and Labour" (Paris: Centre d'Etudes Prospectives d'Economie Mathematique Appliquées à la Planification, 1981).

11. Klein, "Dynamic Competition," p. 86.

12. Steven Wheelright and Robert M. Hayes, *Restoring Our Competitive Edge: Competing Through Manufacturing* (New York: Wiley, 1984).

13. Klein, "Dynamic Competition," p. 78.

14. Ibid, p. 87.

15. Barbara Baran et al., "Technological Innovation and Deregulation: The Transformation of the Labor Process in the Insurance Industry," *BRIE Working Paper* 9 (1985).

16. Ibid.

17. Nathan Rosenberg, *Inside the Black Box: Technology and Economics* (New York: Cambridge University Press, 1982), pp. 254–55.

18. B. R. Mitchell, *European Historical Statistics: 1750–1975*, 2nd ed. (New York: Facts on File, 1981). For a discussion of the politics of this process, see the classic work of Alexander Gerschenkon, *Bread and Democracy in Germany* (Berkeley & Los Angeles: UC Press, 1943; reprinted in NY by H. Fertig, 1966) and Peter Gourevitch's excellent reexamination of the same issues in *Politics in Hard Times* (Ithaca, NY: Cornell Univ. Press, 1986).

19. Annual Reports from IBM, Burroughs, and DEC, for 1984.

20. U.S. Department of Commerce, Bureau of the Census, *Statistical Abstract of the United States*, 1985, 105th ed., p. 522.

21. Alfred D. Chandler, *The Visible Hand: The Managerial Revolution in American Business* (Cambridge, MA: Harvard University Press, 1977).

22. Ibid. See also, Alfred D. Chandler, *Strategy & Structure: Chapters in the History of the American Industrial Enterprise* (Cambridge, MA: MIT Press, 1969).

23. Frederick W. Taylor, *The Principles of Scientific Management* (New York: Harper & Brothers, 1911). For an analysis of the extension and elaboration of Taylorist practices see C. R. Littler, *The Development of the Labour Process in Capitalist Societies* (London: Heinemann, 1982).

24. See L.J. White, *The Automobile Industry Since 1945* (Cambridge, MA: Harvard University Press, 1971).

25. Harry Braverman, *Labor and Monopoly Capital: The Degradation of Work in the Twentieth Century* (New York: Monthly Review Press, 1975), is the best known expositor of this position. However, his argument is now widely accepted in management circles as well.

26. See Hounshell's excellent new history of American production systems for a good discussion of all this: David A. Hounshell, *From the American System to Mass Production, 1800–1932* (Baltimore: John Hopkins University Press, 1984).

27. Boyer and Petit, "Forecasting the Impact of Technical Change."

28. Andrew Sayer, "New Developments in Manufacturing and Their Spatial Implications," *Working Paper* 49 (University of Sussex, Urban and Regional Studies, October 1985).

29. For an interesting perspective, see Yasusuke Murakami, "Toward a Sociocultural Explanation of Japan's Economic Performance," in Kozo Yamamura, ed., *Policy and Trade Issues of the Japanese Economy: American and Japanese Perspectives* (Seattle: University of Washington Press, 1982), pp. 3–46; Yasusuke Murakami and Kozo Yamamura, "A Technical Note on Japanese Firm Behavior and Economic Policy," in Yamamura, ed, *Policy and Trade Issues*, pp. 113–21; Kozo Yamamura, review article in *The Journal of Japanese Studies* 9 (Winter 1983), pp. 202–17, and his "Success That Soured: Administrative Guidance and Cartels in Japan," in Yamamura, ed., *Policy and Trade Issues*, pp. 77–112.

30. Klein, "Dynamic Competition."

31. Murakami and Yamamura, "A Technical Note," pp. 115–116.

32. Private conversation.

33. Two sources for the development of the Honda corporation are: Tetsuo Sakiya, *Honda Motor: The Men, The Management, The Machines* (New York: Harper & Row, 1982); Sol Sanders, *Honda: The Man and His Machines* (Boston: Little, Brown, 1975).

34. Sayer, "New Developments in Manufacturing," p. 19.

35. James C. Abegglen and George Stalk, Jr., *Kaisha: The Japanese Corporation* (New York: Basic Books, 1985), p. 80.

36. Ibid., p. 96.

37. Ibid., p. 98.

38. Chalmers Johnson, *MITI and the Japanese Miracle* (Stanford: Stanford University Press, 1982) is the best available history of the politics of postwar Japanese development.

39. Sayer, "New Developments in Manufacturing," p. 20.

40. David B. Friedman, "Beyond the Age of Ford: The Strategic Basis of Japanese Success in Automobiles," in John Zysman and Laura Tyson, eds., *American Industry and International Competition: Government Policies and Corporate Strategies* (Ithaca, NY: Cornell University Press, 1983), chap. 7. See also Abegglen and Stalk, *Kaisha.*

41. Friedman, in Zysman and Tyson, eds., *American Industry.*

42. Ibid., and David B. Friedman, "The Misunderstood Miracle: Politics and the Development of a Hybrid Economy in Japan," PhD. dissertation, 1986.

43. Sayer, "New Developments in Manufacturing."

44. Charles F. Sabel, *Work and Politics: The Division of Labor in Industry* (New York: Cambridge University Press, 1982). For another interpretation of the Italian case, see Philip Mattera "Small Is Not Beautiful: Decentralized Production and the Underground Economy in Italy," *Radical America* 14, no. 5 (1980).

45. Fiorenza Belussi, "The Diffusion of Innovation in Traditional Sectors: The Case of Benetton," *BRIE Working Paper* 19 (1986).

46. Kathleen Thelen, Research Associate at BRIE, has made this point in her dissertation (in progress) on German Labor.

Chapter 10

1. Robert U. Ayers and Steven Miller of Carnegie-Mellon University estimated the potential savings in metal-working industries resulting from the introduction of flexible automa-

tion at anything from 7 to 30 percent, the highest resulting in products most likely to be produced in smaller batches. See their piece "Robotics, CAM, and Industrial Productivity," *National Productivity Review* 1 (Winter 1981–82). See also Carol Parsons, "Apparel Industry," and Robert Scott, "Motor Vehicles," in Laura Tyson et al., *The Employment Effects of International Trade* (Berkeley: University of California, BRIE, 1985).

2. Michael J. Piore and Charles F. Sabel argue this point in *The Second Industrial Divide: Possibilities for Prosperity* (New York: Basic Books, 1984).

3. This section draws directly on the work at BRIE on factory automation. The work has been conducted by Carol Parsons and Robert Scott. For an in-depth account of the impact of automation in the factory, see Carol Parsons et al., "Revolution in the Factory: The Case of Metal Machining," *BRIE Working Paper* 10 (1985).

4. Although the discussion in this section is focused primarily on manufacturing technologies, a critical aspect of the microchip revolution is that it has opened the possibility of substantially automating white-collar work as well. See Michael L. Dertouzos and Joel Moses, *The Computer Age: A Twenty Year View* (Cambridge, MA: MIT Press, 1981); Tom Forester, ed., *The Microelectronics Revolution: The Complete Guide to the New Technology and Its Impact on Society* (Cambridge, MA: MIT Press, 1981); Tom Forester, ed., *The Information Technology Revolution* (Cambridge, MA: MIT Press, 1985); Gunter Friedrichs and Adam Schaff, *Microelectronics and Society: For Better or Worse* (Oxford: Pergamon Press, 1982); Eli Ginzberg, "The Mechanization of Work," *Scientific American* 247 (September 1982); International Labour Organization, Advisory Committee on Salaried Employees and Professional Workers, *The Effects of Technological and Structural Changes on the Employment and Working Conditions of Non-Manual Workers*, 8th Session, Report II (Geneva: ILO, 1981); Simon Nora and Alain Minc, *The Computerization of Society* (Cambridge, MA: MIT Press, 1980); Diane Werneke, *Microelectronics and Office Jobs: The Impact of the Chip on Women's Employment* (Geneva: ILO, 1983).

Increasingly in manufacturing firms, integrated systems span the divide from factory to office. As in the manufacturing sector, the diffusion of office automation technologies is being driven in the main by a new competitive environment. See also Barbara Baran et al., "Technological Innovation and Deregulation: The Transformation of the Labor Process in the Insurance Industry," *BRIE Working Paper* 9 (1985).

5. U.S. Congress, Office of Technology Assessment (April, 1984), *Computerized Manufacturing Automation: Employment, Education, and the Workplace*, Ota-Cit-235, p. 34.

6. L.J. White, *The Automobile Industry Since 1945* (Cambridge, MA.: Harvard University Press, 1971), p. 39.

7. Carol Parsons, "The Diffusion of New Manufacturing Technologies in U.S. Industry" (Unpublished paper, BRIE, University of California, Berkeley, 1985).

8. Ibid.

9. Ibid.

10. For an interesting perspective on the Lordstown development, see Stanley Aronowitz, *False Promises: The Shaping of American Working Class Consciousness* (New York: McGraw-Hill, 1973, pp. 21–50).

11. Parsons, "The Diffusion of New Manufacturing Technologies."

12. For an article that compares the costs and optimal batch sizes of turning machines ranging in technological flexibility and sophistication from simple and dedicated lathes to NC machine tools to dedicated, highly automated machine tools see A. Gebhardt and O. Hatzold, "Numerically Controlled Machine Tools," in L. Nasbeth and G. F. Ray, eds., *The Diffusion of New Industrial Processes: An International Study* (London: Cambridge University Press, 1974). For a discussion of optimal batch size and programmable automated production equipment see Joel D. Goldhar and Mariann Jelinek, "Plan for Economies of Scope," *Harvard Business Review* (November/December 1983).

13. Goldhar and Jelinek, "Plan for Economies of Scope."

14. Ayers and Miller, "Robotics, CAM, and Industrial Productivity."

15. Personal interview.

16. There is a series of BRIE sector studies that support this general point.

17. The pressure toward product differentiation and therefore flexibility in production is not limited to manufacturing industries. See Baran et al., "Technological Innovation and Deregulation."

18. Michael J. Piore, "The Technological Foundations of Dualism and Discontinuity," in Suzanne Berger and Michael J. Piore, *Dualism and Discontinuity in Industrial Societies* (Cambridge, MA: Harvard University Press, 1980).

19. Ibid.

20. See, for more detailed information, "Trends in Telecommunications Technology," *European Telecommunications: Strategic Issues and Opportunities for the Decade Ahead,* appendix A (Final Report to the Commission of the European Communities, November 1983), p. 54.

21. Jay Stowsky, "Telecommunications Equipment Industry," in Tyson et al., *The Effects of International Trade on Employment* (Berkeley: University of California, BRIE, 1985).

22. Carol Parsons and Jay Stowsky, "Semiconductor Industry," in Tyson et al., *Effects of International Trade.*

23. This point has broad applicability as well; in a range of industries, both blue- and white-collar, microelectronics-based technologies have made new kinds of products possible.

24. See for example Ian Nicholas et al., "Automating the Shop Floor: Applications of CNC in Manufacturing in Great Britain and West Germany," *Journal of General Management* 8 (Spring 1983), p. 35; A. d'Iribarne and B. Lutz, "Work Organization in Flexible Manufacturing Systems: First Findings from International Comparisons," in T. Martin, ed., *Design of Work in Automated Manufacturing Systems—With Special Reference to Small and Medium Size Firms* (New York: Pergamon Press, 1984).

25. The cost of a fabrication line in 1977 is from the United Nations Centre on Transnational Corporations, *Transnational Corporations in the International Semiconductor Industry* (New York: United Nations, 1986), p. 109; the $30.00 average selling price for a 16K DRAM chip was obtained from a personal interview with Alberto Sangiovanni-Vincentelli of the University of California, Berkeley; other 16K DRAM prices were obtained from William Finan and Chris Amundsen, "An Analysis of the Effects of Targeting on the Competitiveness of the U.S. Semiconductor Industry" (Paper prepared for the Departments of Commerce and Labor, and the U.S. Trade Representative, 30 May 1985); the selling price for the 264K DRAM was obtained from *Electronic News,* 11 August 1986, p. 1.

26. This same principle holds true in office automation applications as well. In high-volume paper-processing industries such as banking and insurance, a qualitative leap in the level of systems integration began to occur in the mid to late 1970s. In the place of single-task, batch-oriented machines, multi-task, multi-machine systems began to be introduced, often operating on-line, in real time. The integrated data bases resulting from these linkages afford firms radical new opportunities in everything from the products and services they offer to the organization of their production and distribution systems. See Baran et al., "Technological Innovation."

27. The total number of NC machine tools installed in metal-working has almost doubled since 1978 to 103,000 units. See "The 13th American Machinist of Inventory of Metalworking Equipment 1983," *American Machinist* (November 1983).

28. U.N. Conference on Trade and Development, *The Diffusion of Electronics Technology in the Capital Goods Sector in the Industrialized Countries* (New York: United Nations, 1985), pp. 17, 19.

29. See Wassily Leontief and Faye Duchin, *The Future Impact of Automation on Workers* (New York: Oxford University Press, 1985).

30. Dennis E. Wisnosky, *The Robot as Focus of the Factory of the Future* (Brookfield, WI: Management Resources Assoc., Inc., Robot Population Explosion Seminar, 29 July 1982).

31. Ibid.

32. Kuni Sadamoto, ed., *Robots in the Japanese Economy* (Tokyo: Survey Japan, 1981), p. 26.

33. Kenichi Ohmae, "Steel Collar Workers: The Lessons from Japan," *Wall Street Journal,* 16 February 1982.

34. For a discussion of Japanese industrial policies and their role in the diffusion of technology, see John Zysman et al., "U.S. and Japanese Trade and Industrial Policies," *BRIE Working Paper* 2 (1984). See also the legal brief entitled: Houdaille Industries, Inc., Petitioner: 31 July 1982; "Petition to the President of the United States Through the Office of the United States Trade Representative for the Exercise of Presidential Discretion Authorized by Section 103 of the Revenue Act of 1971," U.S.C. sect. 48(a)(7)(d).

35. Seymour Melman, *Profits Without Production* (New York: Knopf, 1983), pp. 159–72.

36. Parsons, "Revolution in the Factory"; data from ibid.

37. Melman, *Profits Without Production.* See Chapter 5 for U.S. real wage trends.

38. Gebhardt and Hatzold, "Numerically Controlled Machine Tools," found in a cross-section study that the level of diffusion of NC machine tools was highly positively correlated with relative wage rates. At the time of their study (1970) the level of NC diffusion was

highest in the United States, where wages were also higher than in other industrial countries. Since 1970 the relative level of wages in the United States has fallen.

39. For a detailed history of the Defense Department's role in the development of numerical control see David Noble, *Forces of Production* (New York: Knopf, 1984).

40. Andrew Sayer, "New Developments in Manufacturing and Their Spatial Implications," *Working Paper* 49 (University of Sussex, Urban and Regional Studies, October 1985); and Melman, "Profits Without Production."

41. Ibid.

42. "Marketing: The New Priority," *Business Week,* 21 Nov. 1983, p. 96.

43. Baran et al., "Technological Innovation and Deregulation." See also Sayer, "New Developments in Manufacturing."

44. David Friedman, "Beyond the Age of Ford: The Strategic Basis of the Japanese Success in Automobiles," in Zysman and Tyson, eds., *American Industry in International Competition: Government Policies and Corporate Strategies* (Ithaca, NY: Cornell University Press, 1983), pp. 360–61.

45. See Charles Sabel's discussion of the Fordist organizational model in his excellent *Work and Politics: The Division of Labor in Industry* (New York: Cambridge University Press, 1982).

46. James C. Abegglen and George Stalk, *Kaisha: The Japanese Corporation* (New York: Basic Books, 1985), pp. 43–52.

47. Steven Wheelright and Robert M. Hayes, *Restoring Our Competitive Edge* (New York: Wiley, 1984).

48. Ibid.

49. Marc Maurice, François Sellier, and Jean-Jacques Silvestre, "La Production de la hierarchie dans l'enterprise: Recherche d'un effet sociétal," *Revue Française de Sociologie* 20 (April 1979), pp. 331–80.

50. There is extensive work in Italy on these issues. In the U.S. they have been popularized by Sabel, *Work and Politics;* Piore and Sabel, *The Second Industrial Divide.*

51. For a historical parallel to this argument regarding the relations between politically significant producer groups, see Barrington Moore's *Social Origins of Dictatorships and Democracy: Lord and Peasant in the Making of the Modern World* (Boston: Beacon Press, 1966).

52. Other sources worth investigating are Paul Adler's several works, including: "Technology and Us," *Socialist Review* 85 (January/February 1986); "New Technologies, New Skills," *Harvard Business School Working Paper* (May 1984); "Rethinking the Skill Requirements of New Technologies," *Harvard Business School Working Paper* (October 1983). Also worthy is the work of Fred Block: "The Myth of Reindustrialization," *Socialist Review* 73 (January/February 1984); "Technological Change and Employment: New Perspectives on an Old Controversy," *Economia & Lavoro* (1984); with Larry Hirschhorn, "New Productive Forces and the Contradictions of Contemporary Capitalism: A Post-Industrial Perspective," *Theory and Society* 7, no. 3 (1979). In addition, see Larry Hirschhorn, *Beyond Mechanization: Work and Technology in a Post Industrial Age* (Cambridge, MA: MIT Press, 1984); "The Post Industrial Labor Process," *New Political Science* (Fall 1981).

53. Margaret Sharp, ed., *Europe and the New Technologies* (Ithaca, NY: Cornell University Press, 1986).

54. *Financial Times,* 29 November 1985, p. 29.

55. See Berger and Piore, *Dualism and Discontinuity in Industrial Societies;* and Suzanne Berger, "Regime and interest representation: the French traditional middle classes," Ch. 3, in Suzanne Berger, ed., *Organizing Interests in Western Europe: Pluralism, Corporatism, and the Transformation of Politics* (Cambridge: Cambridge University Press, 1981).

Chapter 11

1. This chapter is heavily drawn from three BRIE studies: Michael Borrus et al., "Impacts of Divestiture and Deregulation: Infrastructural Changes, Manufacturing Transition, and Competition in the U.S. Telecommunications Industry," *BRIE Working Paper* 12 (1984); Michael Borrus and John Zysman, "The New Media, Telecommunications and Development: The Choices for the United States and Japan," *BRIE Working Paper* 7 (1984); and Michael Borrus et al., "Telecommunications Development in Comparative Perspective: The New Telecommunications in Europe, Japan and the U.S.," *BRIE Working Paper* 14 (1985).

2. Judith Gregory, "The Future: Clerical Workers" (Paper presented at National Executive Forum on Office Work Stations in the Home, National Academy of Science, Washington, D.C., November 1983); Jean Marion Ross, "Technology and the Relocation of Employment in the Insurance Industry," *BRIE Working Paper* 16 (1986).

3. "The World on Line," *The Economist,* 23 November 1985.

4. Borrus and Zysman, "New Media."

5. "The World on Line," *The Economist.*

6. On this basis also entire industries will be restructured. Nowhere is this more visible than in the reorganization now under way in the financial services industry. Over the last decade the new computer and telecommunications technologies have played a critical role in beginning the blurring of distinctions between financial service institutions by lowering barriers to entry in a number of product lines and making it easier to circumvent regulatory restrictions. See Barbara Baran et al., "Technological Innovation and Deregulation: The Transformation of the Labor Process in the Insurance Industry," *BRIE Working Paper* 9 (1985).

7. Borrus and Zysman, "New Media," p. 4. For the parallel between telecommunications infrastructure and the railroad infrastructure of a generation earlier see Douglass North, *Economic Growth of the United States* (Englewood Cliffs, NJ: Prentice-Hall, 1961). See also Douglass North, "Location Theory and Regional Economic Growth," in John Friedman and William Alonso, eds., *Regional Development and Planning* (Cambridge, MA: MIT Press, 1964), p. 242.

8. Borrus and Zysman, "New Media," p. 4.

9. Ibid.

10. Ibid.

11. Ibid., pp. 4–5.

12. Ibid., p. 9.

13. Ibid., pp. 10–12.

14. See North, "Location Theory"; North, *Economic Growth of the United States.* See also C. Van Woodward, *Origins of the New South 1877–1913* (Baton Rouge, LA: Louisiana State University Press, 1951).

15. BRIE has organized a telecommunications working group directed by Michael Borrus with the participation of senior executives from major user firms. We are exploring together the uses of the new technologies. We expected remarkable results and uses. Even so, we are startled and amazed.

16. Baran et al., "Technological Innovation and Deregulation."

17. See Jeffrey Barstow, "GM's Automation Protocol," *High Technology* (October 1986), p. 38.

18. Private conversation.

19. "Trends in Telecommunications Technology," *European Telecommunications: Strategic Issues and Opportunities for the Decade Ahead,* Appendix A (Final Report to the Commission of the European Communities, November 1983).

20. Michael Borrus et al, "Telecommunications in Comparative Perspective," *BRIE Working Paper* 14.

21. Ibid.

22. Paul David, "Narrow Windows, Blind Giants, and Angry Orphans: The Dynamics of Systems Rivalries and Dilemmas of Technology Policy" (Paper delivered at the Venice Conference on the Diffusion of Innovation, March 1986), p. 5.

23. Ibid.

24. Ibid.

25. See Michael Borrus and James Millstein, "Technological Innovation and Industrial Growth: A Comparative Assessment of Biotechnology and Semiconductors" (Paper prepared for the U.S. Congress, Office of Technology Assessment, March 1983), pp. 57 ff.

26. Borrus et al., "Telecommunications in Comparative Perspective."

Chapter 12

1. William Dickens, Laura Tyson, and John Zysman, *Trading for Jobs: The Impact of Trade on Employment* (New York: Ballinger, forthcoming).

2. Ibid. See also Robert Scott, "Motor Vehicles," Carol Parsons and Jay Stowsky, "Semiconductor Industry," Jay Stowsky, "Telecommunications Equipment Industry," and Carol Par-

sons, "Apparel Industry," in Laura Tyson et al., *The Employment Effects of International Trade* (Berkeley: University of California, BRIE, 1985).

3. *U.S. Industrial Outlook,* 1985 and 1982 Census of Manufactures, preliminary report, SIC 3674 (June 1984).

4. BRIE studies on telecommunications are fully cited in the notes to chapter 11.

5. Eli Ginzberg, "The Mechanization of Work," *Scientific American* 247 (September 1982); International Labour Organization, Advisory Committee on Salaried Employees and Professional Workers, "The Effects of Technologies and Structural Changes on the Employment and Working Conditions of Non-Manual Workers," 8th Session, Report II (Geneva: ILO, 1981); Wassily W. Leontief, "The Distribution of Work and Income," *Scientific American* 247 (September 1982); Wassily W. Leontief and Faye Duchin, "The Impacts of Automation on Employment" (Final Report to the National Science Foundation, 1984); Simon Nora and Alan Minc, *The Computerization of Society* (Cambridge, MA: MIT Press, 1980); Lester C. Thurow, *The Zero-Sum Solution: Building a World Class American Economy* (New York: Simon and Schuster, 1985).

6. See C. Fred Bergsten, Thomas Horst, and Theodore H. Moran, *American Multinational Corporations and American Interests* (Washington, D.C.: Brookings Institution, 1978).

7. Private conversation.

8. *Asian Wall Street Journal,* 10 March 1986.

9. Homa Bahrami and Steven Wheelwright, *Shugart Corporation: Planning Manufacturing Capabilities,* case no. S-MM-8 (Graduate School of Business, Stanford University, 1985). See also Homa Bahrami and Steven Wheelwright, *Industry Note on Small Capacity Disk Drives,* case no. S-MM-6N (Graduate School of Business, Stanford University, 1985).

10. Ibid.

11. Ibid.

12. Ibid.

Chapter 13

1. This definition was developed in Stephen S. Cohen, David Teece, Laura D'Andrea Tyson, and John Zysman, *Competitiveness* (vol. 3 of *Global Competition: The New Reality*), originally prepared as a Report of the President's Commission on Industrial Competitiveness (Washington, D.C.: GPO, 1985).

2. Robert Skidelsky, "The Decline of Keynesian Politics," in Colin Crouch, ed., *The State and Contemporary Capitalism* (New York: St. Martin's Press, 1979), pp. 55–87.

3. See John Zysman, *Governments, Markets, and Growth: Financial Systems and the Politics of Industrial Change* (Ithaca, NY: Cornell University Press, 1983), pp. 91–95, 310–12.

4. This topic is fully broached by Peter Katzenstein in two of his most recent works: *Small States in World Markets: Industrial Policy in Europe* (Ithaca: Cornell University Press, 1985); and *Corporatism and Change: Austria, Switzerland, and the Politics of Industry* (Ithaca, NY: Cornell University Press, 1984). Also see Douglas A. Hibbs, "On the Political Economy of Long-Run Trends in Strike Activity," *British Journal of Political Science* 8 (1978), pp. 174–75; Douglas A. Hibbs, "Industrial Conflict in Advanced Industrial Societies," *The American Political Science Review* 70 (1976), pp. 1034–58.

5. For a discussion of the politics of the corporatist model, see Katzenskin, *Corporatism and Change,* and Andrew Martin, "Trade Unions in Sweden: Strategic Responses to Change and Crisis," Chapter 3 in Peter Gourevitch et al., *Unions and Economic Crisis: Britain, West Germany, Sweden* (London: George Allen & Unwin, 1984).

6. Zysman, *Governments, Markets,* p. 310; Stephen Cohen, "Twenty Years of the Gaullist Economy," in William Andrews and Stanley Hoffman, eds., *The Fifth Republic at Twenty* (Albany: State University of New York Press, 1981), p. 241.

7. Michael Borrus argues this point.

Chapter 14

1. See Mancur Olson, *The Logic of Collective Action: Public Goods and the Theory of Groups* (Cambridge, MA: Harvard University Press, 1965).

2. See Mancur Olson, *The Rise and Decline of Nations: Economic Growth, Stagflation, and Social Rigidities* (New Haven: Yale University Press, 1982).

3. This viewpoint is espoused by Samuel Huntington in Michael J. Crozier, Samuel P. Huntington, and Joji Watanuki, *The Crisis of Democracy* (New York: New York University Press, 1975, pp. 85–91).

4. Zysman, *Governments, Markets, and Growth: Financial Systems and the Politics of Industrial Change* (Ithaca, NY: Cornell University Press, 1983), see John Zysman, pp. 295–98.

5. See Russell Hardin, *Collective Action* (Baltimore: Resources for the Future/Johns Hopkins Press, 1982), for a fundamental critique of the intellectual base of those arguments.

6. Zysman, *Governments, Markets.* The core of this analysis suggests that the dynamic of growth rests on the character of coalition. Gourevitch reaches the same conclusion in *Politics in Hard Times.*

7. See Stephen S. Cohen, Serge Halimi, and John Zysman, "Institutions, Politics, and Industrial Policy in France," *BRIE Working Paper* 4 (1984), pp. 9–12; John Zysman, *Governments, Markets,* pp. 134–39.

8. See Peter Gourevitch, *Politics in Hard Times: Comparative Responses to International Economic Crises* (Ithaca, NY: Cornell University Press, 1986).

9. Laura Tyson and John Zysman, "American Industry in International Competition," in John Zysman and Laura Tyson, eds., *American Industry in International Competition: Government Politics and Corporate Strategies* (Ithaca, NY: Cornell University Press, 1983), pp. 24, 28.

10. Ibid., pp. 28–29.

Chapter 15

1. For a compelling argument as well as an excellent source of reference on the limited spinoff benefits of Pentagon R&D, see Jay Stowsky, "Beating Our Plowshares into Double-Edged Swords: The Impact of Pentagon Policies on the Commercialization of Advanced Technologies," *BRIE Working Paper* 17 (1986).

2. See Kenichi Ohmae, "Japan's Industrial Policy for High-Technology Industries" (Paper prepared for the Conference on Japanese Industrial Policy in Comparative Perspective, New York, 17–19 March 1984), pp. 31–36, 52–56.

3. The recent Houdaille scandal is a case in point. See the legal brief entitled: Houdaille Industries, Inc., Petitioner: 31 July 1982, "Petition to the President of the United States Through the Office of the United States Trade Representative for the Exercise of Presidential Discretion Authorized by Section 103 of the Revenue Act of 1971," 26 U.S.C. sect. 48(a)(7)(D).

4. See for instance Barbara Baran and Carol Parsons, "Technology and Skill: A Literature Review" (Paper prepared for the Carnegie Forum on Education and the Economy, January 1986); see also Richard Gordon and Linda M. Kimball, "High Technology, Employment, and the Challenges to Education," *Working Paper* 1 (Silicon Valley Research Group, July 1985), pp. 84 ff.

5. See Baran and Parsons, "Technology and Skills."

6. Jonathan Kozol, *Illiterate America* (New York: New American Library, 1985), p. 4.

7. See Herbert J. Walberg, "Scientific Literacy and Economic Productivity in International Perspective," *Daedalus* 112 (Spring 1983).

8. Ibid., p. 7.

9. Walberg, "Scientific Literacy and Economic Productivity."

10. See the description of different national automotive production systems in Alan Altschuler et al., "The Competitive Balance," in Alan Altschuler et al., *The Future of the Automobile* (Cambridge, MA: MIT Press, 1984), pp. 145–75; see also chapters 7 and 8 in National Research Council, *The Competitive Status of the U.S. Auto Industry: A Study of the Influences of Technology in Determining International Industrial Competitive Advantage* (Washington, D.C.: National Academy Press, 1982), pp. 109–132.

11. Traditionally, American firms have been slow to recognize the need to retrain existing labor, preferring instead the time tested short-run palliative of massive layoffs. Recently, however, IBM has been making headway in retraining its workers to work with automated production technologies. See the *Wall Street Journal*, 14 April 1986, p. 1; for an account of similar developments in West Germany, see the *Wall Street Journal*, 23 April 1986, p. 1.

12. See Etienne Davignon, Umberto Colombo A.P. Speiser, and John Zysman, "Reviews of Innovation Policies in France" (Paper prepared for the OECD Directorate of Science, Technology, and Industry, 1986); John Zysman, *Political Strategies for Industrial Order: State, Market, and Industry in France* (Berkeley: University of California Press, 1983).

13. Paul Krugman's work, which often reaches quite different conclusions, has been very helpful.

Chapter 16

1. A number of these arguments are drawn from Stephen S. Cohen and John Zysman, "Muddling Through: American Interests in a Changing International Economy" (Paper prepared for the Conference on International Cooperation and Interaction Between Monetary and Trade Policies, Rome, 20–21 March 1986).

2. For a review of the assumptions and dynamics surrounding the birth of the GATT and the LIEO, see John Zysman and Stephen Cohen, "Double or Nothing: Open Trade and Competitive Industry," *Foreign Affairs* (Summer 1983), pp. 1113–39.

3. See C. Michael Aho and Jonathan David Aronson, *Trade Talks: America Better Listen!* (New York: Council on Foreign Relations, 1985), pp. 29, 84.

4. See Stephen S. Cohen and John Zysman, "Countertrade, Offsets, Barter, and Buybacks," *California Management Review* (University of California, Berkeley, Winter 1986); Stephen S. Cohen and John Zysman, "Is the World Bartering Itself Out of One Crisis into Another?," *Los Angeles Times,* 23 March 1986, part IV, p. 3.

5. Friedman makes a similar argument regarding unilateral reductions in trade barriers in the absence of reciprocity. See "Free Trade," in Milton Friedman, *An Economist's Protest* (Glen Ridge, N.J.: Thomas Horton & Daughters, 1972), pp. 168–70.

6. The concept and implications of the "developmental state" are aptly discussed by Chalmers Johnson, *MITI and the Japanese Miracle* (Stanford: Stanford University Press, 1982), pp. 306 ff.

7. T. J. Pempel, "Japanese Foreign Policy: The Domestic Bases for International Behavior," in Peter J. Katzenstein, ed., *Between Power and Plenty: Foreign Economic Policies of Advanced Industrial States* (Madison, WI: University of Wisconsin Press, 1978), p. 139.

8. Stephen Krasner, "Institutional Asymmetries and Japanese-American Economic Conflict: The Case for Specific Reciprocity" (Unpublished paper, Stanford, September 1986), pp. 32 ff.

9. Kozo Yamamura, "Success That Soured," in Kozo Yamamura, ed., *Policy and Trade Issues of the Japanese Economy* (Seattle: University of Washington Press, 1982). Japanese strategies of industrial promotion in both the era of formal closure and the period of loosening of the developmental system are evident in advanced technologies. When Japan lacked basic electronic technologies, American firms were forced to license to Japanese firms in order to have any access to the latter's markets. Texas Instruments, with its strong patent position in generic semiconductor technology, was able to trade its licenses for a permanent share of the Japanese market; its part of the market, however, has not moved significantly up or down over the last years. Even IBM saw its position erode in Japan, despite the fact that no Japanese company could compete with it anywhere else in the world. Formal trade barriers were dropped in the mid-1970s. In preparation the industry was somewhat reorganized and the Japanese government—through NTT and MITI—launched coordinated domestic programs of technology development that allowed Japanese firms to catch up to American companies in basic component products. As the Japanese established parity in the most standard of these products, random access memories (RAMs), production in Japan boomed and export drives into America were fervently revived. Developmental strategies and private coordination did not cease with an end to formal closure.

10. See chapters 2–8 in John Zysman and Laura Tyson, eds., *American Industry in International Competition: Government Politics and Corporate Strategies* (Ithaca, NY: Cornell University Press, 1983).

11. Judith Goldstein, "A Re-examination of American Trade Policy: An Inquiry into the Causes of Protectionism" (PhD. diss., Stanford University, 1983).

12. See Ira M. Millstein and James E. Millstein, "A Sound Approach on Industrial Policy," *The New York Times,* 25 August 1983, p. 23.

INDEX